Potholes on the Path to Healing

Surviving life's traumas with help from God, family, friends, and a bunny named Jack

Judy Ann Meadows

BUNNYRUN PRESS

Potholes on the Path to Healing

First Edition

Judy Ann Meadows

The events and conversations in this book have been set down to the best of the author's ability, although some names and details have been changed to protect the privacy of individuals.

Paperback edition ISBN 9798782152772
ASIN: B09QK87GY8

Praise For *Potholes on the Path to Healing*

"The star of *Potholes on the Path to Healing* is Jack, Mr. Right Rabbit. After dating a couple of truly awful Mr.Wrongs on the L.A. dating scene, Judy decides to get a rabbit for company and lucky Jack gets to share her life - including attending a concert at the Hollywood Bowl where he's discovered by a little girl who yells out, "Rabbit on the loose!" (which I'd wager is the first and only time that line was ever shouted out at the Hollywood Bowl).

"In turn Jack helps Judy through loneliness, cancer treatment, and endures Shirley, the cranky companion rabbit she finds for him. This is a tender and ultimately optimistic tale of surviving a difficult childhood, healing from cancer and cherishing an animal companion."

> —**Barbara Abercrombie**, author of nonfiction: *Writing Out The Storm, Courage & Craft, Kicking in the Wall, A Year of Writing Dangerously,* and *The Language of Loss*, novels and children's books. A teacher in the Writers' Program at UCLA Extension, she also conducted writing workshops for several years in the 1990s at the Wellness Center, a nation-wide cancer support group.

"It is well known that stress can affect the immune system. What Judy's story reveals is how stress can be relieved by caring for a special animal friend. The reader learns a lot about keeping a rabbit as a pet. Bunnies provide companionship and amusement but attending to a pet's needs is a form of 'distraction therapy' when you are dealing with life's challenges. Judy calls these stressors 'potholes' – a very apt description. Just as your car can sustain severe damage by hitting one of these, your body can suffer from the type of serious emotional and physical assaults Judy faced. Without her beloved rabbit Jack and her deep faith in God, Judy would not have emerged centered and at peace."

> —**Katherine Poehlmann, PhD,** author of *Rheumatoid Arthritis: The Infection Connection (Targeting and Treating the Cause of Chronic Illness),* and *Arthritis and Autoimmune Disease*

"This is a poignant memoir covering a stressful period in the author's life caused by the deaths of people dear to her and her own battle with cancer...At a wellness center, she writes a journal to God. Readers in the same situation will find helpful information in this part of the book.

"She never marries, at least partly because of the lasting effects of having grown up in a dysfunctional family...She has other relatives and friends who love her, but Jack, her pet rabbit, may be the dearest of all...One of the wildest scenes in the book is when the author goes to the Hollywood Bowl with a friend and Jack. When Jack escapes, all heck breaks loose.

"The book is easy to read, and the author's sense of humor helps to make it a good experience."

—**Alan Cook**, prolific author of many mystery/adventure novels including the Carol Golden series, and the Charlie and Liz series. Alan also writes history/adventure books for young people. Winner of the Silver Quill award. His *Walking the World* was named one of the 'Top 10 Walking Memoirs and Tales of Long Walks' by the walking website, www.walking.about.com

"*Potholes* is a moving and entertaining true story. Many times, I laughed out loud. When people were mean to Judy, I got mad. And, at a certain point, I cried.

"I think what I liked best was how Judy related to her beloved bunny, Jack. That beautiful bond that Judy had with Jack, his dependable comforting companionship throughout the whole book, helped Judy to navigate the 'potholes' without falling in.

"I will definitely recommend this book to all my friends!"

—**Marilyn Boussaid**, Artist and Poet

DEDICATION

To all who've had to say goodbye to a beloved pet.
I understand and send you love and consolation.

To my family members and friends who showed kindness,
generosity, and emotional support as I faced life-threatening
challenges. I am so grateful.

I hope in reading this book you will realize how much
God loves us.

by Eloise Donnelly

CONTENTS

Chapter 1
Starting My Journey

There was a time when there was a void in my life. It was Fall, 1993. No one to come home to. Something was missing.

I kept seeing friends with their pets. Would a cat suit me? No. A cat would tear my curtains and furniture to shreds. Verna had a dog. Yap. Yap. My neighbors would complain.

After my best friend Dorie died, having battled a very long bout with cancer, my friend Fluff and her husband had a party to commemorate Dorie's life. The McLeans invited all of Dorie's friends to come over to their house, bring food to share, and play croquet in their backyard. Such fun we had!

Left to right: Charles, Freda, Judy, Fluff
Photo by Sandy McLean

Some were very good croquet players. Others sat on the sideline cheering. We were all asked to wear white, to show unity in our love for Dorie. We celebrated her life in this fashion for three years. It was the first year when I met Rascal.

When I took a break from playing croquet, Fluff came over and whispered, "Come with me, Judy, I want you to meet Rascal, my rabbit." Fluff picked him up and set him down on the other side of the room. She held up a carrot, and he came running as she called, "Come, Rascal, Come." He scrambled across the hardwood floors and at the end tried to put the brakes on with his paws. He slid the last ten feet. I was intrigued.

1

Fluff picked Rascal up in her arms and carried him upstairs. She tucked him into a special baby crib. Inside there were soft blankets and a litter box. A water bottle had been attached to the bars. I was dumbfounded. She treated the rabbit like a human being. At the same time, I was jealous of their relationship.

✻✻✻

A few weeks later my friend Francine came over. I mentioned Rascal.

"Judy, let's go to the pet store at the mall and get you a rabbit today," she suggested.

I came home with a new furry roommate, Patches, who was two years old. I named her Patches because she was a black and white spotted rabbit. I really liked her, but she was distant and wouldn't let me pet her very often.

One night she came and nuzzled my leg as if to thank me for giving her a good home. Though I was on the phone I felt emotionally touched. This was the first time she had come to show me affection. I smiled and resolved to pick her up and cuddle her as soon as I was done with the call.

She turned her back. hopped away and went up the stairs.

Then BANG! BUMP! What in the world was that sound?

I dropped the phone. Patches had fallen to the bottom of the stairs. She was lying very still. I thought she had knocked herself out.

I put her in a large plastic dish and took her to an all-night vet. "I think Patches has bumped her head," I said. "What are we to do?"

After listening to Patches' chest, the vet put down her stethoscope. "I'm afraid it's too late," she said. "Patches has had a heart attack." She was only five years old.

I cried so hard when I heard that Patches had died. I thought I couldn't stop. Was there something I could have done to have prevented this from happening?

The doctor said I could take as much time as I wanted to compose myself.

When I got home, I called Francine.

"Come stay the night with me," she soothed. I went to her place. We stayed up until early in the morning, talking. I felt guilty, as if it was my fault that Patches had died.

Should I have done something different? I wondered.

Jean, a mutual friend of ours, met us for breakfast and shared how she felt when her cat had died. This made me feel better.

When I went home, I realized how much I'd loved Patches. I was consumed with guilt, as probably I had been a bad parent.

Maybe if I had kept her confined to flat areas, she wouldn't have fallen down the stairs. Thinking she'd like fresh air, I kept her outside most days. Was this also a mistake?

I put her supplies in my storage, as I could not bear to part with them. I was grateful she'd been in my life as I'd learned to care for something besides myself. If there was a next time, I would do things differently.

✳✳✳

I placed an ad in the paper for a roommate shortly after Patches died, and Mary Ann Simmons arrived early in the winter of 1996. Although I hoped for some company to take the edge off my loneliness, we saw little of each other. She was a nurse on the night shift at the hospital. She left early for work before I got home from my real estate office.

After her shift, she would often stay out with friends until the wee hours. She was sleeping when I awoke, so our paths rarely crossed. She was about five feet tall with black bobbed hair and a plump build, probably because she only ate fast food.

I poured myself a glass of lemonade and opened *The Daily Breeze* newspaper. That's when I saw the article about a grief support group for people who'd lost a beloved pet. It was led by a veterinarian in Hermosa Beach. There was a phone number in the last paragraph. I called it immediately.

A woman answered and said, "There's a meeting next Saturday afternoon. Bring a photo of the pet you lost to share with the group."

Colorful photos of all kinds of animals lined the beige-colored walls of the meeting room. In the middle of the room was a large round table with twelve chairs. I glanced at a few of the photographs

3

on the walls before I took a seat next to a bald man. On the table in front of him there was a photo of a bulldog that looked just like him.

"That's Harry," he said. "He died a few months ago."

That's a long time to grieve for a pet, I thought.

When the bald man finished speaking, the woman on my left told me about her cat.

"She had cancer. I couldn't bear the thought of her dying." She started to cry. "Even though I spent hundreds of dollars on medications and the doctor did his best, she died anyway."

Luckily, I hadn't spent any money to keep Patches alive. Then it was my time to share.

"I came today because my rabbit died ten days ago," I said, holding up a picture of Patches. She was sitting in her litter box, chomping on a carrot.

The six other people in the grief support group stared at me. Although I felt self-conscious I continued talking.

"She was five years old when she tumbled down the stairs. The vet said it was a heart attack. I miss having someone to love, and hope being here will help me heal my grief."

The cat lady put her hand on my arm.

Everyone in the room had such a caring expression. I felt encouraged and continued my story.

"The night before Patches died, she rubbed her body against my leg. She was never affectionate before that night and I wondered if she'd had a premonition that she was going to die. Perhaps that was her way of saying, 'Thank you for adopting me.'

"Last weekend, my friend Francine and I had a memorial service for Patches. We buried her with a few carrots and parsley tips. I hope she'll be happy buried in my friend's yard. I miss her more than I thought I would, especially after I'd put her cage and bunny run in storage."

The cat lady squeezed my hand. "I understand," she said. "The first few days are the hardest. The memories are painful."

The group met once a week, but I never went back to another meeting. Little did I know that losing Patches would begin an earnest and determined search for love and the start of a series of unexpected, often traumatic, events. I didn't realize then what life had in store for me. I was in line for a roller coaster ride, completely unaware of what was to come.

Chapter 2
Looking for Mr. Right

Before I continue my story, let me set the stage. I'm a single lady named Judy who has tried finding love at church, in the Sierra Club, at a hiking club (where I did better on the flatlands than on uphill climbs), at Happy Hour in neighborhood bars, and in encounter groups. I'd even tried polka dancing.

Mr. Right hadn't shown up at any of these places. That is, until a cold winter evening at the Bel Air Church weekly singles' meeting. I was serving myself a cup of punch when I sensed someone's eyes staring at me behind me. Creepy. I turned around and looked up. Way up. There stood a man who must have been 6 feet 5 inches tall, staring at me like a Greyhound dog that had spotted his next meal.

He was very, very, very thin. A whippet of a face. His nose, mouth, and eyes seemed too big for the size of his head. Worse, he had thick caterpillar eyebrows. The pock marks on his cheeks made it appear that he'd been bitten by bees. His long, long, long legs looked like they'd been stretched out on a rack.

"Hello," he said.

"Hello to you." I didn't have anything else to say to someone who seemed so exaggerated. I turned away. Luckily, I spotted my friend Sonya across the room. Without saying goodbye to him or excusing myself, I sprinted in her direction.

That's when I saw HIM! Tall. Handsome. A Pierce Brosnan look-alike. He had striking, bold features. A beautiful mouth. He wore a soft brown sweater looped over his shoulders. He also wore a hat. His movie star presence commanded attention.

He whipped the whippet-faced man right out of my mind. I stopped mid-sprint to stare at this awesome hunk. Then, as if he knew I was there, he looked at me and smiled. My heart pounded so hard, I was afraid he'd hear it across the room. What beautiful eyes he had. I was determined to meet him.

Unfortunately, two women were talking to him. They didn't look like they wanted anyone to interrupt, but I had – *absolutely had* -- to meet him. What excuse could I find to head towards the back of the room where he was standing?

Directly behind him, there was a door. Maybe I could pretend it wouldn't open so I could ask him for help.

"Someone wants to talk with you," Sonya said. She'd come up behind me while I was trying to decide what to do.

"Sonya, you have to see what I see."

I nodded my head in the direction of the handsome hunk.

Suddenly the whippet-faced man appeared and stood to the right of Sonya, blocking my view.

Oh, no! I thought. *How is it that the person that I don't want to be around is always the one to show up?*

"My name is Bernie," he said. The expression on his face made me wonder if he wanted me to pet him. "Would you like to go out for coffee?"

Why had he followed me? I certainly hadn't given him any encouragement. I shook my head, no. Then I looked back over my shoulder to see whether the Brosnan look-alike had seen Bernie approach me. I didn't want him to think we were together. The handsome hunk was gone. I turned my back on Bernie, the better to scan the room, but Mr. Handsome had left.

Darn it.

"Go ahead, Judy. Go with Bernie. We can chat on the phone later this week," Sonya said. I flashed her a *how could you do this to me* look. She shrugged her shoulders and had the good sense to look apologetic.

I didn't like Bernie's approach, but it couldn't hurt to throw him a bone. What were a few minutes of my time? Maybe if I went to coffee with him, just once, he'd go away happy and leave me alone. Besides, I was hungry. I might as well eat.

"Sure, why not?" I said.

"There's a Denny's restaurant around the corner," Bernie suggested.

On my way out the door of the church, I looked around one last time to see if my dreamboat was standing in the parking lot. He wasn't.

At Denny's I ordered hot tea. Bernie ordered a Pepsi. Under the bright fluorescent lights of the restaurant, the harsh shadows made his nose seem even sharper.

"I'm watching my weight, but we can share a hot fudge sundae," I said.

He talked while I concentrated on the taste of the rich dark chocolate. The sugar made me euphoric so that I could relax while ignoring his droning conversation and still savor each delicious bite.

"I write poetry in my spare time," he bragged.

I pushed the empty dish off to the side of the table.

"Plus, I work as a professional writer for the *Saturday Evening Post*," he added.

"I've always liked that magazine," I said. Secretly, I'd always wanted to be a writer. Since I wasn't, at least I could date one.

I wiped my mouth with a napkin and studied Bernie with new eyes. His salt and pepper hair had been chopped off in straggly layers. The ends were frazzled. His bangs fell over his eyes and he kept pushing them back behind his ears. Sure, he looked strange, but weren't writers supposed to look strange? I wondered if I should tell him to fire his barber.

The more Bernie talked about writing, the more I warmed up to what he was saying. I was curious about what it would be like to be a writer. Plus, if I dated him, possibly I'd meet one of his writer friends – someone I might really find attractive.

Bernie was so busy telling me his life story he hadn't eaten his share of the ice cream. He probably thought I was a hog, but I didn't care.

I had a rule: If I didn't like a guy, I'd pay my own way. I placed a $5 bill on the table. Hopefully, he'd get the hint and we could just be friends.

Finally, he stopped talking.

"What are you doing?" he asked. He looked surprised.

"Paying my way."

"OK," he said. He picked up my $5 and continued talking. Thankfully I didn't owe this man any favors now. I could leave the restaurant with a clear conscience.

"Would you like to go to a concert next Friday night?"

I started to shake my head *No*, but he said, "I have season tickets to the Los Angeles Philharmonic. I may have mentioned that I play the piano and love classical music."

I'll never know what possessed me to say yes, but maybe one of his literary friends would also be there and I would meet him. Also, the program featured classics by Beethoven, one of my favorite composers.

***

He picked me up in his old gray Chevy. I sat in the dirty front seat and hoped I wouldn't see anyone I knew. At the concert, he grabbed my hand. His palm was so sweaty I pulled mine away and made a show of wiping it with a Kleenex. That didn't stop him from grabbing it again and again. *Is this guy so stupid that he can't take a hint?* I wondered.

At intermission I excused myself to go to the restroom. I splashed water on my face and looked in the mirror.

"What am I doing here?" I said out loud. I wished I could speed up the night but couldn't think how. When he asked me to go out for a drink afterwards, I said no. He rambled on and on during the long drive home.

On arrival, as he put the car in park, I hastily exited and said, "I think I hear the phone ringing" as I sprinted up the walk. I knew he probably expected a good night kiss or even an invitation to come in for coffee. No way. I had to figure out how to ease him out of my life.

The morning after the concert I woke up feeling lonely. If only I'd been on a date with the Pierce Brosnan look-alike instead of Bernie, how different I'd feel.

Chapter 3
At the Movies

Although I'd vowed never to go on another date with Bernie, he kept calling me. Most of the time, I let the answering machine catch his calls. I didn't return them. Against my better judgment, I finally accepted his invitation to see the new James Bond movie. I loved James Bond and I guess I was still holding out for the prospect of meeting an interesting writer. Also, I didn't want to fight the traffic in downtown Westwood at night or go to the movies alone.

He showed up at my door wearing a suit and tie. Of course, I had dressed casually for a simple movie date. What a pair of misfits we were. Even our clothes weren't on the same page. Not a good start for the evening. I already regretted saying yes. I looked down at my jeans, tank top and flip flops. Darn it. I didn't want to change, as I figured this was our last date anyway.

He drove very slowly. Every time he came to an intersection he waited for people to cross. When he stopped for an old woman who was talking to her friend, I waved my hand impatiently.

"They're not even thinking of crossing the street," I protested. "They're just standing there. You need to keep moving."

"Don't tell me what to do."

"I hate being late."

When we finally arrived in Westwood, he circled around the blocks several times.

"What's wrong?" I asked.

"I forgot to bring the news clipping with me. What's the name of the theater?"

What a bozo, I thought, and rolled my eyes.

I knew my way around Westwood, so I tried to direct him past different movie theaters.

"Turn here, Bernie," I said.

"Stop talking!" he barked.

"No – go this way, Bernie," I shouted.

He shot me an annoyed look.

"You don't know this area like I do," I explained. "If you don't want me to help, then you'd better stop and buy a newspaper. Otherwise we'll miss the movie."

"I know where I am now," he insisted.

He was hopeless. I crossed my arms and stared out the passenger window. We drove around Westwood for another twenty minutes before he finally found the theater and a parking lot that wasn't full.

"You park," I said, jumping out of the car while he waited for the parking attendant. "I'll go stand in line."

There were two long lines in front of the movie theater. I didn't feel like standing in either one of them but at least I was away from that annoying man.

The thought crossed my mind that if I disappeared, then I'd be rid of Bernie forever. I searched in my purse to see if I had enough money for a taxi. It would probably cost me $40 to get home. I certainly didn't feel like spending that kind of money. Darn it, why didn't I ask a girlfriend to go with me instead of Bernie?

I waited in the line with people who'd already bought their tickets. I wanted Bernie to pay for us to go to the movie. No way was I going to treat him. He was lucky that I was letting him take me in the first place. I leaned against the brick wall of the theater and looked around.

Oh my gosh! Was that my Pierce Brosnan look-alike? It must be. He was wearing the same hat he wore at the Bel Air Church. My face felt hot. I was probably blushing a rosy red color that blended in with the bricks. I let out my breath.

I was relieved he didn't recognize me. Thank God. The last thing I wanted was to have Mr. Handsome see me with the whippet-faced Bernie again. He might think we were a couple.

Confidant that he didn't see me, I watched Mr. Handsome talk to the woman standing next to him. She had long black hair and a voluptuous body with breasts that spilled out of the purple flowered fabric of her mini dress.

Oh no! I couldn't compete with her. No way. My only hope was that they were not a couple. Then he put his arm around her. My worst fear was being realized. They seemed to be together. He kissed her on the cheek. I touched my cheek. How I wished that he were kissing me instead.

"Did you get the tickets?" Bernie huffed, out of breath.

I brought myself back to my all-too-awful reality.

"No," I said. "You need to go to the other line and buy them."

Fortunately, instead of being irritated, Bernie meekly did what I told him to do.

As he went to the ticket line, I turned my attention back to Mr. Handsome. Where was he? Had he left? I looked around frantically, only calming down when I glimpsed him entering the ornate door of the theater lobby. He put his hand on the small of Ms. Voluptuous' back and guided her ahead of him. At least he was a gentleman.

Bernie waited in the long line as if he didn't care whether we'd ever get in. His slumped shoulders irritated me. Even though he was dressed in a suit and tie, I was still disappointed in him. How did I ever agree to go on this second date with a man who made me want to run away? Was I still seeing him only because I hoped to meet one of his writer friends?

It took him forever to buy the tickets. Everyone standing next to me had gone into the theater. I stood by myself. Arms crossed. Maybe if the film was sold out, he'd have to take me home. At least then there wouldn't be a chance Mr. Handsome would see us together.

Bernie returned with the last two theater tickets. Darn it. Now I'd have to walk in with him. I'd let him buy my ticket, but I hoped he didn't think that meant anything. If he was expecting a kiss at the end of the night, I'd set him straight.

As Bernie and I walked in, I was a few steps ahead of him, and was acting like I didn't know him. The theater was packed. Everyone was talking and settling into their seats.

Where was Mr. Handsome sitting? My eyes darted around the theater, but I didn't see him or any woman wearing a purple flowered outfit. Maybe they'd bought tickets for another movie.

The only empty seats were in the third row, far down in front of the big screen. I had to lay my head back against the theater seat and strain my neck to see. Being so close to the screen blurred the images. My head ached.

An hour into the film, Bernie tried to hold my hand. "Please understand, Bernie, I'm somewhat of a germaphobe and don't like to be touched. So please, hands off."

To avoid this happening again, I devised a strategy.

"Sorry, Bernie, these seats are just too close to the screen and it really bothers my eyes. I need to go to the back." I left my seat and found an aisle seat in the last row.

I relaxed and let Sean Connery as 007 capture my imagination. He was so forceful. He would have known where the movie theater was located. He would have known the best place to park. He would have flown me to an exotic island in a Lear jet. His strength and masterful mind energized me. I thought Mr. Handsome was just like him, minus the jet. Mr. Bond made me feel so good, it almost made up for Bernie being my date.

After the credits rolled, I found Bernie waiting for me near the exit door. He had that lost dog expression on his whippet face. I stopped smiling. His shoulders slumped. I must have really hurt his feelings when I left him.

"I missed you, Judy," he said. His voice sounded despondent and a little annoyed. "I couldn't hear what you said before you left me. Why did you leave me?"

"I can't sit so far forward in a theater. I get headaches."

"OK," he said, apparently satisfied with the explanation. He led the way to his car.

On the entire ride home he chattered, probably nervous, and tried to get me to engage in a conversation. I was distracted, wondering why I was still dating him. Was it because I was desperate to meet one of his literary friends? Was this fair to him? No, of course not. Although I sort of enjoyed his old-fashioned courting, we were both wasting our time on a relationship that wasn't going anywhere and never would.

I mentally rehearsed what I would say to him. Honesty is the best policy, as the saying goes.

When he pulled up to the curb in front of my condo, he leaned over to try to kiss me goodnight. I was ready for this move, and quickly pulled away from him.

"Bernie, thanks for taking me to the movies. I'm sorry, but this isn't going to work out. I don't want to see you anymore. I hope you meet the right person for you."

"No, please, Judy," he pleaded." Give me another chance. I will show you that I can be right for you after all."

"I know this is disappointing for you, but it's over. The chemistry just isn't there. Thanks again for the movie. Good night."

I reached for the door handle and opened it. Over my shoulder, I said, "You don't need to walk me to the door."

As I glanced back, I could see tears glistening in his eyes. He must have been rejected before. Well, he would have to deal with it again. I sincerely hoped he would find his Ms. Right, but it certainly wasn't me.

I walked up the sidewalk and opened the door quietly, so I wouldn't wake my roommate Mary Ann. A single light in the living room had been left on. It was very quiet, a relief after all that irritating talking. Mary Ann's keys were not on the coat rack. I remembered that she'd gone out with some girlfriends.

Usually I loved being alone, but tonight I felt lonely. Mr. Handsome was probably taking his date out to dinner and I wished it could have been me.

Suddenly I missed Patches. At least my dear rabbit had been someone to love.

Patches (1991-1996)

Chapter 4
Love at First Sight

The morning after my disastrous movie date with Bernie, I had to accept that I didn't enjoy being with him and feeling sorry for him was not a reason to keep dating him. I'd wanted Mr. Right and all I'd ever found was another Mr. Wrong.

Suddenly I got an idea. A relationship with a rabbit like my friend Fluff had with Rascal would be so much more satisfying! I hadn't found Mr. Right but maybe I could find Mr. Right Rabbit.

Dating Bernie made me realize how much I missed Patches, but Patches and I had never bonded. Not really. Not anything like Fluff and Rascal.

Back then, I'd bought the first rabbit I saw. Maybe that's why Patches and I were never close. Fluff had searched for months before she'd bought Rascal. I resolved to do the same.

I would search until I found Mr. Right Rabbit. No matter how long it took. I would search the pound. I would search pet stores. I would search newspaper ads.

I wanted chemistry.

I wanted mutual love.

I would take my time.

"I'm looking for Mr. Right Rabbit," I told my roommate Mary Ann that night. "What do you think about having a pet rabbit around here?"

"I would enjoy having a rabbit here. It's fine with me. Hopefully it would become housebroken so that it doesn't pee all over the place," she stated thoughtfully.

"I'll see that it is litter box-trained within a week," I assured her.

"Do you know anybody selling a rabbit?" I asked a colleague at work.

"Do you know anyone who has a litter of rabbits?" I asked a girlfriend at church.

"I want to get matched up with Mr. Right," I asked my friend Bonnie. When she said she didn't know any available men, I laughed. "I'm not looking for a human, I'm looking for a rabbit."

"Sara, who teaches in the classroom next to mine, needs to give away their family rabbit before she moves to a new house in March. Unfortunately her husband is a 'dog man'," Bonnie said.

"I'll have to think about it," I said. "I don't want to make up my mind that fast."

✳✳✳

Three weeks later in my own good time I called Sara.

"We're moving next weekend," she said. "It's a good thing you called. I thought I might have to take the rabbit to the pound."

On the drive to Sara's house I promised myself that I wouldn't feel pressured. Just because the rabbit would soon be homeless didn't mean it was the right rabbit for me. If the rabbit had a bad personality, I would say, "Thanks, but no thanks." I would give her the number of the rabbit rescue society, so she could put it up for adoption.

I turned left on a tree-lined street in Sherman Oaks. Their sprawling ranch house had a red For Sale sign on their front lawn that said SOLD. A smirking boy about ten years old with long, curly hair opened the front door.

"I'm Rick," he said in a smart-alack voice. "My Mom's been waiting for you."

I checked my watch. Sure, I was fifteen minutes late for my appointment, but I'd driven a long way. Maybe his mother Sara was mad because I'd kept her waiting. Suddenly I felt awkward. What if I didn't make a good first impression?

I followed Rick as he shuffled down a long narrow hall to an enclosed patio. In the middle of the patio was a 21-inch by 31-inch metal rabbit cage set between two wooden chairs.

The first thing I saw was the rabbit's beautiful brown eyes. They followed me across the room. I sat down in one of the lawn chairs and crossed my legs. I couldn't believe how nervous I felt. You'd think I was on a first date. *Get a grip*, I muttered to myself. I was just meeting a rabbit, for gosh sake, and this was only the first one I'd met. I still needed to meet lots of other rabbits before I decided to adopt one.

The rabbit's big brown eyes studied me intently. Maybe he wondered why I was so tense. Or maybe he sensed my desire to please and to leave with a Rascal-like companion.

I wanted to speak with him but didn't know what to say. I leaned over and brought my face closer to the cage. His nose twitched. He stuck it between the bars as if to find out more about me.

I loved that he was curious. I leaned in closer and let him smell my hand.

He turned his back on me and hopped in the opposite direction.

I retreated. My shoulders straight and tight, I sat in the lawn chair and waited to see what he would do next. Then he looked over his shoulder at me. Honestly, I think he might have winked. What a flirt! I smiled and my whole body relaxed. Again, I approached the cage. When I stuck my finger between the bars, he turned his back on me and hopped away.

"What's the matter?" I asked. "Are you afraid of me?" I tried to talk him into coming back, but he huddled in the far corner of the cage. He was shaking.

Maybe he was shy. I wondered if his shyness would be a problem between us. While I waited for Sara, I studied him. He had brown nose markings shaped like the whiskers on his mouth. There was a white spot on his forehead shaped like a crooked arrow. It made him look a bit forlorn.

Up close, his dark beautiful eyes seemed to be saying, "Speak to me. Play with me. Don't leave."

Why had they left him alone in that big bare room? He was so timid. My heart opened. I wanted to cradle him in my arms and comfort him.

What I hadn't counted on was love at first sight.

Don't forget, I reminded myself for the third time, *this is the first rabbit you've seen. You need to meet lots of other rabbits to find Mr. Right Rabbit.*

Sara entered the room. She had gray roots that were two inches deep. Her large stomach bulged over her belt. Only her ocean blue eyes were attractive.

"So glad you could come today," she said. "We're closing escrow on Monday and my husband wants to get this over with."

Why did her husband want to get rid of the rabbit? Did it bite? It was hard to believe it would hurt anyone. Maybe her husband had abused it. If so, I wouldn't blame the rabbit for biting.

Honestly, the little creature seemed exceptionally timid. I wanted to ask why but I didn't.

Instead, I merely asked "Does the rabbit have a name?"

"No," Sara said. "Strange as it seems, even after three years we still call it 'the rabbit'."

They hadn't even bothered to name him! It was as if he wasn't even a part of their family. I felt sorry for the little guy.

"I've decided his name will be Jack," I blurted out. "Yes. He looks like a Jack to me."

"Jack, the rabbit. That's a wonderful name," Sara agreed.

Oh no, I scolded myself. *Why had I named him? Sara might think I was ready to commit.*

"My son's friend gave us the rabbit three years ago at Thanksgiving." Sara sighed. "My son promised to take care of the rabbit, but you know how it is. He's young. He got bored. I had to take over. Kids these days are so irresponsible."

When would she stop calling him "the rabbit"? I asked myself.

Sara kept on making excuses. "I was already taking care of our two dogs, and a cat. They keep me busy. Very, very busy. It was hard to make time to take care of the rabbit." She pointed to a bag of rabbit food in the corner. "I feed him pellets. Unfortunately, we never got around to buying a litter box for the rabbit," Sara said. "Instead, I mix some sand with a little hay in a CorningWare dish."

They hadn't even gotten around to buying Jack his own litter box! Out of consideration for Jack, I didn't give Sara a piece of my mind. I didn't want to ruin my adoption chances.

"I subscribe to the *House Rabbit Society* magazine," I said. "It has articles on how to take care of rabbits and the latest research on how to treat different diseases. It contains listings of rabbits that are up for adoption."

Sara tried to act interested but I could tell she didn't really care about the magazine or how to care for rabbits.

I changed the subject.

"I have lots of bunny reference books at home."

She gave me an odd look and stifled a yawn.

Why couldn't I stop talking about rabbits? I doubt that she was impressed about my knowledge. More likely she thought I was a nut.

I needed to think of something better to say, so I tried, "Can you tell me about Jack's past?"

"Just after my son brought him home, I took the rabbit to live in my kindergarten classroom because I wanted the children to have a pet. The problem was that I couldn't watch him all the time. The kids put their fingers in the cage. They tried to poke him with their pencils. The rabbit was afraid of them. I didn't want him to get hurt."

"You left him at the school overnight?"

"Yes. It was too much of a nuisance to carry him back and forth every day."

"What about the weekends?" I knew my voice was too loud, but I couldn't help myself. I was shocked.

"Each weekend, a different child took the rabbit home. Everyone took turns."

I could only imagine how the children must have treated Jack. They were only six years old. Probably they'd forgotten to feed him or refill his water bottle.

Dang it! I wanted to tell her that she had been a bad parent. A *really* bad parent. She'd left Jack alone in a cold, dark classroom every night. She had given him to families who didn't know diddly-squat about how to take care of a rabbit.

As angry as I felt, I held my tongue.

"After two weekends, I realized that keeping Jack at school was not going to work," Sara continued. "And at the end of the third week I brought the rabbit back here for good. "

"Thank goodness," I said, relieved.

"Do you want to hold Jack now?"

"Yes, of course!"

Sara leaned down and eagerly opened the door of the cage. I knew she wanted me to like him. If I took him, she wouldn't have to worry anymore. She wasn't a bad person. Just clueless. She picked Jack up and rocked him gently for a moment before handing him over.

Sure, she'd made mistakes, but at least she cared. She set him in my lap. I grabbed him around his tummy. He tried to hop off, but I didn't let him. He was frightened. Poor thing. But when I petted him, he hunkered down in my lap. That's when it happened. I fell in love. Completely, madly, truly in love.

"Jack likes you," Sara observed. "I can tell. He's allowing you to hold him. He was that way with me at first, too."

I rubbed his ears, and then I impulsively leaned down and kissed his forehead.

"Are you interested in taking him?" Sara sounded hopeful.

I didn't answer immediately so as not to seem desperate.

"I will give you all his supplies," Sara offered. "And a basketball he likes to play with."

I still didn't say anything.

"Including his cage."

That sealed the deal. "Okay, I will take Jack home."

Sara jumped up and started putting all of Jack's things in a neat pile.

I'd promised myself I was going to meet lots of rabbits, but I hadn't counted on finding Mr. Right Rabbit at the first place.

Her son carried the cage out to my car, while Sara collected the rest of Jack's belongings. We walked towards the front door and heard loud noises on the way, coming from the living room. It was a man's voice yelling, "You lousy bum! You can't hit!" and "Are you blind? That was a strike!"

I asked her, "Is the rule true that unless there are flames and smoke in the TV room, you must <u>never</u> interrupt a man watching a ball game?"

"Oh, yes," she said with a laugh. "That's definitely the rule in this house, but I pray that there will be no fire here until after escrow closes."

Her husband barely glanced up at me before turning back to the baseball game on TV.

"Good luck with the rabbit," he mumbled over his shoulder, his eyes glued to the set. "I'm sure you'll give him a good home."

A better home with me than with you, I thought.

Chapter 5
Jack and I Get Acquainted

I adjusted the rearview mirror of my big Lincoln sedan so I could see Jack in the back seat. The CorningWare dish that served as his litter box had shifted off to one side and Jack had jumped out.

"I'm so glad you're in my life now, Jack," I told him. He looked towards the sound of my voice. Good. I had his attention. I wanted him to hear my welcome speech. I wanted to set a few things straight.

"I... AM... THE... BOSS," I said slowly in a very deep voice. I wanted to make sure he understood every word.

Jack hopped into the CorningWare dish, pushing the hay and sand litter upwards.

"Hey! Be careful, I don't want you to get my car dirty!" I yelled.

I backed the Lincoln out of the driveway. When I drove around the corner, Jack's litter dish again slid across the floor of his cage with him in it. He ground his paws in the sand and rode the dish as if it were a sled. I pulled over to the side of the road, so I could finish my speech.

"I like that you're paying attention, Jack," I said. "Patches, my last rabbit before you, didn't give me any respect. Don't be like her. I would prefer that you be like Rascal. He lives with my friend, Fluff. Maybe you'll meet him someday."

A car whizzed by. I realized that I hadn't parked as near to the curb as I should have, but that was deliberate. I didn't want a passerby to see me talking to a rabbit. They might think I'd lost my marbles and call the cops. Hopefully Jack and I wouldn't get hit on our first date together.

"If you have half of Rascal's good qualities, then we'll get along great."

Jack scratched his ear with his hind foot. *Oh no! What if he has fleas?* I wondered. But he still seemed to be listening, so I continued talking.

"Rascal always does what Fluff wants him to do – no bad lip. Rascal wants to please her. And I want you to try to please me."

When Jack sniffed the air, I sniffed also, hoping there was nothing in the back seat to make him allergic.

Then he peed in the dish. To be polite I turned my gaze away and looked out the front windshield.

After I'd given him the privacy he deserved, and he'd finished his business, I continued my welcome speech.

"Patches didn't give two hoots about me. She'd look at me and then just hop away as if to say, *I don't think so!*"

I recalled the many times this happened. I shook my head. *To think I gave her such a good life and that's the thanks I got.*

Jack licked his paws.

I took a breath and sighed. "That's why I waited so long to find you. I wanted to be sure you would be different."

Jack was still sitting in the dish he'd peed in, but his brown eyes stayed on me. I doubted that anyone had ever taken the time to talk with him as I was doing. I think he liked it.

I'd given Jack the rules. Now it was up to him to follow them. Hopefully he would prove to me that he was different from Patches. Hopefully he would confirm that I'd made a good decision.

I put the car into gear and started driving us home.

"If you behave," I yelled over my shoulder, "we'll have good times together and I can promise you I'll be better than your last owners. That's for sure.

"I will <u>not</u> leave you alone for extended periods of time. I will <u>not</u> allow naughty children to poke pencils at you. I will <u>not</u> keep you locked up in your cage like Sara did. At our home, the cage door will always be open. There will be fiberglass fences in the living room, so you can run around free. But I'm warning you, Jack, do not chew on my furniture. Do not chew the electrical cords, or the phone cords."

On the way home, I stopped at the Centinela Pet store. They would have all the supplies we'd need. So Jack wouldn't be too hot, I parked in the shade. I cracked open the window an inch.

"Now you be good," I commanded. "I'll be right back."

I walked up and down the aisles looking for rabbit supplies. First, I spied a real litter box, but remembered that I had one in storage that belonged to Patches. No more CorningWare dish for *my* rabbit. Next, I grabbed some cat litter deodorizer to sprinkle in the litter box underneath all the Timothy and oat hay that Sara had given me. That should stop any smell.

On one aisle, I purchased a small shovel and a bottle of white vinegar to clean the litter box. I bought a small spray bottle to fill with water and give Jack a squirt in the face if he was tempted to chew on my furniture. This painless discipline method is a tip I learned from reading *House Rabbit Society* magazine. It had worked on Patches.

When I returned to the car, Jack was asleep. When I started the car, he woke up. He looked so cute. There was no doubt that he was Mr. Right Rabbit.

We pulled into my parking space at the townhouse and I carried Jack and his cage past the pool to his new home. As I turned the key in the lock, I heard my telephone ring. The answering machine clicked on.

"Judy, hello, hello…Hello, Judy?" It was Bernie's voice.

I didn't have time to mess around with him. Making sure Jack was settled into his new surroundings was much more important. Bernie would have to wait.

"Judy, Judy…. Are you there?"

The answering machine clicked off. I wouldn't be calling Bernie back, as usual. At some point, he had to give up on courting me and realize it was a lost cause. I made myself clear about wanting to break off the relationship after the movie date.

He just didn't want to believe it.

I hung the car keys on the coat rack in the entrance hall. Then I held Jack's cage up, so he could see the square-shaped living room. On the far wall there was a gas fireplace and across from it a television.

"Here's your new home, Jack," I said. "Do you like it?"

He hopped around in his cage.

"Is that a yes?"

He stopped hopping and looked up at me.

"Sorry, Jack, I know you've been stuck in that small stinky space for over an hour. You probably need to run around."

He hopped again.

"But you'll have to stay in your cage for a while longer." I said. "I wasn't expecting you to come home with me. I have to get everything ready, so you can live here."

I set his cage down next to the patio door.

"You're heavy, Jack. I'm going to have to leave you here while I set things up."

From behind the bars of his cage, Jack watched me set up four fiberglass panels to be used as fences that I'd bought at Plastic Mart the day before. Each fence stood three feet high by seven feet wide. I connected four of the fences together to form walls. His new rectangular fortress measured 12 X 20 feet. The coffee table was in the center of the room.

I wondered if I should move the books, magazines, and remote controls to another location, but decided to leave them where they were.

This would turn out to be a mistake.

I put Jack's cage inside the fortress. I opened the metal door. He shot out of it and hopped across the floor. When he reached the fiberglass, he didn't stop. His nose bumped up against it and he fell backwards. I laughed out loud.

Next, I had to clean out his cage.

"This smells terrible. I'm giving Sara's CorningWare dish to the Goodwill," I explained. "Dishes are meant to be used for food, not poop."

I looked over my shoulder to see if Jack was listening. He was smelling his new home. Then he nudged the fiberglass wall, but it was solid and didn't move.

Now that he was safely inside the fortress, I felt I could leave him alone. I went to my storage bin, located above my car in the garage. After rummaging behind old escrow files, car wax, and tiles from a kitchen remodel, I finally located Patches' old litter box. It was made of heavy plastic and twice as big as that stupid CorningWare dish.

When I returned to my condo I noticed Jack had gone back into his cage. I set the plastic litter box on the patio outdoors. I poured baking soda on the bottom of the box, then lined the box with newspaper. An advertisement for an Easter church service made me smile.

"That's *your* holiday, Jack," I announced.

I tossed some Timothy hay and oat hay on top of the newspapers. Finally, I refilled his water bottle from my own filtered water pitcher. I suspected that Sara had given him hard city water, but I was determined that only the best was good enough for my Jack.

"Good night," I whispered tenderly when I finished fixing up his new home. "Sweet dreams."

I slept soundly.

❋❋❋

24

The next morning, I woke up to find the newspapers in Jack's cage completely soaked. The water bottle had dripped all night.

Jack had also peed outside of the litter box all over my living room floor. I had to fix the water bottle. I would have to train him to pee inside the box. I sighed. This was going to be a busy day. I'd forgotten how much work caring for a rabbit could be.

My stomach growled. I was starving, but first things first. I grabbed a banana and gobbled it down. After this meager breakfast, I drove to the pet store and bought him a new bottle. At the recycling bin in the parking garage I scavenged some dry newspapers.

At home, I swept up the area around the fences. One of them opened and Jack bolted across the living room. Freedom! He ran so fast I couldn't catch him. I just saw his bobbed tail disappear behind the sofa. Then I heard a rustling noise. I peered over the top of the sofa and saw him chewing on the slipcovers.

"Bad boy!" I yelled.

Still, I decided to let him stay there while I changed the newspapers. He probably liked the dark and I needed some time to fix everything up.

After attending to Jack's needs, I prepared a bacon, lettuce, and tomato sandwich. I ate it much too fast and burped. My stomach hurt. When I went to capture Jack, I noticed teeth marks on the sideboard. One of the lamp wires had been attacked as well. It was amazing how much mischief one little rabbit could get into in such a short time!

A rabbit can get electrocuted when chewing on electrical cords. And besides, I had to protect my possessions. I scooped him up and put him in the cage while I went shopping.

I drove to Linens & Things, where I bought plastic dowels to wrap around the cords. I bought masking tape at the Dollar Store.

"It's a good thing you're confined to the space in your enclosure," I said to Jack after I finished rabbit-proofing everything I could think of. I shook my finger at him.

"If I have to protect everything in my house," I scolded, "I won't have time for anything else."

Jack knew I was talking to him and he seemed to nod his head. I felt happy believing that he understood me.

That belief didn't last long. Over the next few days he chewed the coffee table's other leg. He also chewed on the remote controls and magazines on the bottom shelf. Good thing I had bought a lot of masking tape. I taped all the edges and feet of the wooden table. I resolved to study my bunny books to find out what kind of expendable toys could substitute for my belongings.

That night on my way to bed I congratulated myself on what a good decision I'd made when I'd brought Jack into my life. However, those good feelings towards him didn't last. No matter how often I tried to train him, he continued to pee inside his cage.

"Jack, I've told you a hundred times already – you need to pee in the litter box!"

❊❊❊

Every morning I sprinkled baking soda under the litter to avoid odor. I took the soiled paper from the bottom of the cage and buried it in the litter box. This was how the experts advised to train a rabbit, but it wasn't working. It had taken Patches three days to figure it all out. Was she that much more intelligent than Jack?

I'd thought Jack was smart, but now he was acting like a dumb bunny. Why wasn't he learning? Was his brain defective? Either he didn't understand what I wanted, or he was being stubborn and simply refused to use the litter box. Either way, I felt annoyed.

There was no returning Jack. I would have to cope. The life expectancy of a rabbit is three to five years. Long years if he was a dumb bunny and I had to put up with it.

After I finished cleaning up his mess, I put aside my annoyance and picked him up in my arms. When I tried to pet him, he struggled to free himself. I felt disappointed. He seemed friendlier when I first met him at Sara's home. Maybe I'd been too hasty in my choice. I should have interviewed more rabbits.

I was beginning to think that Jack hadn't listened to my lecture in the car on the way home. He wasn't following my rules. I don't know what the bunny experts think about giving verbal commands, but I was certain that I had received Jack's full attention in the car. Of course, he'd been listening, and therefore was just choosing not to obey me yet. I was not giving up on him. I was going to win.

Mary Ann was really pleased when Jack came to live with us and when I was away for the weekend she offered to take care of him. Her payment was a little reduction in her rent. In the evenings she had a pathway from the front door to the kitchen to have a snack, so having a big enclosure in the living room didn't bother her.

❊❊❊

Because I didn't have a choice in the weeks that followed, I ordered myself to be patient. Each day I held him in my arms and petted him anyway. Eventually he stayed still for longer and longer periods of time before he wrenched himself from my grasp and scooted off.

I was taming him. He had potential after all. Encouraged by his progress, I praised him often.

"I want you to be as good as Fluff's rabbit, Rascal. Maybe you'll get to meet him," I reminded him.

Jack licked his paws and then used them to wash his face. In that moment, I felt so much love for him. He was so endearing, I resolved to quit comparing him to other rabbits. I would love him for who he was.

Bernie continued to call me despite all the times I turned down his invitations to go out. Honestly, I didn't want to date him, but sometimes I was really lonely and needed to hear a human voice.

One day while on the phone with Bernie I watched Jack out of the corner of my eye. He jumped up in the air and twirled in circles. He landed on his hind feet and danced a little jig. I clapped.

Jack scooted underneath the coffee table. All my papers scattered across the room.

"What are you doing, Jack?" I yelled.

"Who's Jack?" Bernie asked.

"I've got a new rabbit and I don't want any flak from you," I snapped. "I've got to go," I said curtly, and hung up before Bernie could reply.

That afternoon Jack used the litter box for the first time! That night I let him lie on my lap and we watched the *Mary Poppins* movie together. The happy music relaxed both of us. Jack hunkered down, and I leaned back on the sofa. All was well for an hour. Then suddenly, he peed on my shirt.

"You forgot to get up and go to your litter box," I shouted at him.

Then I made myself calm down and said in a quieter voice, "We were too relaxed. Isn't that right?" I dropped Jack to the floor quickly. He ran to his litter box. I guessed that maybe he was embarrassed.

"Don't worry, Jack. Next time we watch a movie together, I'll put a towel on my lap."

There were times when Jack didn't like me the way I wanted him to like me. One night when I was holding Jack on my lap, he started struggling. The tighter I held him, the more he resisted. I alternated scolding him with pleading with him.

27

Then Eureka! It hit me. I was acting just like Bernie, who was trying too hard to please me.

I prayed, "OK, Lord, show me how to do this differently."

That's when I realized I had to back off and let my relationship with Jack unfold at its own pace.

by Eloise Donnelly

Chapter 6
Mr. or Ms. Right?

That night, Bernie called, and this time I picked up the phone, ready to remind him again that we had broken up. But he opened with, "Judy, I never did read you any of my poetry.'

That surprised and intrigued me. I took the bait.

"Okay, Bernie. Read me one of your poems." I had wondered why he didn't make this offer before. Maybe he was too shy. Or maybe that was just a line he used to impress me when we first met. He never did introduce me to any of his writer friends. *Let's see whether he's bluffing*, I thought.

His short poem was a small cut above "Roses are Red, Violets are Blue." No author likes to be told his work stinks, so I told a fib so he'd stop.

"Very nice, Bernie, but I prefer classical poems."

"Don't hang up, Judy. I have just the thing."

I heard the sound of book pages turning on his end of the line. *What would he choose?* I wondered. There was nothing on TV. Might as well listen to poetry after a long day at work. He was probably looking for a suitable romantic sonnet. Keats? Shelley? Shakespeare? Emily Dickinson?

When he started to read Longfellow's "Song of Hiawatha" I nearly laughed out loud at this silly choice.

"By the shore of Gitche Gumee, By the shining Big-Sea-Water...," he droned.

I knew that this was a very long poem and couldn't sit through all of it. When he got to "...At the roots of his long tresses. And he reeled and staggered forward." I interrupted and said, "Speaking of tresses, I really need to wash my hair."

Enough was enough. My hair truly needed attention, and it was getting late.

"Thanks for the poetry. Bye now."

After I hung up, I looked over at Jack. He was watching me. Had he been listening to our conversation? I didn't want him to be jealous.

"You're more important than he will ever be," I said. "To prove it to you I'm going to feed you a special treat. A carrot. Won't that be nice?"

Jack stood up on his hind legs. Obviously, he understood the word "treat." What a smart rabbit. I smiled watching him nibble his carrot treat.

Near the door I saw Jack's basketball. Sara had given it to me because she said Jack liked to push it around with his nose. I bounced the ball inside Jack's fortress and it rolled across the floor. He pushed it with his nose just as Sara had described.

"Since you like basketball, maybe you're a boy," I said.

The truth was, I didn't know his sex. It's difficult for ordinary people to determine the gender of a rabbit. Their genitalia are hidden. When we'd first met, I'd had a hunch he was a boy. That's why I'd named him Jack.

*** ***

For a few days, he continued to push the basketball around with his nose. So cute! Then one morning while I was eating my yogurt with blueberries, he humped it. I almost choked on my blueberries.

"Jack! I thought you were a respectable rabbit," I chided.

He stopped humping and looked up with a puzzled expression. I didn't say anything. He started humping the basketball again.

"Stop!" I yelled.

He stared into space, like he was in an ecstatic trance. Then he humped the ball again.

"STOP!" I yelled, louder.

This time, the sound of my voice didn't make a difference. He didn't stop. He handled that basketball with practiced finesse, like he'd been doing it very, very often. When he finished he gave a gleeful shudder.

"Yikes! You are one horny bunny!"

He looked so satisfied, I couldn't help but laugh. Although the humping disgusted me, I also felt relieved. At least he was behaving like a boy. He had to be Mr. Right Rabbit. I didn't need a Ms. Right Rabbit. I needed the veterinarian's professional opinion. It was time to get his gender confirmed once and for all. If my initial impression was correct and he was a boy, that would explain why he was peeing all over my home. He was marking his territory. I'd have to get him neutered.

✳✳✳

When I opened the door to Dr. Rosskopf's reception room, a loud squawk greeted me. I backed up against the wall and Jack's carrier banged against the chair. A giant parrot jetted across the room, grazing the top of my blond curly hair. I ducked. It was as if I'd walked into Alfred Hitchcock's horror film, *The Birds*. Good thing I didn't drop Jack's carrier.

When I regained my balance, I closed the office door behind me. With one eye fixed on the bird, I found a seat for Jack and me. I set his carrier on the empty plastic chair next to mine.

"AAWRRKK!" the parrot screamed. He'd perched himself on top of the bookcase and took turns glaring at me and everyone else in the reception room.

"Whose bird is this?" I demanded. "Why isn't he in a cage?"

"He belongs to one of the staff here," the receptionist explained.

"Ridiculous," I muttered under my breath. "He really scared Jack and me."

With both eyes on the parrot, I cautiously backed up to the doctor's sign-in sheet. I would have made it there without incident, except that I bumped into a very large man with a goatee and a bald head. He wore a six-foot-long striped snake around his neck and shoulders like a shawl.

Yikes! This place is dangerous! I thought, reevaluating my decision to come here.

I signed in and my name was called ten seconds later. Thank God. The chaos of the waiting room had spooked me. I followed the nurse down the hallway to an examination room.

Dr. Rosskopf whisked in with a smile. He'd been Patches' doctor.

"Hello, Judy. Good to see you again. What do we have here?" He leaned down and petted Jack. "I'm glad to meet you," introducing himself to Jack in soft, low tones.

I watched Jack's whole body relax. I guess he liked Dr. Rosskopf. The doctor whipped out a lighted instrument and examined Jack's eyes, ears, and teeth. Using his fingers, the doctor tapped Jack's tummy. I knew he was testing to see if there were any hair balls present. Then he set Jack on the scale. He weighed six pounds.

"Just right," Dr. Rosskopf said, "No need for him to gain any more weight."

"I want to know if I should call him Jack or Jacqueline," I asked.

He turned Jack over and probed his bottom with his fingers. "Yes, he's a male."

"How can you tell?"

He continued holding Jack on his back. "Do you see these two balls?"

"I think so," I said, although they were so tiny I couldn't be sure.

"When a bunny is newly born, it's easy for doctors to make a mistake in their diagnosis," Dr. Rosskopf said. "But Jack is three and a half years old. It's easier to get an accurate reading."

The last thing I wanted was oodles of bunnies. If the doctor made a mistake there could be dire consequences. I sighed. On the walls of the exam room were photos of his patients (including rabbits) with their owners. They were all smiling, which gave me the confidence that his diagnosis was correct.

"Neuter him, please," I said. "One rabbit is enough."

The neutering procedure took three hours. Afterwards I took Jack home. While he slept off the anesthesia, I cleaned the basketball before giving it to Chris, my pre-teen neighbor.

I fixed myself a hamburger, sweet potato, and broccoli for dinner. I was just sitting down to eat when the telephone rang. I wondered why people always waited until the dinner hour to call but I answered the phone anyway. I couldn't bear to let it ring and not know who was calling.

"Oh, Judy, hello. It's so good to talk to you!"

"I can't talk now, Bernie," I said, and hung up the phone.

***

Two days later a letter arrived. I recognized Bernie's scrawl but opened it anyway and skimmed through the paragraphs. You'd think that a writer should be able to write something interesting. But no. The letter was boring. I had to face facts. The chemistry between Bernie and me stunk like an old tennis shoe. Time to get rid of him. I burned the letter.

Unfortunately, burning the letter didn't erase my memories of him. I hated how he looked at me with adoring eyes. Creepy. His sweaty palms were gross.

That night he called again. He started talking before I could say anything. He was so excited and passionate with his feelings that he started panting.

"Be careful, you might hyperventilate, and that's not good for you," I warned. "Time to face reality, Bernie. I thought I made myself clear on the night we went to the James Bond movie. We're through."

Finally, that got his attention.

"How can you do this to me, Judy? I care about you so much. How come you kept taking my calls? You let me read poetry to you. Why did you lead me on for weeks? Why did you waste my time?"

"Bernie, I'm sorry if it seemed that I misled you, but I'd never had a chance to listen to your poetry, and I was curious about hearing it. Now I need you to accept that the feelings are not mutual. We can be friends, but not more than that. I need to hang up now. Please continue going to the singles' groups. Hopefully, you will find a woman there who is just right for you."

He was definitely Mr. Wrong. I felt sorry for Bernie. That's probably why I had accepted his calls. But pity is not a good foundation for a relationship. I assumed that he had been searching for love a lot longer than I had. I prayed that he would find someone compatible and turn his attention away from me.

Three days later another one of his letters arrived. I burned it without reading it and threw the ashes down the toilet.

Chapter 7
The Neighbors Meet Jack

Jack and I always went to the mailbox together. That day, I wrapped everything except his head in a blue towel. Then I put him under my armpit and carried him like he was a football. On my way back from the mailbox I ran into Diane, my neighbor. As usual, her blond hair was perfectly styled.

"Did you get anything interesting in the mail?" she asked.

"I've got another rabbit," I said, ignoring her nosy question.

She looked more closely at the bundle I held and saw Jack.

"Someone mailed you a rabbit?" she remarked, incredulously.

"The postman didn't bring me the rabbit." I said, thinking, *What a dopey question!*

"Why on earth did you get another rabbit?" she said.

"I like rabbits," I said, defensively. "They make good pets."

"Cute little critter," a man's voice interjected.

I looked behind Diane. Her husband Fred smiled. Diane puckered her lips as if she'd just bitten into a sour pickle. That distasteful expression was one I was used to seeing. She turned it on Fred.

"How could you say that?" she scolded. "What's going to happen when Judy goes out of town?"

"Don't worry," I quickly assured her. "I won't ask you to take care of Jack. My roommate Mary Ann will."

"That's a lot to ask of someone."

"He's not a dog. He doesn't bark. She won't have to take him for walks." I managed to stop myself from rolling my eyes, but just barely.

"My friend told me that rabbits are messy. And they smell!"

"They invented pet deodorizer," I protested.

"Pet deodorizer!" she retorted, adding, "I'm allergic to perfume."

"We're going inside now," I said, putting an end to an argument she seemed determined to continue.

Diane gave me a look that made it clear that she was not pleased. Fred, like a shadow, followed her to their mailbox.

"Who does she think she is, ordering me around like I'm a child?" I muttered under my breath. I picked up the *L.A. Times* and whacked it angrily against the wood fence.

"I have the right to have any pet I want. After all, it isn't a pig. Or a pony."

The next day, Trudy, another neighbor, stopped me on my way to the mailbox. She had frizzy bleached blond hair and a heart-shaped face.

"Did you get a pet?" she asked.

"Have you and Diane been talking about me?"

"No, I saw you carrying a cage." When Trudy spoke, her head bobbed left and then bobbed right.

"Yes, I got a rabbit. I named him Jack."

"Cats are much better pets," Trudy asserted, an opinion I didn't welcome or share.

I centered myself. Speaking with Trudy while she bobbed her head made me feel like I was standing on a raft in the ocean.

"Cats claw the furniture," I said.

"Rabbits *chew* the furniture."

"I'd rather have a chewer than a clawer. Besides, I bunny-proofed my unit."

"Cats make better pets," Trudy repeated. "Mine have wonderful personalities. If you come to visit me, wash your hands first. Saucer and Homer won't be happy if you smell like a rabbit."

I didn't say anything. Trudy always had to have the last word.

The next day I ran into Robert, who lives two doors down from Trudy. He was walking his Saint Bernard dog that reminded me of a big bear.

"I hear you have a rabbit," he said.

"Have you and Trudy been talking about me?" I said, a bit indignant. *Gosh, news sure travels fast around here*, I thought.

He ignored my question. Instead, he warned me sternly. "You'd better be sure your rabbit keeps out of sight or it will be Bear's next meal."

I looked at the big slobbering beast. As usual, he was wearing a muzzle. A few months earlier, Bear broke his leash and snapped at a child in the complex. I looked Bear in the eye. Was it my imagination or did he have a killer look aimed straight at my leg? Thank goodness for the muzzle. Bear tugged on his leash. I stepped backward. My fear invigorated him, and he pulled on the leash. It appeared that he wanted to lunge at my leg.

"Hold on to your dog!" I shouted.

"You need to be more careful," Robert said.

"You're the one who needs to keep your distance," I said, authoritatively. "I'm just taking a walk and minding my own business."

"You'll have to keep your rabbit locked up," he demanded.

"Oh yeah, my rabbit's a real killer," I said. But the sarcasm was lost on this dufus.

"Bear and I have our rights," he insisted.

"I don't relish the possibility of my rabbit or me being mauled by Bear. Neither will the police."

Robert gave me an angry look and shook his head. I stared at him and Bear, standing my ground until they turned and walked away in the opposite direction.

✳✳✳

Later that night, Mary Ann was bursting with good news. She had gotten a promotion to an administrator position at the hospital. It meant a higher salary, but she would have to travel on business for two to three weeks at a time. She liked to travel, so that wasn't a problem for her. I hoped I could match my schedule to hers so that she could take care of Jack whenever I was gone.

by Eloise Donnelly

Chapter 8
Finally – Mr. Right?

For the last two months, I had attended eight singles' events at several churches and so far, I hadn't met anybody interesting. Hope springs eternal. Thank God, the ninth event turned out differently.

It was a blustery Sunday evening. My friend Cora met me at Brentwood Presbyterian Church. We both drove our own cars. Our agreement was that if we met anyone interesting, we'd be free to stay and talk afterwards. Wasn't that the purpose?

Cora arrived before I did. She had saved me a chair and waved me over. We were both excited to hear that night's speaker, Dr. Neil Warren. He was a psychologist and author of several relationship advice books. He was testing his theory that certain personality characteristics can predict compatibility and lead to more satisfying long-term relationships. In a few years, he would launch E-Harmony.com and build it into a membership site with 33 million members, but this was well before that.

Dr. Warren talked about a questionnaire that he'd developed. Cora leaned over and whispered in my ear.

"I might fill that out," she said. "Maybe that will help, because I never meet anyone at these events."

"The only person I've met is Bernie," I said, making a sour face. "And you know how I feel about *him*."

"Will you fill out the questionnaire if I do?" Cora asked.

"I'd like to meet Mr. Right," I said. "But don't know if I want to do it this way. Besides, this costs money."

"Probably not too much," Cora said. "I have a hunch it will be worth it."

I looked around the room. I recognized many people from other singles' events. The meeting started promptly at 7:30 P.M. Dr. Warren talked about how to meet the love of your life. He stressed compatibility and promised that the E-harmony program would help us find the right mate.

When Dr. Warren finished his talk, everyone clapped. A few people rushed up to the refreshment stand. They nibbled on cookies and carrot sticks.

Then I saw HIM. Mr. Handsome! Six months had passed, and I hadn't forgotten him.

I remembered his fetching smile and wavy brown hair. My Pierce Brosnan look-alike must have sensed me looking at him. He turned toward me and smiled. My heart fluttered. I smiled back. Maybe tonight we would finally meet.

"Look over your shoulder to the back of the room on the right," I whispered to Cora. "That's him."

"Wow! He's a knock-out," Cora exclaimed. "Go get him!"

I met him at the refreshment stand. We each got a glass of lemonade and a cookie.

"Come, follow me," he said.

I did. He led me out the door to the patio where we found a table and chairs.

"My name's Martin. What's yours?"

"J-Judy," I stammered. I had dreamed of this meeting but now that it was happening, I was nervous.

"I noticed you right away. You're new here, right?" he asked.

"No, I've been here three times before, but not when you were here. I've been going to different churches around town to meet new people. I saw you before about six months ago at Hollywood Presbyterian Church, but you were preoccupied with a lady."

"I make my way to different groups," he said. "Is it working for you? Are you meeting people you're interested in?"

"Now that I've met you, I feel I can say yes to that question."

He laughed. Such a rich baritone. I suspected that he had a great singing voice.

We sat outside on the patio. We talked about art and music and movies and sports until they turned off the lights. I told him about my real estate career, and enjoyed answering his many questions. He lived in Pasadena and worked for an allergy doctor. They did research and allergy testing. I loved that he was helping people overcome their illnesses.

"I'd like your phone number, so I can get to know you," he said.

"How about giving me your number, too?"

"That's not a good idea," he croaked.

I wondered why. *What was he hiding?* I decided not to challenge him. There was no denying my attraction. I didn't want to ruin my chances.

"I'll call you tomorrow and we'll plan something," Martin offered.

"Okay," I said. Except for his not giving me his phone number, Martin had made a good first impression. I felt positive chemistry. How different he was from Bernie, thank goodness.

***

The next morning, I woke to a message from Bernie on my answering machine. I had to say one thing for the guy, he was persistent. In a weird way, I admired him, but I didn't call him back.

Martin kept his word. He said he'd call, and he did at 9:00 A.M. I was leaving to go to work, but when I heard his voice on the answering machine, I picked up the phone.

"I'm going to be in your area later today," said Martin. "How about a late lunch, say, 2:30?"

"Hopefully I can clear my schedule," I said. There was a big smile on my face that I was grateful he couldn't see.

I finished my real estate calls quickly and raced home. It was 2:15 P.M. I changed into shorts and a ruffled blouse. Refreshing colors. Feminine. He brought out the girl in me.

Just as I flipped on my sandals, the doorbell rang. I looked at the clock. 2:30 on the dot. When I opened the door, he was wearing a bright short-sleeved shirt that showed off his bicep muscles. I could picture him in the gym working out and that made me feel happy.

"I'm ready. Bye, Jack."

"Jack? Who's Jack?"

"My rabbit."

"Hopefully next time we go out, I'll meet him."

Martin wanted to meet Jack? That was more than I could say for most men. This was a plus.

He drove an Oldsmobile convertible. The top was down. He opened the door on the passenger side and I slid into the seat that smelled like new leather.

"We're going to Jerry's Deli," he said.

"I love it!" I put on my sunhat, so my hair wouldn't get messed up. Riding in his convertible was fun. I could see everything I couldn't see in a regular car. I felt free, like it was the start of a new and exciting adventure.

At Jerry's Deli, I ordered a pastrami sandwich, coleslaw and pickles. He ordered a salami and cheese sandwich with a large Coke. We were surrounded by a young, hip crowd. I heard that movie stars sometimes ate there but I didn't recognize anyone. Or maybe I was just too busy gazing into Martin's eyes.

He told me about his recent trip to Spain. We had both been to Europe, but he traveled more than I did. We had other things in common, too. We were both tennis players. We both liked to bike and roller skate.

"Looks like we'd have fun together," I said.

"How about tennis on Thursday afternoon?" he suggested.

"Don't you have to work?"

"Yes, but sometimes when the doctor isn't in, I can take the afternoon off."

On the drive home, I felt all warm and fuzzy. We'd made plans to meet again. What more could I want? I leaned back on the leather seat and closed my eyes. The warm California wind blew across my face. I was happy.

Suddenly the car jerked. I opened my eyes and saw him taking an exit that wasn't mine. I put my hand over my heart. It was beating fast with fear of the unknown.

"Where are we going?" I said. But if he heard me he didn't answer. He pulled off to the side of the road. The gravel spun underneath the tires and we skidded to a stop.

"Sorry!" Martin gagged and grabbed a box of Kleenex from the back seat.

"What's happening?" I tried to control the anxiety in my voice.

Martin didn't answer. He jumped out of the car and raced over to the curb. Then he bent over and lost his lunch in the rose bushes. I covered my eyes. The sound of his retching scared me. No wonder he was so thin. If he lost his meals every day, he must have some kind of sickness. *Could it be contagious?* I wondered.

When Martin returned to the car he looked sheepish. His skin was pale and clammy. He leaned over the driver's seat and grabbed his water bottle.

"Maybe it would be a good idea to wash off the rose bushes," I suggested.

He smiled awkwardly. "I have a delicate stomach. I should be more careful about what I eat," he admitted.

On the ride home, I tried to overlook the smell of vomit that was still lingering on him. Martin used a mouth wash spray and chewed on a mint. It seems he was prepared. Apparently, getting sick after eating happened often.

He walked me to the door of the condo complex. Despite being sick, he was a gentleman.

That's why I melted in his arms when he hugged me. I wasn't going to let the lingering scent of vomit ruin the strong attraction I had felt.

"I'm looking forward to playing tennis on Thursday," Martin said. He turned away quickly. I watched him walk down the sidewalk to his car. He had a nice slim body, but he was walking so fast I wondered if there was a fire somewhere. Could it be that he had another date? Probably he wanted to miss the rush hour traffic on the freeway.

"Drive safe," I called after him.

I found Jack in the living room hiding behind the stereo. I got the broom and with the brush ends scooted him out. When I picked him up he tried to jump out of my arms.

"Calm down, Jack," I said. "I want to tell you about Martin. He's very interesting to be with. Maybe Thursday you'll meet him. "Hopefully," I said under my breath, so Jack wouldn't hear, "he isn't still seeing that girl that I saw him with at the movie theater."

✸✸✸

It rained the next day, a rare event in sunny Southern California. I already missed Martin. Too bad it wasn't Thursday already. I jumped when the phone rang. Maybe it was him.

"It's about time you answered your phone," a man's voice demanded.

"Martin?" I asked, hopefully.

"Have you been listening to my messages?"

"Bernie? Is that you?" It was hard to disguise my dismay. Now I was starting to worry that I had a stalker to deal with.

He started telling me about his job. He totally ignored that I'd said another man's name and told me about an article he was writing. I interrupted him after two minutes of non-stop talking.

"Please don't call me anymore, Bernie. I'm in a relationship now. I really hope you find someone who is right for you."

I hung up quickly to avoid an awkward discussion.

Mr. Right?   by Eloise Donnelly

Chapter 9
Playing Tennis with Martin

The next morning, I woke up happy. Today I would be playing tennis with Martin.

When I arrived at the office I canceled a showing for one of my properties. I wanted to be sure I had time to look my best. I raced home. When I walked in the door of my condo I saw the red light flashing on my answering machine. I pushed the button to play the recorded message.

"Hello, Judy," Martin's voice mumbled.

I smiled. Today was going to be so much fun.

"I'm so sorry," he continued. "Something has come up at work and I can't meet you today. I'll call you soon."

"What a flake!" I yelled as I hung up. I knew Martin was too good to be true.

Startled, Jack looked up from his food bowl. The loud noise scared him and he ran and hid behind the sofa. I followed him. When I leaned over the back of the sofa Jack's big brown eyes looked up at me.

"I'm sorry for yelling," I said. "It's just that Martin backed out at the last minute and I was angry."

I picked Jack up with one hand on his head and another on his bottom. He squirmed a little bit but settled down when I sat in the rocking chair.

"You don't know how much I was looking forward to this date with Martin," I said. "But he's acting suspicious. Why didn't he give me his phone number on Sunday night? Now he canceled. What do you think, Jack?"

Jack didn't answer, of course, but I knew he sensed my disappointment. Instead, he snuggled down in my lap and eventually dozed off. "What a comfort you are, Mr. Right Rabbit," I whispered into Jack's ear after he fell asleep.

❉❉❉

On Friday morning, the phone rang at 2:00 A.M. If that was Martin, he could darn well wait until later. I turned off the phone and went back to sleep. On arising, I hit the message button. "Come fix our pipes. The water heater broke."

It was a woman's frantic voice. I erased the message. I was used to people misdialing the Roto-Rooter number by scrambling the last four digits of mine. It was really annoying to get these mistaken calls at all hours.

An hour after breakfast the phone rang again. Hopefully this time it was Martin. Unfortunately, it was the same woman who'd called me in the middle of the night. She was furious.

"Why didn't you return my phone call? What kind of outfit are you anyway?" she yelled.

Barely stifling my anger, I said, "You called a private number by mistake. Dial more carefully and you'll get Roto-Rooter."

That night when the phone rang near midnight, I answered it hoping it would be Martin. Surely, he was missing me by now.

"Roto-Rooter?"

"No, I am a real estate agent and you are ruining my sleep!" I shouted. "If you want to buy or sell your house, call me back. Otherwise pay attention when you dial and stop calling me."

I disconnected the phone.

The next day when the phone rang again, I answered without waiting to hear who it was on the other end of the line.

"You're dyslexic. You have transposed the last four digits of Roto-Rooter's phone number."

I waited for the caller to apologize but he didn't say anything. "You want 0940, not 9040," I said, hoping to clarify my comment.

It wasn't until after I hung up the phone that I realized that I wasn't sure who was calling. It could have been some clumsy, careless idiot misdialing Roto-Rooter or it could have been Martin. If it *was* him, I missed my chance to talk with him.

If it *wasn't* him, why wasn't he calling? Hadn't we had a good time? What if he didn't like me as much as I liked him? Worse, what if he was out with other women?

✳✳✳

After the church service at Bel Air on Sunday morning, I was listening to the organist and noticed a woman who had moved to sit beside me. "Hi, my name is Mariella, and I always stay to hear this last piece, as I enjoy playing both the organ and the piano."

My ears and heart perked up. This was definitely an answer to prayer.

"Hi, I'm Judy. It's nourishing to the soul to hear this music. I'm just wondering – if you're not married, maybe you'd like to join me tonight at the singles' group here at 7:30. There's someone I'd like you to meet."

As agreed, that night we met in the parking lot and walked in together. I spotted Bernie and we went over to him.

"Mariella, I'd like you to meet Bernie. He's also an accomplished pianist."

Bernie's eyes lit up and he reached out his hand to her.

"Hi, Mariella. Is this your first time here?"

They were chatting happily, so I excused myself to sit with some friends and listen to the speaker talk about "Finding the One."

✳✳✳

Out of the blue, Martin called.

"Sorry I had to cancel our date at the last minute, Judy. Something came up.–I can't help being busy at work," he explained. "Let's start over. Do you want to play tennis on Saturday?"

I felt my resolve soften. The sound of his voice made me want to be with him again. He certainly had a lot more potential than Bernie.

"When?" I asked.

"Let's say 10:00 at the Alta Vista Courts in Redondo Beach on Julia Avenue. I'll call for reservations. Afterwards we'll go out for lunch. A restaurant on the beach. Deal?"

"I could be interested," I teased, sipping my iced tea, stalling for a moment. "It does sound like fun. But how do I know if you'll be able to keep our date?"

"Do you want to play or not?" he asked, with a shade of annoyance in his voice.

"I'm not sure if I want to play since I don't want to be stood up by you again."

Would this be a repeat of what happened before? I knew he was becoming irritated, but I didn't care. I remembered the girl I'd seen him with at the movies. Maybe she was the reason he hadn't called for three weeks. I wasn't interested in being his backup plan.

"I assure you I will meet you at the courts," he insisted, lowering his voice to a more soothing tone. "Besides, I've missed you."

My heart sped up and I smiled.

"I've decided to give you a second chance," I replied. "I'll meet you there."

On Saturday morning, I woke up anxious with anticipation. I dressed in light cotton sweats. They were loose, but they showed off my long, shapely legs.

There were several cars in the parking lot. I saw his distinctive convertible and parked next to it. He jumped out of his car and greeted me with a quick hug.

"This is a perfect day to play. I reserved court #3," he said, pointing off to the right. "Over there."

His hug made me feel warm inside. I only wished it lasted longer.

"Let's have a go at it," I said. "I haven't played in a few weeks. I hope I'm not too rusty."

When we rallied, he hit the ball hard. I returned the ball hard. We played two sets. He beat me 6-1 on the first set. By the second set, I'd warmed up and he only beat me 6-3. Obviously, he was a better player, but if we played regularly, I'd be able to give him a run for his money. I felt invigorated.

"You play well," he commented as we walked to our cars. "Usually the girls I play with don't get any games off me."

I wondered how many girls he played tennis with. Hopefully, not too many.

"I played on tennis teams," I said. "Elementary school through college and won some tournaments. I've saved a few trophies to use as bookends."

He laughed. Then he put his arm around my shoulders and pulled me close. His shirt was slightly damp, but he smelled good.

"The Good Stuff Restaurant has limited parking," he said. "Why don't you leave your car here and we'll use mine?"

The restaurant was on 12th St in Hermosa Beach, on the Strand next to the ocean. We sat outdoors on the patio. We watched people with brightly colored swimsuits and flip flops walk by. I ordered an avocado and tomato sandwich with an iced tea. He ordered a turkey wrap with lettuce. No bread.

"I'm learning what to eat," he insisted. "Last time I was allergic to the salami I ate. We don't want any of that, do we?"

"Right," I agreed. "Hopefully you won't lose your lunch again. It's really helpful that you have such a flexible schedule at work, so you can get lots of tennis in."

"I work 40 to 45 hours a week and often if there are no patients, I stay and do research for the doctor."

I smiled. My job gave me a flexible schedule too. That would make it easier to date him.

"I'm learning how to help people prevent disease by abstaining from foods that cause food allergies," he continued.

"That sounds like a noble venture."

We were having our second glass of tea when suddenly he croaked, "I'll be back in a moment." He jumped up and ran toward the men's room.

Yikes! Was he going to throw his food up again? While I waited for him to return, I read a book that I kept in my purse.

Five minutes later, when he returned I asked, "Are you OK?"

"We've had lots of tea. Time to go," he said.

"But we haven't finished eating," I protested.

"I thought you'd be done by now," he complained. When I didn't say anything, he sat back down in his chair.

"Are you married?" I asked bluntly.

"What makes you ask that?" he stammered.

I could tell from the look on his face that he was indeed married. "Just a hunch. That's all."

"Everything's fine. Let's just enjoy our time together," he said.

What kind of an answer was that? But I didn't care. I wanted to be with him and until my suspicions were confirmed, I didn't want to know any more.

He pointed at the book sitting on the table next to me. "What are you reading?"

I knew he was changing the subject, but I let him.

"*The Late Great Planet Earth* by Hal Lindsey," I said." He prophesied that Jesus will return soon for those who've already accepted Christ as their Savior. He will take them up to heaven. Have you accepted Jesus as your Savior?'

He blinked his eyes and cleared his throat. "I'm not really interested in Jesus and all of that."

"Then why are you going to all the church groups, if not to meet Christian people?"

"You know the answer to that," he said. "I meet wonderful women – like you."

I warmed to those words, but if I was going to continue to date him, I was going to have to work on his belief in God.

"Are you ready to take a walk now?" he asked.

"Yes, let's do it," I replied.

He left a skimpy tip on the table.

We strolled along the ocean boardwalk. Roller skaters and bikes whizzed by. There was a volleyball tournament happening. We sat on a bench and watched the players shoot the ball back and forth across the net. He put his arm around me and tried to kiss me. I pushed him away, gently but firmly.

It had been a long time since I'd dated anyone I liked as much, but I didn't want to get hurt. He was still too much of a mystery.

"There's a lecture by Nathaniel Branden at the Santa Monica Auditorium a week from Tuesday," he suggested. "He'll be talking about growing your self-esteem. Is that of interest to you?"

"I've heard of him but never attended one of his workshops," I replied, "Yes, I'm curious."

"Let's meet there. It starts at 7:00 P.M. and it costs $15."

I wondered why he wasn't picking me up and that he expected me to pay my own way. All my doubts resurfaced, but I liked him too much to say or do anything that would make him take back his invitation.

He drove me back to the tennis courts to pick up my car. When we arrived, he turned off the ignition to kiss me. This time I let him, and we kissed enough to steam up the windows. His hands traveled down my neck. I decided I'd had enough.

"Time for me to go, Martin."

"I'm just getting started," he blustered.

"Yes, but I'm done for today."

His face looked anguished. I didn't mean to laugh but couldn't help myself. Why is it when you let a man go to first base with you, they think it's an invitation for a home run?

I opened the car door.

"Bye, Martin. See you a week from Tuesday."

My heart throbbed all the way home. It was a good thing I left when I did. We had such strong chemistry, but I didn't believe in sleeping with a man before marriage.

By the time I reached home I felt wonderful. It had been a fun day. The only wrinkle was when I'd asked him if he was married and he'd changed the subject.

I shrugged my shoulders and picked up Jack. We rocked together, and I told him about my day with Martin. "I like him *so* much better than Bernie," I said. "I hope you will, too."

Chapter 10
The First Pothole: Hopes Dashed

The day I was supposed to meet Martin for the Nathaniel Branden lecture, I woke up excited. Not only would I learn some new things, but I would finally get to be with him again. With rush hour traffic, it was a one-hour drive to the Santa Monica Auditorium. Luckily, I found one of the last spots in the parking lot.

There must have been 300-400 people there. Most of them were much younger than I – in their 20's and 30's. Martin hadn't told me where to meet him, so I looked around. When I didn't see him, I took a seat in one of the back rows, so I wouldn't miss him when he came in.

I pulled my sweater tight around my shoulders and then sat on my hands. The air conditioning had been turned on high and I was frozen. Hopefully sitting next to Martin would warm me up. I didn't have to wait long. Five minutes later I saw Martin. I raised my hand to let him know where I was.

He saw me but didn't acknowledge me. Instead, he put his left arm around a young woman's shoulders. She had long flowing black hair and stood about five feet eight inches tall. Dressed in a polka dot outfit, she looked like a high fashion model. An older version of the younger woman stood on the other side of Martin. She had brick-red bobbed hair and she held on to Martin's other arm. Then I recognized the women's outfits. They looked like they'd been bought at Chico's, a high-end clothing store where I shop. At least they had good taste in clothes.

Upset didn't even begin to describe how I felt. *Devastated* would be a better word. He'd invited me here on a date. Then he'd arrived here with two women! Was the younger woman a girlfriend here with her mother? What a twist of fate that could be.

Eureka! My instinct told me that the younger woman was his wife and the reason he didn't give me his phone number is because she could have answered the phone, and his goose would be cooked.

Finally, he looked around and saw that I was still standing. I used my hand to indicate the empty seat I'd saved for him. He looked away. Then he looked back, his eyes pleading with me to stay where I was. I couldn't believe he wasn't even going to come over and say hello.

For a moment, I considered walking over to the three of them and hugging Martin. Even better, I imagined myself saying how glad I was that he'd finally arrived. It would serve him right to have to explain me away to his wife as his occasional date. There could be fireworks and she might have a meltdown.

Deciding not to embarrass myself, I sat down. I must have had a stunned look on my face because the stranger in the seat next to mine said, "I saw you were interested in that man with his two lady friends."

I nodded, "I *was* interested."

"Do you want to go sit with them?" the stranger asked.

"No!" I replied, my voice dripping with sarcasm. "I want to sit on *top* of him. He deserves a piece of my mind."

"Oh," the stranger said, nodding knowingly. "I get the picture."

"Yes," I admitted. "The picture is really clear now."

Overcome with a variety of emotions, I turned my face away. A tear dropped from my eye.

The stranger reached for my hand and squeezed it.

"Everything will turn out for the best," he said. "You'll see. You're better off without him."

"Thanks, I sure hope so."

I thought about leaving the lecture, but I'd paid good money for a ticket. I guessed that when Martin mentioned that he was going to this lecture, both his wife and mother-in-law were curious and eager to go, so he decided to bring them, unaware that it might hurt my feelings.

During the lecture Nathaniel Branden talked about his new book *The Psychology of Self Esteem.*

"Raising your self-esteem is the most important factor for a fulfilling life," Branden said. "It affects your work, relationships, love – everything."

I needed to raise my self-esteem, so I wouldn't keep dating the wrong men. Why had Martin come to this lecture? Why had he invited me and his wife, the fashion model, and his mother-in-law? Did he think we all needed more self-esteem? He was the one who was married and still looking for other women.

I tried to focus on the lecture, but my eyes strayed to where Martin, his wife and her mother were seated near the front of the room. I was curious to see how they treated each other, but they were sitting too far away.

Why was he spending time picking up women at singles' groups in churches when he had such an attractive wife at home? Besides me, how many other women had he charmed? I was angry at myself. How could I have let myself get involved with a man who wasn't available for a long-term relationship? It's a hard lesson to learn – that a single woman dating a married man is a big mistake.

After the applause ended, I jumped out of my seat. I was determined to approach Martin and his family. Unfortunately, I didn't move fast enough. Martin and his wife and mother-in-law had disappeared. I felt disappointed. I would have to let go of my fantasy that he was Mr. Right.

When I arrived home, I picked up Jack and squeezed him tight. "I've been so foolish," I said, shaking my head, "So, so foolish. Thank God, I have you to come home to. At least you are my Mr. Right Rabbit."

✹✹✹

The next morning Martin called at 9:00 A.M. "Did you like the lecture?" he said.

"It would have been more meaningful for all of us if I'd met your wife and mother-in-law," I said.

"I'm so glad you didn't approach us. My wife would have understood. Our marriage is an 'open relationship'. However, my mother-in-law doesn't know that."

"An *open relationship*? How does that work? That you can have a wife and women on the side?"

"Yes. That's our agreement. We don't have affairs. We just have good times with whomever we're with."

"No wonder you refused to give me your phone number," I scolded. "No wonder you stood me up for our date on Thursday. You can't commit to being in a relationship because you're already in one. And you hedged when I asked if you were married," I said, my voice getting louder and louder. "How come you weren't honest with me? Then I could have made up my mind after knowing all the facts."

"Whoa!" he said. "One thing at a time. On Thursday, I couldn't meet you because Clarisse's mom was ill and needed to go to the ER. I was the only one able to take her."

"Clarisse? Is that your wife's name?"

He didn't say anything.

"Your arrangement with Clarisse might work for the two of you, but this is where I quit."

I knew I had to give this man up even though it would be difficult, since I was so attracted to him.

"I get that you're having a problem with me being married," he asserted, "But what difference does it make?"

"I refuse to be the *other woman*," I declared firmly.

"Even if you got married, I'd still be around for you," he offered.

"Nope. When two people are Christians, marriage is a sacred covenant between them and God. They give up all others and remain true to their spouse. You can call what you're doing *open marriage*," I stated, "I call it *adultery*."

"Sorry you feel that way. We could have had some good times together."

"Don't call me anymore," I said.

A few minutes later the phone rang. My heart pounding, I picked up the phone.

"Roto-Rooter?"

"Wrong! Number!" I snarled, enunciating each word, and slammed the receiver down.

I looked at Jack. He tilted his head, as if to comfort me. Nowadays, he always seemed to know how I was feeling.

"I'll be okay, Jack. I have you. I'll be okay."

As we cuddled together in the rocking chair, I confided to Jack, "I'm learning a lot about how I look at men right now and I need more wisdom about how to interact with them. I need to know how to determine more quickly who are the right men to have in my life."

❈❈❈

.Jack began to doze off as we rocked. I had wanted to believe that Martin was The One for me, even though I suspected otherwise. On our dates I had told him a lot about my dysfunctional family and my unhappy childhood. I didn't want his pity, so I downplayed the abuse somewhat in favor of more pleasant memories, like seeing my Aunt Ruth.

When Mom would ask me, "Would you like to go visit Aunt Ruth today?" I immediately would have a warm glow in my heart and an eagerness to see my beloved aunt. This was a rare treat, since it was an hour's drive to her home near the beach.

Aunt Ruth had often remarked that Andrea, Deborah, and I were the daughters she never had. At her home I'd sit on her lap at the piano with my little hands on top of hers and as she'd play, we'd sing our favorite hymns. She had a lovely voice.

Later we'd be sitting in her rocking chair and cuddling when we'd get interrupted by Uncle Joe who always seemed to be angry. She'd stop whatever we were doing to help him, and then return to me. When he left the room I'd whisper to her, "Can you ask him not to be so mad at you?"

"It's okay, Judy. He doesn't really mean it."

I didn't believe that. I think he *did* mean it. That really bothered me. I loved her so much. She was a surrogate mom to me. I wanted to muster the courage to tell Uncle Joe to stop, but for a kid aged six, seven, or eight, the words wouldn't come out. I didn't know how to protect her from him.

There were times he'd say, "Ruth, you're losing your mind."

After he'd left the room I'd tell her, "Don't worry, lots of people, including my Mom, lose their keys. You'll be okay."

But unfortunately, he hammered that thought in her mind. Years later as she was forgetting things more and more, Andrea and I would go visit her in that place where she lived before she died. I'd bring my cassette player and we'd sing hymns and she would smile and mouth the words with us.

We were so glad to visit and be there for her then, because we both remembered how loving she was to us as children when we really needed her.

Martin had been such a good listener while I poured out my life story. I didn't mean to unload on him, but it felt so good to express my feelings after so many years of keeping them bottled up. I would notice his body language for crossed arms, stifled yawns, sidelong glances at his watch, but didn't detect any signs of boredom.

Was I deceiving myself that he was really listening? Or was he covering his thoughts about his other girlfriends through lots of practice pretending to be interested? Maybe with that kind of skill he should have been a therapist.

Or a bartender.

Broken heart pothole   Photo by K. Poehlmann

Chapter 11
The Second Pothole: Skin Cancer

My two sisters. My parents. My brother. Me. We were all at risk. Skin cancer ran in my family. Dr. Winter, a dermatologist in Laguna Beach, treated all of us.

I had fair skin that never tanned, but that didn't stop me from frying my skin in high school and college. The sun always made me turn a bright red – never the beautiful bronze I longed for. By the time I graduated from college, Dr. Winter found my first skin cancer. She burned it off with liquid nitrogen and cautioned me about further damage from sun exposure.

After I moved north to Los Angeles, I found a new skin doctor for my monthly checkup. I sat in Dr. Chai's waiting room and thumbed through a *Reader's Digest*. All four walls of the waiting room were filled with photographs of Tahiti, Rome, Paris and other exotic vacation spots that I'm sure my money had helped pay for.

After Dr. Chai burned off the latest bump on my face, tears sprang to my eyes. In the mirror above the examination room, I saw that a new scab had formed. I felt disfigured. I was tired of financing Dr. Chai's vacations. My skin cancer wasn't getting any better.

I knew that skin cancer could spread to other parts of the body. Then it could be fatal. But what was my alternative? I didn't know any other way to treat this deadly disease.

I still had scabs on my face when I attended a deacons' luncheon at my church a week later. At least it wasn't a singles' group. It didn't matter how I looked. I was standing in line for the buffet lunch when I noticed the fair complexion of the woman standing directly in front of me.

"How beautiful your skin is," I commented.

"I work for a dermatologist," she said. "Hi, my name is Shari, and this is my husband, Sherman."

We all shook hands. After we filled our plates, Shari invited me to join them at their table. Between bites of meat lasagna, I pointed to the latest scab on my face.

"I'm so upset." I said. "I wish I could find a cure."

Sherman and Shari looked at each other as if sharing an unspoken secret. I was puzzled.

"Have you thought about laser resurfacing?" Shari asked.

"How will that help my skin cancer?"

"Sherman and I both had skin cancers, but now they are gone," Shari said.

"Totally gone?" I couldn't believe what I was hearing.

"Totally gone. You should do it, too. I work for Dr. Ahmed in Century City. If you'd like, I'll give you his phone number," she said.

I readily agreed. If this laser treatment worked the way she said it would, I didn't care what it cost. To be cured! Dare I hope? I would hate to be disappointed, but it sounded like a good possibility. That night I could hardly sleep. I was too excited. The next morning at exactly 9:00 A.M. I telephoned for an appointment and got one for a week later.

✳✳✳

There weren't any photographs of beautiful foreign locales hanging on the wall of Dr. Ahmed's reception room. A good sign? Hopefully it meant he wouldn't be too expensive. I looked around and noticed that all the other patients were also women.

The nurse led me to an examination room. Dr. Ahmed came in immediately. He was a distinguished-looking man with silver white hair and eyebrows. He had a taut, tanned face. I wondered if he'd used the laser procedure on himself.

Extending his hand and smiling, he said, "Hello, Judy. Shari mentioned that you were coming in today."

I shook his hand, saying, "I'm so looking forward to hearing how you can help me."

I sat up straighter. I was excited but apprehensive. What if the treatment ruined my skin? Before he could say anything else, I blurted out my story.

"As a teenager, I wasn't careful, and got second degree burns on my nose. Gosh, what a dork! I used zinc oxide and wore a plastic guard attached to my sunglasses."

Dr Ahmed smiled and nodded knowingly. He must have heard this story before.

"Then in college while sunbathing on the roof of my dorm, I used baby oil and fried myself on tin foil. It was a popular fad at the time, and now I regret my foolishness," I said.

I hoped I hadn't damaged my skin so much that he'd turn me down as a patient.

"I hate seeing a dermatologist every month," I continued. "I'm tired of my eyes looking like slits. When I'm out in the bright sun I

59

can't see well. Can you help me?" Finally, when I didn't have any breath left, I stopped speaking.

Dr. Ahmed leaned in toward me and with his index finger he lifted my brow. Next, he gently poked the skin around my eyes. Then he sat back and shared his assessment.

"The laser procedure will take off the top layer of your skin. It will feel baby soft. If you're careful, you won't have to worry about skin cancer anymore. The laser procedure will raise your eyebrows and make you look younger. It should also lessen the puffiness beneath your eyes. Yes, I think this is the right treatment for you.

"The laser resurfacing for the face costs $2,700. The treatment under and over the eyes costs an additional $3,900. The total cost for both procedures will be $6,000," he said.

Of course, he wanted me as a patient! He would earn $6,000 off me. I gulped. What should I do? I didn't want to spend lots of time interviewing other doctors. I'd have to gather funds from my various bank accounts. It would be a hardship, but worth it.

I nodded agreement. "Yes. Let's do it."

"You will need someone to watch over you for five days after the procedure," he said. He pushed his glasses back on his nose and made some notes on my file. He was very handsome. No wonder there were so many female patients lined up to see him in the waiting room. I looked at his left hand. Was he wearing a wedding ring? He was. Too bad. I would have liked to date him.

He looked up from his notes. I hoped he didn't see me blush.

"You'll be wearing bandages, so stay away from the bank," he said. "The security guard will think you're holding them up." He laughed at his own joke.

Bandages? Enough to scare a security guard? Dr. Ahmed must have seen the horrified expression on my face because he added hastily, "You will look like a mummy for a few days, but after awhile you will look beautiful. And no more skin cancer."

"I can handle looking like a mummy for a short time, but I will have to find some place for Jack and me to stay and for that person to care for me."

"Is Jack your husband? Why can't he take care of you?"

I laughed. "Jack is better than any husband. He's my pet rabbit and he wouldn't be able to cook meals for me. I really want this procedure, though. I'll call my friend Francine tonight. She house-sits and might be able to watch over Jack and me."

I booked the procedure with Dr. Ahmed and crossed my fingers, hoping that Francine would be available. Mary Ann had just left on a lengthy business trip. Dang. Bad timing for me. But I was determined to get this treatment as soon as possible.

Francine wasn't a professional nurse. I first met her when she was a caregiver for my best friend Dorie, who was dying from cancer. Francine lived with Dorie for the last six months of her life. Dorie felt safe with Francine because she anticipated all her needs without her having to ask. That was important because Dorie was a generous soul who never asked for much in life.

Whenever I visited Dorie, she asked me about myself. Never once did I hear her complain about her pain. Even when she lost her long, thick hair to the cancer she was still more concerned about how I was doing.

I knew Dorie must be anxious and fearful about dying, despite being in so much pain. We'd been very close and shared so much over the years. When she didn't tell me how she was really feeling, I felt sad. Left out. I knew she didn't want to burden me, but I wanted to be there for her.

Somehow being with Francine made it easier for Dorie and me to spend a lot of time together. Francine knew we were close friends, so she knew when to disappear and leave us alone. But when Dorie needed Francine for pain management, she was always nearby to respond.

When Francine read passages from the Bible, like *"Casting all your care on Him, for He cares for you,"* her soothing voice comforted both of us. When Dorie tried to hide her pain, Francine held her hand and encouraged me to hold her other hand. Francine was such a good listener. I hoped Dorie confided in her when I wasn't there.

Francine loved health food and exercise so when Dorie slept, she walked her dog Barnabus through the rolling hills north of Sunset Boulevard. Sometimes I went with her. As soft-spoken and intuitive as Francine was, her dog Barnabus was the opposite. He barked loudly and lunged at people.

The first time I met him, he jumped on me, almost knocking me over. A very large Dalmatian, he weighed more than 70 lbs. His ears stood up straight, which I saw as a sign of aggression, and I was always afraid he was going to attack me. His watchdog alertness intimidated me.

Barnabus's dark brown eyes matched Francine's. He had smooth fur that was soft to the touch, but I never petted him unless she was there. His long legs ran up the rolling hills, dragging us along behind him.

Whenever Francine pulled on the leash to slow him down, he sped up. When he saw another dog, he growled and barked and pulled against the chain. Francine struggled to hold on. What would happen if he got loose? I was always afraid he would. Then what?

One day, a friend knocked on Dorie's door.

"Hi," he yelled. "It's Dick here. I'm coming in."

He opened the door a few inches slowly and peeked inside the room to see if we were home. Barnabus raced across the hardwood floors and lunged for Dick's legs. Luckily, Francine stepped between Dick and the beast or he would have bitten off a hunk of Dick's flesh.

Knowing that Barnabus would be there with Francine made it challenging to ask her about letting Jack and me stay with her for a few days. I couldn't think of anyone else who could take care of us. I really wanted to have the laser procedure. She was my only hope.

❋❋❋

I had booked the procedure without knowing whether Francine would consent. That's how excited I was. I telephoned her that night with an offer to compensate her for her care.

"How about $50 a day plus enough food to feed Barnabus and me?" she suggested.

Good grief! Barnabus was a huge dog. He'd eat more than Bernie and Martin combined. Why should I pay for her dog's food? Somehow, I had imagined that she would put us up as a personal favor. But I was mistaken. I was also desperate.

"I guess that will be OK," I agreed. After all, she was in the caregiver business and knew the going rate.

"Jack will need to stay outside during the daytime," Francine said. "He can stay in the enclosed patio at night."

"Francine, I need assurance that Jack will be safe while I'm staying with you. Barnabus can be an aggressive dog and no way do I want your dog to attack and harm Jack. Frankly, I'm always afraid he will jump up on me and knock me down. After all, I'm paying you to take care of me and that also includes Jack. Either you guarantee our safety, or I will find another suitable place for us." It was a gamble to say this, but I was willing to take it.

"Yes, I can understand your concerns and I'm well aware that Barnabus can be rather unruly at times, but I promise that he will behave. I will do everything possible to assure your safety. I'd like so much for you to stay with me," she replied.

"Okay, then, I feel confident that it will work out now, knowing you will have our safety as your top priority."

"It's set then. I'll expect you to arrive with Jack on Sunday afternoon. We'll get you all settled in, and I will drive you to the doctor's office early Monday morning for your procedure."

I hung up the phone hoping I'd made the right decision. If anything ever happened to Jack, I knew I'd never forgive myself.

Chapter 12
Convalescing at Francine's

Jack had only lived with me for a few weeks and I wanted him to be as comfortable as possible when we took our trip to be with Francine for my convalescence. On Sunday afternoon I went to the storage area underneath the stairway in my living room, where I'd kept most of Patches' supplies.

The wood frame for the two six-foot bunny runs would sit on top of cinderblocks and Jack's cage would be placed on top. The open cage door would connect with the enclosed bunny runs providing a protected space. Being six inches off the ground, the assembled structure would keep him safe from raccoons and other pesky animals in that area, and from Barnabus, a dog big enough to traumatize Jack if he happened to venture outside his cage. All of this would be set up in Francine's backyard.

Jack had stayed inside at my home, but now he'd have to get used to being outdoors during the day for the next week. Would he be able to cope with living outside in a strange place? I wanted peace of mind both for him and for me while I was recovering from my facial procedure.

I pulled it all out. The panels were heavy to move, and I was soon out of breath. Even though it would be a lot of work to transport the bunny runs, Jack would be able to move back and forth and get a limited amount of exercise this week.

It took me three trips to carry all the equipment to my car. From inside his cage Jack watched me work. On the third trip he shot out of the cage and raced along the carpet. I caught a glimpse of his tail as it disappeared behind the buffet in the dining room.

Smart rabbit. He knew something was different. He probably thought I was taking him to the veterinarian. I looked behind the buffet and saw him cowering.

"Hey Jack, what's up?" He looked up at me with his big brown eyes. His ears perked up. I leaned over to pet him, but he ran out from the other side of the buffet and retreated into his cage. I closed the cage door.

"I'm not giving you away," I assured him. "You're going on a little vacation, that's all."

My explanation must have satisfied him because he began to eat his hay. While he ate, I went upstairs to take a shower and wash my hair. This would be the last shampoo until the following Saturday night.

I changed into shorts, flip flops, and a cotton blouse. To complete my ensemble, I put on a straw hat over my wet hair. In the mirror, I saw what might have been a character from the Beverly Hillbillies TV show.

I snapped shut my suitcase. In another small bag, I packed my camera, tape recorder, and favorite cassette tapes. They would help me endure the long hours of being cooped up during my convalescence.

Although I owned a large Lincoln Continental, the rabbit equipment had taken up a lot of space. I packed the six-foot bunny runs and fiberglass panels in the car. One run stuck out of the passenger window in the front seat and through the driver's side backseat window. The other stuck out of the backseat passenger's window and through my window so that I had to move my seat very far forward.

My nose was almost at the dashboard. I wasn't sure how I'd drive but decided to think about that later. At least both runs were in. This diagonal direction of the bunny run meant I had to squeeze my suitcases on either side. It was a tight fit.

"Come on, Jack. Time to go." I opened the cage door. He wouldn't budge. When I tried to pull him out of the cage he slipped out of my hands and ran away from me.

"Stop, Jack!" I yelled.

He didn't listen. He raced around and then hopped through the pet door that led to the patio. When I went out to the patio, he raced past me and back into the house. There he hid behind the sofa. I found him curled him up in a furry ball. He must have been really scared.

"It's OK, Jack. You're safe." This time he let me pick him up. I held him in my arms and rocked him. He was shaking. Hoping to calm him down I sang "Mary Had a Little Lamb." He relaxed into my lap.

"Everything is going to be OK," I said. "Think of this as an adventure."

When he'd calmed down completely, Jack let me put him in his cage. I carried him out to the car and was pulling out of the driveway when I realized I'd forgotten some things.

In the house, I collected towels, bags of hay and dry food pellets. Then I saw his stuffed bunny toy and I picked that up too. Arms full, I stumbled back to the car. It looked as if we were going to be gone for a year, not just six nights.

I backed out of the driveway. With all the stuff packed into the back seat, I couldn't see out the rear-view mirror. If a policeman pulled up behind me, I wouldn't see the patrol car's lights.

I turned on the radio. The relaxing sound of "Mahler's Symphony No. 1" made me feel as if we were going for a drive in the country. Jack looked up at me as if to say, *This is going to be a nice vacation.*

✹✹✹

Francine lived in West Los Angeles on a street north of the upscale Montana Avenue shops. All of the homes on the wide street had been built in the early 1950's. There were one-story houses with flat shake roofs. Her house was white with deep forest green trim and shutters. An Ozzie and Harriet neighborhood. She even had a white picket fence enclosing the back yard. The manicured lawns had lush eucalyptus trees that looked as if the gardeners regularly tended them.

I parked on the street because I didn't want to block her driveway. Jack looked up at me expectantly.

"We've arrived," I announced. Jack jumped around excitedly in his litter box. I picked up his cage and together we went up to the front door.

At the sound of the doorbell, I heard Barnabus race across the vinyl floor. When he reached the front door, he barked. The loud noise made my heart pound. In his cage Jack raced around in circles. To stop him from being afraid, I carried his cage to the side of Francine's house hoping Jack couldn't hear the barking.

Jack looked frightened. What should I do? The barking grew louder. Where was Francine? She knew we were coming and should have locked Barnabus up.

We cowered at the side of Francine's house for about a minute, but it felt like ten. I heard her open the door and call my name. I left Jack in his cage and I ran to the front of the house.

"Where's Jack?" she asked, smiling. It seemed like nothing bothered her. Despite all the commotion, her round face and big brown eyes looked serene.

"I left Jack over there," I said, pointing to the side of her house. "He's very afraid."

She looked confused. Behind her, Barnabus pawed the floor like an angry bull. His bark became a growl. *What if she couldn't hold on to him?* I thought, visualizing a vicious attack.

"Sorry, Judy, I thought Barnabus was outside," she said. She tugged the dog's collar with all the strength in her petite frame. After she yanked him away, she slammed the door.

"I'll be back in a minute," she yelled through the closed door.

I heard her escort Barnabus out to the back yard. If she was being too laid back, this arrangement might not work, but what choice did I have? Mary Ann was out of town and unavailable. Jack and I were stuck.

I went back to the side of the house where I'd left Jack. I took him out of his cage and held him in my arms.

"She knew we were coming," I whispered. "She should have locked the dog up before we arrived. I won't let anybody hurt you."

Hoping to signal that I was protecting him, I rocked Jack's small body in my arms. He wouldn't stop shaking.

I looked at my watch. Five minutes passed. Then ten minutes. Finally, I heard her open the front door again. I didn't hear Barnabus, which meant it was probably safe to return to the front door.

My hair was a mess. Jack was keeping his ears close to his head, which meant he was still frightened. Surely we both looked frazzled, but if Francine noticed, she didn't say anything. I decided to set her straight.

"Rabbits can have a heart attack from fright, Francine. This isn't a good beginning to our time together." I knew my voice was caustic, but I couldn't stop myself. "You knew we were coming. Barnabus should have been out of sight and restrained. He scared both of us."

At least she seemed remorseful to see me upset.

"I'm so sorry, Judy. Follow me."

My anger dissipated, I followed her to an enclosed patio. She pointed at a rug.

"Put Jack's cage there," she said.

I looked through the sliding glass door and saw Barnabus. He was pacing back and forth outside. He wasn't barking, just whining loudly as if to say, *I want to come in and be with you.*

I took a towel out of my bag and placed it over the side of Jack's cage. I didn't want him to see Barnabus.

"Francine, please play some classical music," I asked. "It will calm both of us."

She rifled through her cassette tapes and finally chose one and slid it in the cassette player. I heard violins and flutes playing. I took a deep breath. I loved *Sanctus* by the Cambridge Singers. Jack cocked his ear as if to hear the music better.

Together Francine and I unloaded my car. It took us four trips. The whole time, Barnabus ran underfoot. I almost tripped over him as I set the bunny runs on top of the cinder blocks under a shady tree outside the bedroom where I'd be convalescing.

On our last trip out to the car, I opened the gate. Barnabus dashed past me. I couldn't stop him before he ran into the street. Francine ran after him.

"Stop!" she yelled. Barnabus stopped in the middle of the street. Then he saw a lady walking her poodle. Naturally, he raced up to them and barked.

"Aieeee!" the lady screamed as if screaming might do any good. A car suddenly turned onto the street.

"STOP!" Francine screamed as if *her* screaming might stop Barnabus or maybe the car or maybe both.

The car's horn honked loudly but the driver didn't stop.

The lady with the poodle put her hand to her throat and opened her mouth but no more screams came out. Francine stamped her foot.

"Come!" she yelled. Thank God, Barnabus obeyed and ran back toward the curb. The car swerved, barely missing him.

I let out my breath. My heart was pounding. That was a close call. The car only missed hitting him by a couple of inches. I might not like Barnabus, but I certainly didn't want him to be killed. More than that, I didn't want it to be my fault that he'd died.

"Mind your dog!" the poodle's owner demanded. "I could have had a heart attack."

Francine and I looked at each other. We both snickered but managed to contain our laughter until we reached the back yard. We were laughing so hard we fell onto the lawn in a heap. Barnabus barked happily while he ran back and forth between us. All the animosity I'd felt earlier disappeared.

After I finished unpacking everything, I took Jack on a tour of Francine's house. In the back yard, I showed him the bunny run that I'd set up under the oak tree.

"This is where you'll be living in the daytime," I said. "I'll be living on the other side of that window."

I placed Jack's cage down at the beginning of the bunny run. I opened the cage door.

"Meet me at the end!" I shouted. I ran alongside the wooden wire pathway. He followed my lead. When he reached the other end of the wooden wire bunny run, I held out an apple slice.

"Good boy!" I praised.

He gobbled up his delicious treat. He'd never tasted an apple before. I placed more apple slices in his food bowl at the other end of the bunny run. He raced down the wooden wire pathway into his cage to eat them.

"Apples are good for you," I said. "I'll make sure to feed you more."

Francine came outside. She'd changed her clothes and was wearing a long plaid skirt with a bright red top and boots. She looked like a Christmas stocking.

"Jack, I'm going out to dinner with Francine," I explained. I was concerned that he might be frightened because this was his first time being alone here. I didn't want him to think that I was going to abandon him, the way that his previous owners had.

"We'll be back soon."

On the way to dinner we stopped at the ATM and I withdrew enough money to pay Francine for her caretaking fees.

"Let's go to El Torito," I suggested, after I paid her the cash. "I'm treating."

Framed photographs of folk dancers livened up the restaurant's entrance. A hostess dressed in a colorful Mexican peasant blouse and ruffled skirt led us to a table near the dance floor. The piped-in Latin American music made me want to dance, but we were there to eat.

I gulped down my salty, sweet margarita. All the stress of the day fell away. Everything was going to work out. The waitress took our order. Francine had a cheese burrito. I stuffed myself on a tostada, chips, and guacamole. This would be the last solid food that I could eat until the doctor took the bandages off. For dessert, we split a chocolate mud pie with ice cream.

I excused myself to go to the restroom. My meal had been delicious but messy. Out of the corner of my eye I saw Martin near the front entrance. He had a new girl with him. He must be cheating on his wife again. I took a detour and walked toward the couple.

"My goodness," I said, feigning shock. "Isn't this something to find you here?" I smiled innocently.

The expression on his face looked like he'd swallowed a turtle. He looked over at the girl as if to reassure her that I was just an acquaintance. Nobody special.

"We had such good times together," I mused, wistfully.

"Oh, uh, hi, Judy, how are you doing?" he stammered.

I glanced at his girlfriend. "Martin and I were very good friends for quite a while," I said to her with a wink, adding in a low voice, "If you know what I mean."

The girl appeared to be confused as she looked up at Martin with a peeved expression on her face. I wondered if she knew that Martin was married, and for a moment I debated whether or not I should tell her. Martin took her arm and pulled her away from me and led her towards the bar.

"Nice seeing you again, Judy," Martin called back hurriedly over his shoulder. He was uncomfortable and that made me happy.

Since the bar was on the way to the restroom, I followed them, hoping to make him even more uneasy. He leaned over and whispered in the girl's ear. I wanted to save the girl from feeling as much pain as I had felt when I had found out about his wife. Then at the last minute I decided that it wasn't my business.

"The food is great here," I murmured as I passed them on my way to the restroom.

"I saw you talking to that couple," Francine commented when I returned to our table. "Did they upset you?"

"He's someone I used to date, but I stopped seeing him when I realized he was married and stepping out on his wife."

"Oh, one of *those*," she said. "Good riddance. You sure don't need a man like that!"

"What I feel badly about is that he's probably lying to this new girl, too. I chose not to tell her the truth, but maybe I should have."

The waitress had brought our bill and I paid it. On the way out, I saw Martin and his new girl arguing. Hopefully she'd asked him some hard questions and learned the truth.

When we returned home, Jack was very happy to see me. He ran back and forth in his bunny run. I picked him up.

"Remember Martin? I set him straight tonight."

Maybe it was my imagination but I'm sure Jack smiled. I hugged him.

"Jack, you're going to spend the night on Francine's patio where it's nice and warm," I said. "No mean animals can bother you there." I picked up his cage and took him inside.

I had set up his 12 X 14 foot fiberglass fortress on Francine's patio before dinner. When I set Jack down, he raced across the floor, but couldn't see the other side of the fence, so bumped his nose.

"Oops," I chided him gently, "Be careful. Watch where you're going."

I unpacked his stuffed rabbit and cylinder tube and set them down inside the structure that I had brought from home and was now in Francine's patio. I picked up Jack and pointed to the cylinder.

"That's where I want you to hide from the prying eyes of Barnabus," I said. "I even brought your stuffed toy."

I placed him back in the fortress expecting him to be excited about his toys, but he ignored both. Instead, he jumped into his litter box and ate some hay.

In the other room, I heard Barnabus whine. Oh, no! He knew that a rabbit had invaded his home turf. Francine jumped up and closed the doors.

"I'll have to introduce you to Barnabus," I explained to Jack. "You have never met a dog before, much less a huge Dalmatian. Don't be scared. I'm here to protect you."

"I'll try playing some classical music," Francine said. "Maybe that will settle Barnabus down. It worked before for you and Jack."

It didn't work

Barnabus whined louder. However, the music calmed

Jack and me. He ignored the dog's whining and played with his stuffed bunny.

In the other room I could hear Francine talking in a low voice. It took her twenty minutes to quiet Barnabus. She stuck her head around the door.

"Ready, Judy?" she asked, tentatively.

"Just a minute. I have an idea that will make it easier for Jack to meet Barnabus."

I picked Jack up backwards, so he couldn't see where we were going. In the living room, Francine was holding Barnabus by his collar, but it looked as if he might drag her over to where we were standing. Instinctively, I put my hand protectively behind Jack's head.

"Hold on to him!" I shouted. The huge dog was whining again, louder than before, as loud as a police siren.

"Hold on! Don't let him attack us!" I looked anxiously for an escape route.

"I have him under control," Francine asserted. "You and Jack don't have to worry."

"I thought I was going to have to make a run for it," I said with a nervous laugh.

Holding Jack firmly, I walked slowly and cautiously toward Barnabus. He was still tugging on the leash, but Jack couldn't see him and remained calm. I turned Jack's face around, so he could see Barnabus.

The huge beast pulled back his head and lunged. Oh my gosh! My heart almost stopped beating. Jack hid his head in my oversized sweater. I couldn't imagine what his little bunny heart was doing.

"Barnabus!" Francine yelled. "STOP!"

She grabbed his neck with both hands. When he continued to lunge, Francine clamped her legs around each side of his giant body.

Jack dived under my armpit. Only his little patootie stuck up in the air.

Francine's legs wrapped around his body seemed to control Barnabus. He quit whining and finally lay down on the floor quietly. I rocked Jack. A couple of minutes passed

"Jack, shall we try this once more?" I asked hesitantly. This time we stood across the room. Slowly, I tried to turn Jack's head around again, but he wouldn't look at Barnabus.

"I'm going to take Jack out to the patio," I announced to Francine. "We've all had enough excitement for one day."

In the middle of the night I woke up and decided to make sure Jack was doing okay. He was awake. His eyes followed me when I entered the room. He was nestled between his towels and seemed to be expecting me. The backyard lights gave off an eerie glow.

I wrapped my blanket tighter around me and picked him up gently for some cuddling.

"My procedure is today. I hope you'll recognize me when I'm wearing bandages."

I wasn't sure that Jack understood what I was saying but he fell asleep in my arms. Everything was going to work out.

by Eloise Donnelly

Chapter 13
The New Me

"I've never had a serious treatment done on my face before," I told the nurse.

I was lying on the operating table. No makeup. The nurse had pinned back my hair with ugly bobby pins. A sheet covered my body up to my collar bone. The bright surgical lights made my eyes squint. I must have looked terrible.

Dr. Ahmed appeared over me. When he smiled, my heart fluttered. Even though he had white hair, for a moment, I thought he could be an older version of Pierce Brosnan.

Good grief, I thought. *I seem to have an obsession with this male ideal for a human Mr. Right.*

"I've been doing this for 25 years," he assured me. "I'll take my time and do a very thorough job for you." He squeezed my hand.

I focused my eyes on a big round clock on the sterile white wall. It showed 9:05 A.M. If I didn't wake up for several hours, I'd know he'd been very thorough.

"I hope you have lots of warm blankets for me when I wake up," I mumbled. "I hate being cold."

I'd given him a cassette of Pachelbel's Canon to play during the procedure. In the background, the violins relaxed me with this beautiful music. The doctor's handsome face was the last thing I saw before the sedative knocked me out.

✳✳✳

When I woke up, the same violins were playing another selection. It was almost as if no time had passed. I looked over at the clock. I'd been sedated for two hours. I reached up my hand to touch my face and felt bandages. The skin underneath the bandages felt hot, as if I'd fallen asleep in the sun for hours. A nurse handed me a mirror. My skin hurt so badly that I hesitated. Then I shrugged my shoulders. I might as well get it over with. I forced myself to look into the mirror.

Gauze and tape covered nearly every centimeter of my face and neck. It stretched up a few inches above my hairline and was tied in a big bow. Where my eyes should have been, there were two holes shaped like eggs. Below my nostrils, two smaller holes allowed me to breathe. Across my mouth, a mean slit grimaced. That little bit of my skin that wasn't bandaged looked bright red. This awful jack o'lantern mask matched how I felt inside.

"You'll be wearing this mask for five days," Dr. Ahmed explained. "But don't go to a bank while you're wearing bandages. The security guard will think you're holding them up."

I nodded weakly. He had used this same joke for 25 years. He must have forgotten that he told it when we first discussed the procedure.

Maybe this was his idea of doctor humor, but I didn't laugh. A bank robber would have been an improvement over the unhappy clown face I saw in the mirror.

I tried to give him a smile, but I couldn't. The bandages were too tightly wrapped. I couldn't move any facial muscles. I took a deep breath. Heat radiated off my skin. I put both hands on either side of my head as if I could stop the burning, but I couldn't. I felt miserable and a little sorry for myself.

Francine gave me a ride home from the doctor's office. I nodded off. That's how tired I felt. Too tired even to visit Jack. He'd have to wait to see me until after I got some rest. I slipped into the bed, careful to keep my face up. Francine fetched some ice cubes and a washcloth. She placed the ice pack on my head.

Aaaahh… The cold relieved some of the burning. I felt somewhat better. She stuffed hand towels around my face and neck so the ice wouldn't leak onto the sheets, and left more ice cubes in a bowl on the bedside table. Then she tiptoed out and gently closed the door. As I drifted off to sleep, I remembered that I should have asked her to visit Jack while I was away. I napped.

***

The noise of a lawnmower woke me. Francine's gardeners had arrived.

Oh, no! Jack was outside. In the bunny run. I looked out the bedroom window. He was crouched down in his litter box as if that would help him escape the loud noise. Jack was not used to such a racket. It was always quiet at our home. I had to rescue him.

Forgetting the cold pack on my face, I bolted towards the bedroom door. The ice pack fell to the floor. I didn't pick it up. I had to hurry. Jack needed me. I rushed out the back door and across the lawn. When Jack saw me, he ran in circles around the inside of his litter box.

"Jack don't worry – it's me. I'm here to take you into the house where it's quiet." I reached down inside his cage and with one hand under his furry chest and the other hand under his rump, I lifted him up and out of his litter box. Together we headed towards the patio.

Even before I opened the patio door, Barnabus began barking at us. Oh, no! To get to the living room I would have to pass by him. Where the heck was Francine?

What if Barnabus didn't recognize me behind the bandages? What if he thought I was a burglar?

Slowly, inch by inch, I opened the patio door. Jack wiggled in my arms.

"Shhh. Stop it," I commanded, firmly but in a reassuring tone. "I'll protect you."

To keep Jack safe, I turned around and entered the room backwards. I couldn't see Barnabus, but I heard him bounding across the vinyl floor. I braced myself for impact.

Barking loudly, the beast jumped on my back. His huge paws almost knocked me over. I yanked my head around to scold him but before a word came out of my mouth, he pushed against me. I held strong but the skin on my face beneath my bandages pulled tight.

"Arrggh!" I screamed. "Barnabus – STOP! You're hurting me!"

My yelling scared Jack. He jumped out of my arms, but I caught him midair and saved him before he hit the floor. The last thing I needed was Barnabus biting poor little Jack.

With my left hand, I thrust Jack high over my head. Then carefully I shuffled past Barnabus and towards freedom. When I reached the living room, we would finally be safe. With my right hand, I grabbed the door handle.

When Barnabus jumped again, Jack and I slipped through the door before his paws landed on us. Thankfully, his paws landed on the wood frame.

I sat down on the sofa, laying Jack down on the corduroy pillow beside me. To make sure he couldn't escape, I held him firmly. My whole body was shaking. I started to cry. Salty tears fell inside my bandages, stinging the skin stretched across my burned face. I moaned.

"Oh my gosh! That was a close call."

Jack relaxed into my arms. I must have held him for an hour. It was hard to know the time. I didn't have a clock.

Because the gardeners were still working outside, we remained trapped inside the living room. Why wasn't Francine here? Of course, I understood that she had things to do. I didn't expect her to stay home and wait on me hand and foot. On the other hand, I was paying her, wasn't I?

My back ached but I sat up straight, my ears cocked to the door. Vigilant. Waiting. Waiting. Waiting.

✳✳✳

Finally, an hour or so later Francine strolled into the house. I was upset but there was no way she could know that from my facial expression hidden by bandages.

She smiled and handed me a large bag. I looked inside. There were a dozen cassettes and some audio books on tape. "How very thoughtful – thank you! The heat radiating off my face makes it hard for me to focus when I read. Now I have something to occupy my time."

Francine sat down on the sofa next to Jack and petted him.

"I've had an awful time with Barnabus," I confessed. "I didn't realize this was the day the gardeners were coming. I rushed outside to rescue Jack, but when I came inside, since Barnabus was in the patio, I had to pass by him on my way to the living room. He jumped on me and almost knocked me down. You do understand, since I'm paying you, that this is a business arrangement, and if either of us were injured, you'd be responsible for our medical bills."

"Oh, Judy, I'm so sorry for the hassle you went through today. I'll figure out where to put Barnabus when I leave next time."

I continued, marginally satisfied with her apology.

"It's really important for my peace of mind that you get Barnabus under control. I'm surprised that you've never gone to a dog trainer, to learn how to get him to behave, so that he won't jump on people," I chided her.

Francine gave me a look that told me she was offended.

"I'm surprised that this bothers you so much," she griped.

Then she paused, and admitted, "Perhaps you're right. I've noticed that some people seem afraid of him." Then came the usual excuse. "But he's such a sweet dog!"

Obviously, she didn't grasp how serious this was, and probably because I was her first overnight guest, she hadn't dealt with this before. She was clearly unaware of how intimidating Barnabus could be. She could not imagine the ordeal Jack and I had gone through.

"Do we need to have another understanding about our personal safety, maybe this time in writing?" I demanded.

Francine's nostrils flared, but she held her temper. I don't think anyone had ever reprimanded her before.

"Okay, I will leave Barnabus in my bedroom when I leave, if that makes you more comfortable," she promised.

"It's not just a matter of comfort. My procedure was very expensive. I have to be super careful during recovery. Another episode like today's and my skin could tear and be ruined forever. Jack could have a fatal heart attack. Please understand that this issue with Barnabus is a lot more serious than you think, but thank God it's only for a week."

❋❋❋

The next day, Barnabus whined and clawed her bedroom door, but at least Jack and I felt safer. For the next four days, Jack and I stayed out of the dog's way.

In the morning, I brought Jack into my room to visit me. I placed him on a bath towel and together we listened to the books on tape and music on the audio tapes Francine had given us.

Nights were hard. Jack slept in his cage on the patio and I missed him. My face hurt. The ice pack the doctor prescribed was cold and dripped. Sleep didn't come easily. To relax, I listened to the tapes. Most nights I didn't doze off until two or three o'clock in the morning.

By the time I woke up each day about 9 A.M., the ice packs had melted. Cold damp water soaked my pillowcase. Each morning Francine brought me clean, dry bath towels. I wrapped one towel around my head and put another on top of the pillowcase.

Francine carted off the soaked towels and put them in the dryer. Then she brought me juice, yogurt, or a protein drink. Our routines began to be in synch.

By Thursday, I was well enough to visit with Jack in the backyard. The warm sun felt wonderful. I fed Jack a piece of banana. He ate it quickly, then looked at me expectantly. He wanted more. I showed him my empty hands.

Once he realized he wasn't going to get any more banana, he turned his back on me and ate some hay. The sun went behind a cloud and made me feel chilly. I wanted to spend more time with Jack outside.

I was sick of looking at the four walls in my bedroom. I hadn't heard Barnabus bark or whine, so maybe Francine had taken him for a walk. I decided to take a chance.

I bundled up Jack for a trip to the living room. Our first fifteen minutes there were peaceful. No sooner did I think we would continue sitting quietly than I heard Barnabus nudge open the bedroom door. Obviously, Francine had left the door ajar, which is why he was now bothering us. I was angry that she hadn't kept her promise. He sauntered towards the couch, sniffing the air.

Oh no! I'd better not take a chance with Jack's safety. I was sitting on the low sofa. What if Barnabus grabbed Jack off my lap before I could stop him?

I stood up on the couch cushions holding Jack above my head. The cushions were soft, and it was difficult to maintain my footing. Afraid that I'd topple over, I took a chance and sat down again, despite my concerns.

Immediately Barnabus put both of his huge front paws on the couch. He towered above us. I leaned over Jack, protecting him with my whole body.

"SIT!" I shouted to the beast. "You're supposed to leave us alone."

To my surprise, Barnabus listened. He sat down on the floor next to where we were sitting, but his body swayed back and forth. Saliva dripped from his gaping mouth. His teeth were big and sharp. His breath smelled foul. I maintained stern eye contact.

"Sit still!" I commanded.

Once again, Barnabus surprised me by staying put. I sighed. Maybe there was hope. It was cold outside. I really wanted us all to be friends. If Jack and I could trust Barnabus, maybe we could all spend more time together in the warmth of the living room.

Suddenly Barnabus shifted. He leaned over and sniffed my arm. I felt warm liquid seep down into my lap. Jack was so scared that he'd peed on me.

"Lucky you," I said to him. "I have to pee and I can't get to the bathroom until Francine comes home."

I dared not move. Next time, Barnabus might do more than smell my arm. He might move quickly to bite Jack. It was a standoff! The longer I sat there, the more uncomfortable I became. I was desperate to go to the bathroom. Jack's pee smelled. It was sticky. Barnabus kept slobbering. The skin on my face hurt.

I looked at the clock and watched the second-hand move. It was 4:15 P.M.

Time passed slowly. Very slowly. Where was Francine? My back ached from sitting in one position for such a long time.

At 4:45, Francine breezed into the house, cheerful and clueless. It had been a long and stressful half hour for both Jack and me. I burst out crying.

She clucked like a mother hen as she escorted her big baby, Barnabus, to the bedroom that she'd promised to lock him in before leaving the house. *Is she really that absent-minded?* I thought. A tongue-lashing would have to wait. I had bigger priorities.

I handed Jack to her and raced to the bathroom, explaining, "Emergency. Gotta pee."

Whew! What a relief. Now it was time for some tough love.

"Francine, what's with Barnabus being loose? He was supposed to be locked away from us when you're not home. I'm glad the week is almost over. You have tried to help me with ice packs and bringing tapes, and I appreciate your hospitality, but you have not done well with the safety measures we agreed on."

"Guilty as charged," she said meekly. "I'm putting in the effort, but Barnabus is a handful."

"That's a feeble excuse. All you needed to do was close the bedroom door tightly behind you. I strongly suggest that you spend the money I'm paying you to hire a dog trainer."

I didn't give her a chance to protest. I was in no mood to argue. I was angry and felt icky. I took Jack back to my room to clean up.

As I left the room I stated with strong emphasis, "If there's another problem here, I'm going to ask for a refund of the money I paid you. All of this trouble with Barnabus was not ever supposed to happen. We had an agreement at the beginning that you would provide a safe place for us."

I plopped Jack down on my unmade bed where he sat and watched me change my clothes. When I was clean, warm, and dry again I picked him up.

"You're such a good boy."

I put his furry face next to mine and nuzzled it. His whiskers made me want to sneeze.

"I do love you."

Jack licked my cheek. He didn't seem to mind that a bandage was in the way. Although I couldn't feel his little tongue directly on my skin, I felt his love traveling directly to my heart.

In spite of all the hassle, he'd forgiven me.

By Eloise Donnelly

Chapter 14
Goodbye to Barnabus

On Saturday, the fifth day of my convalescence, it was finally time for the bandages to come off. Francine drove me to Dr. Ahmed's office. Carefully, he peeled the gauze away. When he finished, he handed me a mirror. Oh my gosh, my face was fiery red!

Now I understood why my face had been radiating heat all week. The laser had removed the top layer of my skin. Although I wasn't thrilled that I looked like a cooked lobster, I was relieved to know why my face had felt so hot all the time.

"Stay out of the sun," Dr. Ahmed warned. "Use lots of this 45+ sunscreen for protection." He handed me a sample. "Wear a hat at all times outdoors, even if the sun isn't out. Your skin is going to itch. Do NOT scratch. It is very important not to injure your face. No matter how much it itches, you must keep your hands away from your face. At night, wear light cotton gloves so you don't accidentally scratch in your sleep. It will take a few months for the redness to diminish."

Francine drove me back to her house to pack up my clothes and Jack's stuff. He was outdoors in his bunny run.

"Time to go home," I called to him. He ignored me. That hurt my feelings. Jack didn't understand the pain I'd been through.

"I'll deal with you later," I promised. "Right now, I have to finish packing."

The week had been an ordeal. I was tired. I forced a smile and a cheerful attitude and thanked Francine again for her hospitality. Francine helped me greatly as she loaded most of my gear, probably feeling guilty for all the hassle with Barnabus I'd had that week. She understood that I really needed assistance with packing so as to not injure my face in the process.

After I loaded Jack, his cage, bunny run elements, fiberglass panels, and our luggage into the car, I waved goodbye. I relaxed my insincere smile and turned the key in the ignition.

"Let's go home, Jack."

✳✳✳

After struggling with the big, bulky fiberglass panels for Jack's fortress I decided that I needed another type of pen in case I needed to travel with him in the future. The answer was a folding plastic-coated wire frame that could be braced against an inside or outside wall. The enclosure gave plenty of room for his litter box, water bowl, food dish, a cutout box and tube for hiding, and other toys.

I could drape netting over the top to protect him from hawks.

His permanent pen in the living room would be sturdier, leading to his outside pen on the patio through the pet door.

Two weeks after the procedure I was still hiding away in my house. My only company was Jack and my roommate, Mary Ann. She was back in town and I was grateful for her help. She was nice enough to do some shopping for me. As a nurse, she had seen plenty of skin conditions, so she was very understanding about my treatment.

One afternoon on my way back from the mailbox, my nosy neighbor Diane stopped me.

"What did you do to your face? You shouldn't be out in the sun. If you're not careful, it's going to blister," she scolded.

Just my luck. Before going outside, I had looked out the front window to be sure no one was around, but Diane had appeared out of nowhere.

"It's no big thing," I replied defensively.

"No big thing? Your face looks like a fire engine."

"I think I hear the phone ringing," I said, my fingers crossed. Hopefully Jesus would excuse my little fib. The last thing I needed was Diane gossiping about me with the other neighbors.

I went upstairs to look at my face in the bright light of the bathroom mirror. My skin was still red. Maybe not fire engine red exactly, more like a beefsteak tomato. I didn't want anyone to see me looking like this. I was afraid they'd say I'd made a mistake by having the procedure done and make me explain why.

Childhood memories of being called an ugly duckling assaulted me. "You're unattractive and dumb. You're going to have to improve your character to compensate," Mother often said. Maybe she'd meant well, but it had hurt my feelings.

Was that true? Was I still an ugly duckling? I went back into the bathroom and examined my face in the mirror again. My eyes looked refreshed. My skin was tighter, younger. Surely, I looked better. Or was I kidding myself? Dr. Ahmed had assured me the redness would fade over time. Maybe I was just too impatient to see the final result.

The real test would come this weekend. Before the surgery, I'd signed up for a Cinema Retreat at St. Andrew's Abbey, hoping some single men would be there. Maybe I shouldn't go, but I'd already paid a deposit and if I was a no-show, I would lose my money.

The night before my retreat, I dreamed about my dear friend Dorie when she was dying yet was surrounded by her loving family and friends.

I woke up suddenly. The clock said 3:00 A.M. She'd been gone for four years, but I still missed her.

What would happen if *I* had a crisis or serious illness?

Would *my* friends be there for me? Or would they abandon me?

I picked up the big Teddy bear Dorie gave me and let myself cry.

I fell asleep with my arms wrapped around my bear.

Chapter 15
Retreat at the Abbey

The next morning, saying goodbye to Jack wasn't as hard as I thought it would be. He knew I loved him. He would be able to handle my being gone for the weekend. He might enjoy some alone time. Mary Ann promised to feed him. I cleaned out his cage and gave him a farewell hug.

I knew the way to St. Andrew's Abbey. I didn't need a map, having gone to many retreats over the years. The Abbey is a Roman Catholic Benedictine monastery in the northern foothills of the San Gabriel Mountains. Originally located in China, in 1952 they were forced to leave when the Communists took over. They relocated to Valyermo, California in 1955.

The monastery still abides by the Rule of St. Benedict. The monks ascribe to "seek nothing but the love of Christ." Their retreats allow lay people like me to experience their ordered way of life.

I wasn't a Catholic. I was a Presbyterian, but Father Francis allowed me to join the Abbey as an Oblate in 1996. He knew I wanted to bring the Rule of St. Benedict into my daily life.

To reach the Abbey would take over two hours. It's a long way but I like driving through the desert and leaving the city and all its cares behind. After a few freeway transfers, the roads became smaller. Now that I was driving on a two-lane road, it felt like I was on vacation.

I passed antique shops, thrift shops, and a Hungarian sausage factory. I couldn't believe how many car repair shops I saw. Maybe in the heat of the desert lots of cars broke down. I sure hoped mine wouldn't.

On the last part of the drive I always stop at Charlie Brown's Farm. They make good coffee and offer real cream. On my return trip, I would stop again to order a date shake and a barbeque beef sandwich to eat at home. Yum.

The last turn onto Longview Drive winds through the hills towards Valyermo. The road leading up to the Abbey is lined with apple trees.

I drove past a sign that read:

♥ *NO HUNTING EXCEPT FOR PEACE* ♥

I pulled up to the stone building and parked in front of the stairs leading up to the retreat office. Brother Benedict greeted me. I checked in and they assigned me room #14.

It's always the luck of the draw when you opt to share a double room. Those rooms are available for couples, but some of us on a budget try to cut corners. I've been really lucky so far with a compatible lady.

Looking around my assigned room, I noticed that my roommate had already arrived. She had put her suitcase on the bed near the patio. I set my suitcase down on the floor next to the other bed. We could coin-toss for the bed later.

I opened the curtains and sliding glass door and breathed in the hot air of the desert and the scene before me, which refreshed my soul.

A wild rabbit hopped by. *Jack, are you sending me a message?* I mused. *Will you send me another one before the weekend is over?*

The intense heat of the desert made my face itch, so I decided to drive to a pharmacy in nearby Palmdale. I bought ice and Benadryl. The cream is to be used topically on the skin and there's also a liquid version for children. I purchased two bottles of the liquid planning to double the dose for adult use.

When I returned to the room, my roommate was there and introduced herself as Crystal.

"This is my first time here," she said. "I found the Abbey on the Internet and decided that coming to a movie retreat was a good idea, but I had some doubts until the office said there was air conditioning. That's a must in the Mojave desert."

"Glad to meet you, Crystal. I'm Judy. I've been coming to these movie retreats for the last fifteen years, and they're lots of fun."

Crystal suddenly exclaimed, "Oh, my! Forgive me, Judy! I didn't ask you which bed you'd like to have."

This is definitely going to work out, I mused. I explained to my courteous new friend that I didn't have a preference.

She pointed to my face.

"I recognize *that* look," she said, with a knowing smile. "No fun being a lobster is it?"

"Right, but I don't think lobsters have pain and itch that goes with facial resurfacing. That procedure was done a week ago," I replied. "I bought ice and Benadryl to help me get through recovery."

"What a coincidence! I had the same procedure two years ago to remove a lot of ugly acne scars."

I was highly relieved that she had confessed this as I realized that she would be sympathetic to my situation. As we talked, I dumped the ice into my ice chest. I placed some ice in a washcloth and pressed it against my face.

"Aaaahhh," I sighed as the cold pack alleviated some of the itching. Afterwards I slathered on a thin layer of Benadryl. I also drank a few ounces of it.

Once the pain and itching became bearable, I put some fresh ice in a washcloth. Then I wrapped a hand towel around it to prevent the ice pack from dripping on me during Vespers. Crystal and I left together so I could show her the location of the Chapel.

Singing the songs helped me feel God's presence. I felt peaceful. Transported. This was why I'd come on the retreat.

After Vespers, when I strolled into the dining room, Bob and Wendy Avery nodded in my direction. I knew them from past retreats. Since the first part of the meal was in silence, I sat at a different table.

The buffet, as usual, made my mouth water. I was hungry. I heaped fish, rice, and mixed vegetables on my plate and took a small glass of wine. When I finished my meal, I returned to the buffet to get some chocolate ice cream. I ate it quickly because my face was starting to itch again. I would have to return to my room to freshen up my ice pack.

Going back to the room I retrieved more ice from the cooler and drank a little more Benadryl even though I couldn't tell if it was helping yet. When I reached the lounge, the opening credits of that night's film, *Saving Private Ryan,* rolled on the screen. I slipped into a seat at the back of the room.

An hour into the movie, I snuck back into my room and drank some more Benadryl before returning to my seat. The Benadryl, even though it was the children's version, was making me sleepy. The glass of wine I had at dinner might also have contributed to my feeling a little light-headed. If a police officer gave me a drug test, I probably wouldn't have been able to walk in a straight line. Good thing I wasn't driving to my room later.

This was a *long* movie. At the two-hour mark, once again I slipped out of the lounge to refresh my ice pack. I drank a little more Benadryl. Between using it topically on my skin and drinking some, I was feeling relief.

The clapping at the end of the movie startled me. I sat up quickly. Oh my gosh, I had dozed off. I didn't have the slightest idea about what had happened in the last hour of the film. I hoped I hadn't snored. During the discussion, I didn't say anything since I'd missed most of the movie.

"After you leave the lounge, remember the rule of The Grand Silence," Father Gregory, the retreat leader, announced when the discussion ended. "Please be considerate of others. No talking until after breakfast tomorrow morning."

That night as we were getting ready for bed, Crystal whispered, "I'm a sound sleeper so I probably won't hear if you need to dig into the chest to get more ice."

"Thanks," I whispered back. Even so, since I wasn't sleepy now, and out of consideration for her, I decided to fill my plastic bowl with ice and take my pillow, blanket, Benadryl, book, alarm clock, and room key to the lounge. She protested briefly but not energetically. Crystal was too drowsy to argue and let me do as I wished. I settled on the couch alongside the window.

I recalled another shared room experience where my roommate Carla confessed that she snored "like a fork in a blender" and told me to bump her leg if the snoring woke me up. No sooner did Carla drop off to sleep than the rattling fork sound began.

I bumped her leg. She turned over. All was well for a while. Then she snored again, so I did what she asked and bumped her leg again.

The third time I bumped her, Carla sat up in bed and yelled, "Judy, fleas are attacking me! This is the third time I've been bitten!"

Realizing that this could go on all night, I decided to find another place to sleep. I assured Carla that it was just her imagination, that the Abbey was very clean and bug-free, and that I was the so-called "flea" who "bit" her with a gentle bump, per her instructions.

After that, I gathered up some bedding and a pillow and headed for the couch in the lounge. Although the couch was made for sitting, not sleeping, I managed to get some rest. I was grateful that Carla's yelling hadn't disturbed the other retreaters during the Grand Silence.

Crystal was a much better roommate. Very considerate, although here I was, back on the couch. I resolved to splurge on a single room from now on.

I read for awhile and thought about Jack. I realized how much I missed him and wondered how he was doing without me. Usually we cuddled in the evenings. I missed his furry body against my face and fell asleep dreaming of when I'd see him on Sunday night.

At 4 A.M. and out of ice for my washcloth, I tiptoed back to the room and found Crystal fast asleep. I quietly put more ice in the bowl and returned to the lounge. I filled my washcloth, cooled down my burning face, and applied more Benadryl. I slept until my alarm went off at 7:15.

The theme for this film retreat was "Death and Letting Go of the Past." Over the weekend, we watched three more movies on this theme and it was perfect, just what I needed. I felt like I was in transition. At breakfast that morning I sat with Wendy. I was holding an ice cube with my left hand and eating my cereal with my right.

"I noticed your skin is very red," Wendy said. "Either you have a mighty bad sunburn or had a facial procedure."

"The latter. Now I'm wondering about the consequences."

"What do you mean by 'consequences'?"

"I don't want people judging me for doing it," I admitted.

"Nonsense," she said in a firm voice. "If people think less of you, then they are not your friends."

I felt a tear glide down my cheek. "As a young girl, I had acne scars and they embarrassed me. The laser removed them, but I still feel scarred on the inside."

"When you're finished eating, let's take a walk before the movie starts," Wendy suggested. The morning film was *Sophie's Choice*.

"Good idea," I agreed. "I have some extra bread to feed the ducks." We walked over to the pond together. The ducks saw us coming and waddled over, clucking and eager to eat our treats.

"Lately I've felt like a freak," I confessed while we fed the ducks. "Having this fiery red face this weekend doesn't help."

Photo by Teresa Lin

"I see the beauty of you on the inside," Wendy said in a gentle voice. "I know what it's like to feel the way you do right now. I once had lots of scars, but on the inside. The only way I could let go of that kind of negative self-talk was to ask God to help me through it."

"How does that work?"

We sat on a bench. She took my hand and began praying, "God, be my strength. God, be my wisdom. God, be my courage."

I'd heard these words as a prayer before, but somehow on that day, with the sun warming us, holding her hand, I felt a shift inside my heart.

"Thank you, God, for speaking through Wendy," I said out loud to the Lord, after she'd finished praying. In that moment, I felt as if I'd let go of my inner revolting self. Time to change my self-concept.

The surgery had removed my skin cancer and external scars. Now Wendy with her comforting words was helping me heal inside. God had removed the blackness of my doubts. Could I allow myself to accept this and embark on the process of becoming a swan?

✳✳✳

That afternoon, during the movie discussion, instead of shrinking into the woodwork, I raised my hand and shared my ideas about the film, *Lorenzo's Oil*. It was fun.

After the discussion, I asked Crystal if she'd like to join me to explore the grounds. I lathered SPF 70 sunscreen on my face and put on a floppy hat. We strolled along the Abbey's gravel road and visited their Arts and Crafts Center where Father Maur's newest ceramic creations were on exhibit.

Next, we visited Father Eleutherius' garden. In the early 1940's, he'd planted poplar seeds. Now they'd grown into lovely, tall trees. Beneath their shade, we found two plastic chairs. I let the steady cool breeze and the sound of the rustling leaves bring me God's peace.

I opened my Bible and prayer journal. This was the perfect place for meditation, prayer, and relaxation.

If only Jack were here. He would love this garden.

✳✳✳

That night we saw the film *Titanic* with Leonardo DiCaprio. What a romantic story, and thank God, the itching on my face had lessened considerably. I didn't have to drink Benadryl now, so I was able to stay awake for the entire film.

I watched the love story in *Titanic* with a sense of gratitude, even though my own love life was very quiet. It was as if God had given me a new set of eyes.

During the movie discussion, Crystal talked on and on about the themes she had noted in the movie. I sensed she was rather insecure and trying to prove how intelligent she was in order to impress Brad, an interesting single man I'd met at dinner the night before. I left the group to gather my things for another night on the couch.

Brad turned around. He cocked his head and smiled at me as if to ask, *Where are you going?*

I would have liked to get to know him better, but right now I needed to return to my room.

"I'll be back," I said, without any explanation.

By the time I had collected my belongings and lugged them back to the lounge, the movie discussion had ended. Bob and Wendy were the only people in the lounge. I poured myself a cup of tea and joined them on the couch.

Behind me I heard a man's voice say, "Hi, Sunshine."

I turned around and saw Brad.

"Wow – that's the first time I've ever been called Sunshine."

"You are glowing from the inside out," he said, touching my arm. "Let's just say you have a sunny disposition. What's with the bedding, if I may ask?"

"I'm roommates with Crystal," I explained. "Even though she insists that she's a sound sleeper I've chosen to come here so I can read late, get water and ice if I need it without worrying about making noise."

"Crystal is a brilliant woman but sometimes it's hard to get a word in edgewise," Brad observed.

We all chuckled knowingly. She had indeed dominated the discussion.

After a half hour of pleasant conversation, Bob and Wendy excused themselves. Brad lingered behind. He told me he was a fitness coach who lived in Encino.

“I imagine the ladies are always flirting with you,” I said. “If you were my coach, I would have a hard time concentrating.”

He laughed. “None of the gals have dropped the bar bells on my feet. That means I’m not too much of a distraction,” he joked as he stood up. “I’ll let you get some sleep,” he said. “It was nice talking to you, Judy.”

“I liked talking with you, too,” I said. What I didn’t say was that I liked him as a friend. No need for him to be Mr. Right. I was content for him to be Mr. Right Friend.

In fact, in that moment, I was remembering that back during my dating days some of my girlfriends dated wonderful men. I was glad for them, yet disappointed that those men didn’t ask me out. I seemed to attract men who were not right for me and I chose to drop them after just a few dates.

After my challenging times with Bernie and Martin and the men before them, I was finally realizing that maybe meeting Mr. Right would not be happening for me. No more need to go to all those singles’ groups anymore. *Knowing this, can I live with this conclusion?* I mused.

Yes, I will be just fine, as long as I have many friends and family and especially my beloved rabbit, Jack. All of them love me. And God loves me.

I turned off the light on the table next to the sofa. I hated having to sleep in the lounge and I missed Jack terribly. Yet I felt grateful. God had revealed to me what really mattered. That night I slept better than I had in months.

***

I awoke refreshed. I realized how grateful I was to go to the Abbey that weekend. It was not just about seeing movies but I thank God that I could be there to meet Him and learn more completely how much He cares for me; that I could trust Him to provide the strength, hope, and direction I would need to guide my footsteps in the days ahead.

After breakfast, Bob, Wendy, Brad and I exchanged phone numbers and promised each other that we’d attend a concert at Westwood Presbyterian Church together. It was one of those friendly

"I'm so glad I met you" exchanges, but I doubted any of us would follow up. Maybe we'd see each other at next year's film retreat.

I took one last look at the peaceful grounds and smiled when I saw another wild cottontail. "Thanks, Jack, for telling this rabbit to come say hello to me," I whispered.

On my drive home, I stopped at Charlie Brown's Farm for my ritual date shake. I ordered a big slab of ribs and ate one gooey portion in the parking lot. The leftovers would be for dinner. I had earned this delicious treat.

✳✳✳

I dropped my luggage on the floor of my condo's entryway.

"Hi Jack, Mama's home," I called out to him. "I really missed you. I wish you would have been my roommate, but Crystal was a good second best."

Jack looked up at me as if he didn't know me. I reached over to pick him up, but he ran away and hid behind the couch.

"What's wrong, Jack?" I said in a low and soothing voice. "Have you forgotten me already? It's only been two days. Are you mad at me because I didn't bring you with me?"

I guess my sweet talk helped because when I tried to pick him up again, he let me.

"Tonight, let's you and I have our very own film festival. We're going to watch *Babe* together," I said. "Babe is almost as cute as you are, but he's a pig."

Jack nestled into my arms and closed his eyes. Now all we needed was some buttered popcorn.

Chapter 16
Jack Escapes

The morning after the retreat I called Blue Shield Health Insurance. The switchboard operator put me on hold. As I had a long list of things to do, I turned on the speaker phone while I waited.

I set Jack's grooming brush, Laxatone medication, and syringe on the table next to the phone. The Laxatone stopped hairballs from collecting in Jack's stomach. Unlike house cats, domesticated rabbits can't cough up hairballs. It is necessary to monitor their eating and make sure they get enough fiber in their diet.

I fed Jack different kinds of hay, and that usually did the trick, but rabbits will eat everything in the house from stucco to cardboard to curtains. They chew constantly to keep their teeth sharp, not because they are hungry. That's why they need Laxatone.

I noticed this morning that he'd stopped eating. While I was at Francine's, I fed him the medication, yet hairballs must have formed anyway.

Today I would increase the dosage, giving him 0.4 cc's instead of 0.2. If he still didn't eat in the next two hours, I'd have to take him to see my vet, Dr. Rosskopf, since hairballs are a serious condition.

I finally caught Jack and picked him up. I settled him on my lap. I brushed him and cuddled him. I wanted to calm him before I gave him the medication.

I picked up the syringe and measured the dose of 0.4 cc's, but when I aimed the syringe towards him, he twitched suddenly and flipped it up. The semi-liquid medication squirted on my shirt with some going up his nose. Jack sneezed.

I heard a voice on the speaker phone.

"Hello? Hello? Anyone there?"

"Just a minute," I yelled. "I have to wipe Jack's nose."

"Do you want me to call you back?" asked the voice, clearly puzzled by my excuse.

"No – please, no!" I shouted, "I'm here. I don't want to wait on hold again."

I set Jack down on the floor. He was happy to escape the syringe. He raced across the vinyl floor and slid into the piano pedals. I was laughing when I picked up the phone receiver.

"Sorry," I said. "I was feeding my bunny some Laxatone and it got into his nose by mistake."

"Is he going to be OK?" said the voice on the other side of the line. She introduced herself as Glenda from Blue Shield.

"Yes, he's fine. I'll have to deal with him later. Here's the reason for my call. For 20 years, I went to Dr. Chai for facial skin cancer treatments. Those cost your company lots of money. But I have good news. He will never send you another bill. I had laser resurfacing. Since I won't need any more office visits, I'm hoping Blue Shield will pay for the laser treatment."

"How much was your bill?" Glenda asked.

"$6,000."

"That's a lot of money. I'm not sure we can approve that expense. I wish you had checked with us before you had the surgery."

"Think of how much money you'll save," I protested.

"I'll look into it, but I can't guarantee anything. Don't get your hopes up. Laser resurfacing is usually considered a cosmetic expense and we don't cover that."

"It wasn't cosmetic," I said. "I have had skin cancers removed over many, many years that cost Blue Shield a ton of money. Now that payout is over."

"Have your doctor send me the paperwork. Make sure he tells us why you needed the procedure." She gave me the fax number.

After I hung up with Glenda I filled another syringe with more of the Laxatone. Jack was hiding. I finally found him behind the couch. I dropped to my hands and knees. The dust from the couch's fabric made me sneeze.

I crawled over to him. He was chewing on the dust ruffle.

"Bad boy!" I scolded as I grabbed him and almost knocked the lamp off the end table.

"Jack, I'm so sorry for what happened," I said after I caught him. "Mama was distracted. I shouldn't be on the phone while I'm trying to help you."

I rocked Jack in my arms, but it took him several minutes to settle down enough to accept his weekly dose of Laxatone.

"Good for you, Jack," I said, as he licked the sweet medicine off his mouth.

✷✷✷

That afternoon I bought Jack new supplies. I climbed the steps, carrying a bag of rabbit food in one hand and an extra-large bag of hay in the other. I set the food and hay down at the top of the steps. Sweat was dripping from my brow. I wiped it off with my sleeve and retrieved a peppermint spray from my purse that I use to refresh my face. I dropped my purse, and my wallet and papers fell out.

Suddenly, out of the corner of my eye I saw a rabbit streak by.

A rabbit? How could that be? I mused in disbelief. Then reality struck.

"Jack! I left you locked in the living room. What are you doing outside?"

My neighbor Diane was on her way back from the mailboxes.

"Judy, is that your rabbit?" she shouted.

"I'm afraid so," I yelled as I ran after Jack. The front door to the condo common area was open. Oh my gosh! If he ran through that door, something disastrous could happen.

He could be run over by a car.

Or be attacked by a dog.

Or get lost.

I needed to catch him, and quickly. It was a matter of life or death.

Jack zigzagged away from the front of the condo complex door and raced towards Ginger's unit. A cat sitting on top of her patio fence hissed. Jack ran around in circles.

I stamped my foot.

"Jack!" I yelled "HOME!"

He stopped running in circles and looked at me to see if I was serious. I saw him debate whether he should obey me or keep playing. Fortunately for him, he ran towards home.

I chased after him. Oh my gosh, he moved fast. I probably wouldn't have caught him, but he ran a few laps around Diane's flower pots, giving me enough time to grab a broom leaning against the front door of my condo.

Gripping the handle like a baseball bat, I stomped over to where Jack was hiding behind the biggest flower pot.

"Mama is serious. Playtime is over," I commanded in my most authoritative voice.

He peeked out from behind the pot.

I gave him *the look.*

He decided I meant business and raced past my feet and hopped through the front door into our living room.

Then I noticed how he had escaped. He had scratched or chewed a huge hole in the screen door. I shook my finger in his face.

"Oh, Jack, I'm glad to have you home safe but you're a *very* expensive bunny."

I didn't even know whether Blue Shield would pay on my laser procedure claim and now Jack was costing me more cash to repair the door. I needed to pay attention to what he was trying to tell me. Maybe he wanted fresh air. He couldn't tolerate being inside all the time. Maybe that's why he'd gotten hairballs.

Now back in his enclosure, he was eating some of his hay. At least I wouldn't have to spend more money taking him to the vet for escape injuries.

✻✻✻

The next morning I bought a mini doggie door at Home Depot. Dave, the resident handyman, came over that afternoon. It took him two hours to install it, and another hour to repair the hole in the screen door.

After Dave left, I said, "Jack, I'm going to teach you how to use the mini doggie door." Jack didn't look happy. I must admit that I didn't have any idea if a rabbit could go through a doggie door. I had never tried to train Patches to use one.

I fetched a stuffed bunny from the living room. I always kept a few on the couch, much like other people keep throw pillows. While Jack watched, I made the stuffed bunny hop through the mini doggie door. He didn't look impressed nor did he move to go through the door himself.

Every morning for a week I made Jack watch the stuffed bunny hop through the door. The first day of the lesson, I stuck a stick through the hinges, so it would stay open. By the third day he looked at me as if to say, *Why must I watch a stuffed bunny? Are you nuts?*

I wondered if Jack would ever learn.

✻✻✻

On the seventh day of trying to train Jack, I said, "Enough now. I have run out of patience. You must learn on your own how to hop through the doggie door."

I removed the stick. With my fingers, I pushed the tiny door, so it swung back and forth. As usual, he looked at me with his beautiful brown eyes but did nothing.

This is where the term "dumb bunny" must come from, I thought.

I'd done all I could. I hoped he would figure it out someday. That afternoon I was on the phone with a friend, when I glanced over to see Jack approach the doggie door. He pushed on it. It didn't open. He pushed harder. It opened. He hopped through to the other side.

I interrupted my friend mid-sentence, yelling "Hooray!"

"What?" she asked, puzzled.

"I have to go. Jack went outside, and he doesn't know how to get back inside."

I hung up the phone. Sure enough, Jack was scratching the outside door in frustration. I made the stuffed bunny go through the doggie door from the outside. After watching the stuffed bunny two more times, Jack followed his example.

"Good boy!" I praised, after he went in and out of the doggie door several times in a row.

"Jack, you learned how to do it. I'm so proud of you. You're a smart bunny after all."

He looked up at me, pleased with himself.

Once he learned to come and go, he spent most evenings out on the patio. He amused me as I watched him push his head against the doggie door as if he were going to play with it. Sometimes he circled around the patio and then through the living room. I cheered him on.

***

Two weeks later, I received a letter from Blue Shield containing a check for $3,000. Thanks be to God. Now I would be able to pay for the bunny door and the expense of installing it plus paying Dave to replace the screen.

Chapter 17
Jack at the Hollywood Bowl

To avoid the service charge on all tickets, I would drive to the Hollywood Bowl box office on the first Sunday in May to buy tickets for all the concerts I wanted to attend during the summer. I'd already asked my friends to commit to the concerts they wanted to attend, so I bought tickets for them, too.

Waiting in line, I saw all ages and races of people. One lady looked like she'd just come from church. She was wearing long gloves and a hat and coat even though it was warm outside. A boy with tattoos on his shaved head seemed to be talking to himself until I noticed his ear phones.

Even people who've never visited Los Angeles have probably seen the landmark dome structure of the Hollywood Bowl on television or in films.

Photo by K. Poehlmann

It's located on 120 acres in the hillsides of Bolton Canyon. It is the largest natural amphitheater in the United States with a seating capacity of approximately 18,000. Since its official opening in 1922 it's been the summer home of the L.A. Philharmonic Orchestra. In 1991 it also became the home of the Hollywood Bowl Orchestra. Audience members are invited to bring food and drink to enjoy during the performance, making a picnic of the event.

I'd been buying tickets since 1975. Every year I scanned their brochure. They offer an amazing variety of symphonies, jazz programs, recitals, big screen movies, spectacular fireworks, and famous performers such as Frank Sinatra, Barbra Streisand, Abbott and Costello, Ella Fitzgerald, and Andrea Bocelli.

That night as I pondered my selections for the year, I debated whether to take Jack with me to the box office or not. I shuddered to recall his escape earlier that week near home and my high-speed chase to capture him. I decided not to take a chance. Suppose he escaped again but dashed into the street to be lost or (gasp!) killed? No, he would not go with me to the box office.

But how about to the performance? Oh, my! If he escaped in the huge Bowl crowd I would never find him. Someone would grab him and take him home, maybe for dinner! No, Jack was much safer at home. I couldn't risk losing him when I needed him so much.

Exhausted after a long day at work, I dozed off on the couch, dreaming that I was getting ready to go to the Bowl.

❋❋❋

In my dream, my friend Catherine drove up from San Diego to go with me. After 30 years of being a high school art teacher, Catherine had recently retired. Now she was teaching women how to do arts and crafts and belly dancing. I looked forward to some interesting conversations.

The concert was at night, so we spent the earlier part of the day at the beach. We walked out to the end of the pier. Looking in the baskets of the fishermen, I saw tiny fish, probably bait. To me, fishing was a waste of time. Yet the men all seemed content. We stopped at Giuliano's deli to pick up some sandwiches and sodas for the Bowl.

We'd had such a good time. I never expected the evening to be any different.

Well, was I wrong. When we returned to my condo, I pulled the picnic basket off the top shelf of the laundry room. "Jack is going to join us tonight," I said.

"You can't be serious?" Catherine said. "Are you really going to take that rabbit?"

I did not like the way she said that rabbit. It reminded me of Sara, his first owner.

"Sure. He's never been to the Hollywood Bowl before. It will be an adventure."

Catherine's resistance irritated me, and I became even more determined to take Jack with us. Secretly I wanted to get away with something, to go against the rules and not get caught. If Security checked our baskets and discovered Jack, we might not be able to get in, but I was willing to take the risk.

I was already aware that Catherine was not keen on animals, but she would only be with Jack for a few hours, and I had hoped she'd be pleasant about it. She didn't have to carry him. I was the one who'd be doing all the work.

I put Jack in the picnic basket. It had a loose weave, so air could circulate inside. Jack would be able to breathe, and the box was big enough to hold him, his litter box, water container, and food bowl.

Just in case he peed, I put a towel underneath the litter box. I stuffed my sandwich and soda into my dark blue backpack.

Catherine carefully packed her food in her purse. When we walked to the car I wondered if I was making a mistake, as Jack hopped around inside the picnic basket. He plus all his gear must have weighed ten pounds. I felt like my arm might come right out of its socket. Every time he moved his weight shifted from one side to another. It felt awkward.

I wondered if I would end up regretting taking Jack with us. I had almost decided to take him back home, but just then Catherine opened her big mouth.

"You'll see, taking him may not be as much fun as you think," she said.

That clinched it. Jack was going to the Bowl. At 6:00 P.M. we parked my car and walked from the parking lot to the park-and-ride station at the Veteran's building in West Los Angeles. I sat on a seat in the front of the bus. It faced the aisle and I held the 1½ by 2½-foot picnic basket on my lap. When I peeked inside the lid, Jack looked up at me with his big brown eyes as if to ask, *Where are we going, Mama?*

As I reached in to pet him, Catherine sniffed. Her nose scrunched to the left. Her eyes narrowed. "I hope I don't have to smell that rabbit all night."

I wished she'd quit acting like her night was going to be ruined just because I was carrying an animal.

"Catherine, that rabbit has a name. His name is Jack. I changed his litter box this morning. He doesn't smell."

The bus dropped us off at the main parking lot of the Hollywood Bowl. Catherine was greatly surprised by the crowds of people. Many were standing in long lines to buy beer, wine, sandwiches, and roast chicken. Others were waiting in line to get their tickets at the box office or crowding into the Hollywood Bowl store to buy souvenirs. Still others were waiting in line for the restrooms. There were vendors selling balloons and necklaces that blinked in the dark. We joined the hundreds who were walking towards the turnstiles. Many carried picnic baskets and backpacks.

"Follow me," I ordered Catherine, and led her to the end of the queue. The security guards lined us up like soldiers. Everyone had to wait their turn. Security guards were spot-checking picnic baskets and bags.

"What if he checks your basket?" Catherine asked me apprehensively as we approached the turnstile. "I can't believe I might miss this concert because of that rabbit!"

My heart beat harder. I wondered if I should stash Jack under my jacket. If he didn't move, I might get away with it.

"Hey, Catherine. This is going to work out. Stop being so negative!"

What I didn't tell her was that if they discovered Jack, I had a Plan B. I would give Catherine her ticket and hide Jack's basket behind the women's restroom, where he'd be safe. Or I'd hide him behind the booth selling CD's. When it was our turn, I smiled at the security guard.

"Can you smell my sandwich?" I asked.

The security guard gave me a suspicious look. He glanced down at the basket and glanced back up at me. I thought for sure I'd been caught. Surprisingly, he waved me through the turnstile. I let out a sigh of relief!

The cement walkway was about 50 feet wide. On the edges of the walkway people had set up picnics. They sat on the ground sipping wine, beer, or champagne from glasses or plastic cups. They ate chicken, lasagna, salads, and gourmet treats on expensive china or paper plates. Some even had candles in candelabras. I would not last long if I had to sit on that hard cement. Looking at the picnickers' faces after several glasses of wine, they probably weren't noticing the hard surface.

The festive party atmosphere made me feel hungry. I thought about our measly sandwiches. Maybe next time I'd buy a better picnic lunch instead of bringing Jack.

When we strolled past some concession stands, I smelled popcorn. We both wanted some. "Catherine, I'll pay for the popcorn if you carry it."

After I paid the vendor, I popped handfuls of the salty treat into my mouth while we walked. Some kernels made it. Other kernels fell to the walkway leaving a trail behind us. We walked past several more picnic areas, but they were all full.

"Let's go directly to our seats," I said. "That way we can finish eating before other people sitting around us on either side arrive."

"Why do we need to do that?" Catherine asked.

"Because I can't eat with Jack's basket on my lap. I can set it on an empty seat."

"Oh, wait. Let's get some wine first," said Catherine. "Over there, they're giving out free samples." A lady poured each of us a small glass. I chugged down my wine, so I wouldn't have to carry it, then tipped the lady a dollar. By the time we reached the escalator I felt tipsy.

"I don't think I can manage the escalator," I said. "Let's walk instead."

We climbed the steps. And more steps. So many steps. Up and up. With every step the basket grew heavier and I grew hungrier. The wine had given me a headache. I didn't know if I was going to make it to our seats. They were up at the very top. The cheap seats are in what they call the "nosebleed section."

We hadn't even arrived at our seats and all I could think about was how long it would take to leave once the concert was over. It didn't seem possible, but Jack was growing even heavier. I had to make frequent stops to catch my breath. "We need to leave before the encores." I said.

"Oh, no! Is that really necessary?" Catherine complained.

"Do you want to walk home? With this huge crowd, and the exits so far away, if we stay for the encores, we'll probably miss the last bus."

Finally, we made it to our section. Just as I feared, our seats were in the middle of a long row. When all the seats filled up there would be nowhere to put Jack except on my lap. Hopefully, I still had a few minutes left before everyone came.

I was famished. I set Jack on the bench in the row ahead of us. I opened the top flap of the picnic basket so he could breathe and grabbed my sandwich out of my backpack.

At 7:45 the rows around us had almost filled up. I chewed faster but still had one half of my sandwich left when a family sat in the row ahead of us. Their five-year-old, a Shirley Temple look-alike peered into my picnic basket, which was still on her seat.

"A rabbit," she shrieked. "A real rabbit!"

Her family stood up. They crowded around Jack who looked up at them with fearful eyes. I cringed. He wasn't used to strangers, especially children. Plus, I didn't want everyone within earshot to know that I had snuck in an animal. If someone reported me, I could still get kicked out.

"Can I pet him?" the girl asked.

"Yes, carefully. Away from his eyes. Only on his back."

Eagerly she stuck her hand in the basket. I held my breath. Fortunately, Jack remained still and let her pet him.

"O-o-o-oh. His fur is so soft," she murmured.

Catherine and I finished eating our sandwiches.

"I need some ice cream," she said.

"I'm not going down that hill with Jack," I responded. "No way. Not me. I'm not going down that hill for anything, not even to pee." But I really wanted some ice cream. Hopefully she'd bring me some.

I scanned the concert program. Tonight, they were playing Tchaikovsky's 1812 Overture. There would be fireworks. I felt excited that the USC Trojan Band would play again.

By the time Catherine returned, all the seats except hers were filled. Although I'd hoped she might surprise me with some ice cream, she didn't. Darn it, I should have asked her.

I picked up the picnic basket off her seat, so she could sit down. There wasn't enough room to put Jack on the ground in front of me. I had no choice but to put the basket, all ten pounds of it, on my lap.

My knees bumped the wooden partitions of the row ahead of me. The music hadn't even started, and I was already cramped. How would I ever make it through the next two hours? This was going to be a very, very long night!

The conductor, John Mauceri, arrived. I stood with the heavy basket in my arms to sing the National Anthem. When I sat down again I tried to arrange my legs in a more comfortable position. I would not be able to move again until the intermission.

The orchestra played two movements of the 1812 Overture. The conductor put both arms in the air to greet us.

"Hello to all of you up there in a different area code," he said.

Everyone in the nosebleed section cheered and waved.

"Hey, John," I yelled. "Thanks for noticing us!"

The wooden benches were so hard that my butt became numb. When this was over, I'd be lucky if I could walk. Catherine was smart to bring a cushion. I regretted that I hadn't rented one.

Once when the music played softly, Jack chose to change positions. The litter box slid inside the basket and rustled the hay. Someone behind us whispered, "What's that noise?" I lifted the lid and put my hand on Jack's body to quiet him. By intermission my whole arm had lost circulation but at least I'd kept Jack quiet.

During a break in the music Catherine sniffed and whispered, "What's that sweet smell in the stands above us?"

"Some people like to party," I said.

Catherine gave me a blank look.

"They're smoking marijuana," I explained quietly.

"Oh, my," said Catherine. "Will they get in trouble?"

"I doubt it," I said. "Security guards are too plump. They never climb up this far."

Suddenly laughter broke out behind us, as we heard a wine bottle break. The man behind me stood up, turned around and shook his fist at the noisy partiers. It would have been better for him to have bought a more expensive ticket as these antics are common in the nosebleed section.

When the first half was over and as the applause died down the lights came on for intermission. We stood up and stretched our legs. Figuring that Jack would appreciate a break, I took him out of the litter box and placed the basket on my seat.

"Can I hold him?" the Shirley Temple look-alike asked.

I tried to hand him over to the girl, but Jack didn't want any of that. He wiggled free and jumped out of her arms and plop, he landed on little girl's mom's lap. She shrieked. Then Jack hopped again over the shoulders of another woman. Every time he hopped, it looked like he was flying through the air.

"Yikes!" I yelled.

"Rabbit on the loose!" screamed the little girl.

If I could have hidden under my seat, I would have. I felt mortified, but I loved Jack more. I had to catch him. I could tell where he was by the confusion in the stands below me. People yelped. Others raised their legs.

One lady yelled, "It's a rat!"

Ten rows below us he landed on the lap of a rather large lady who was eating a strawberry tart. Squish! Tart filling was all over her and Jack. Luckily the lady grabbed Jack and held him until I finally reached them. Jack had strawberry jam on his face and paws. I gathered him up, tart mess and all, and returned to my seat, eyes focused on the ground. I heard people giggling. The man behind me had a peeved look,

"Oh, so that's what we heard," he grumbled.

"Would you change seats with us?" I asked a couple sitting on the aisle.

Fortunately, they agreed. We traded seats. I placed the basket on the steps and stretched my legs out sideways at an angle.

"I like the aisle seats better," Catherine said. "The man behind us complained about the noise but he was smacking his gum the whole time, so he deserved what he got. What a hypocrite."

"Thanks, Catherine," I said. "You've been a good sport tonight."

In our new seats I was able to take Jack out of the basket and keep him on my lap. During the fireworks he burrowed his head into my sweater. The USC marching band played their trumpets and Jack pushed his head even deeper into the soft fabric.

At the end of the program, I needed to go to the restroom. The instant the music stopped, and the applause began, we left. Other people were leaving also. We made it back to the bus in record time.

After we settled into our seats on the bus Catherine said, "I thought for sure that Jack was gone forever. Did you see everyone's reactions? You'd think they'd never seen a rabbit before."

We both laughed.

"I don't think either one of us will forget tonight," I assured her.

"Jack sure gave us a night to remember," Catherine agreed.

On the bus on the way home, I dozed. When we arrived at Veteran's Park at midnight, I woke up.

✻✻✻

At the same moment, I woke up from my nap. The dream I'd had was so vivid that for a moment I was disoriented and realized that I was *not* on a bus, but on my couch at home. The clock said I had been asleep for an hour. All that exciting action in just one hour? Was it really a dream? I rushed to check on Jack. He was safely in his cage. What a relief!

I mulled over the elements of my dream and how a bunch of real-life events had come together to form a fantastic story.

Excitement about receiving the Bowl brochure in the mail.

Deciding whether to take Jack to the box office with me to buy the tickets.

Imagining what might happen if Jack escaped during the performance.

Jack's escape through the hole in the screen door a few days ago.

Recalling how his first owner, Sara, referred to him as "the rabbit."

Imagining what it was like when Sara's young students took turns caring for him, probably letting him run wild and get into mischief. How scared he must have been sometimes.

My shoulder muscles were still a bit sore from lugging bedding and a heavy ice bowl to the lounge at the Abbey. That would explain the sensation of carrying the heavy picnic basket.

My deep-seated desire to defy all the many rules my parents laid down for me as a child took the form of sneaking Jack past the security guard.

All this was quite an interesting blend that was like elements of an action movie. For a moment I was tempted to write up my wacky dream as a screenplay.

I made dinner and read for a while. Before heading upstairs to bed, I checked Jack's cage again and smiled, knowing that he was safe.

"I'm so glad you're still here with me. I would feel so bad if something ever happened to you.

"Good night, Jack. I hope you enjoyed the concert, even though it was just a dream."

I climbed the stairs to my room, saying, "Now, Lord, I can spend my usual quiet time with You. The day was both exciting and exhausting and I'm glad You were there with me guiding my footsteps."

As I laid out my clothes for church the next morning, I remembered that the first Sunday of the month is Communion Sunday. When I get to church on time, I get to hear the trumpets blow.

I then spent the next hour reading my Bible and praying to my Heavenly Father.

Good night, Abba Father.

Fireworks at the Hollywood Bowl
during the *1812 Overture*

Chapter 18
Celebrating My Birthday

After my sister Andrea died in 1994, I became even closer with her daughters Claire, age 31, and Becky, age 38. Two weeks before my 57th birthday in August, Claire called to say that she and Becky wanted to throw me a birthday party. I was nervous about seeing my family. I had kept my laser procedure a secret from them. I was afraid they wouldn't understand if they knew. I didn't want them to judge me or think I was being vain.

"Yes, I'll come," I told Claire. "Thanks – it sounds like fun." Maybe they wouldn't notice anything different about the skin on my face.

❄❄❄

On the morning of my birthday, I woke up excited. I went into the bathroom and flipped on the overhead light. As I brushed my teeth, I caught my reflection in the mirror above the sink. There was still some redness on my face from the laser treatment, but all the lines around my mouth, eyes, and forehead were gone. My eyes didn't look like slits anymore. They looked large and luminous. Gone was my gray hair. I'd colored my hair blond. With the layers of skin removed, it was as if I'd cast off the ugly duckling persona. I had turned into a lovely swan, both outside and inside.

At 11:30 I found Jack staring into the mirror-like glass of the stereo.

"Jack, we're going to my birthday party. None of my relatives have met you. I need to make you beautiful."

I picked Jack up, carried him to the couch and placed him between my knees. I cut a piece of red Christmas ribbon and tied it into a big red bow around Jack's neck. He shook his head hard.

"Jack, you need to cooperate. I want you to make a good first impression."

I set Jack on the floor and went into the kitchen to cut up vegetables so he could have a snack while the rest of us ate my birthday lunch. By the time I returned to the living room, Jack had loosened the bow around his neck and was chewing it. I grabbed the ribbon out of Jack's mouth. Then I tied another bow around his neck. I put him on the floor and returned to the kitchen to pack Jack's food in a plastic bag.

I was only gone five minutes. By the time I returned to the living room Jack had again torn the bow into shreds and it hung off his neck.

"Bad boy! You're not helping me at all." I untied the remains of the bow. "I'm very disappointed in you."

Again I set Jack down on the living room floor.

"I'm going to pack our stuff in the car. Do you think you can manage to behave yourself while I'm gone?"

He hopped away. I shook my finger at his departing rump and commanded, "Now you keep out of trouble."

After I finished loading the car, I returned to the living room for Jack. I couldn't find him.

"Jack," I yelled. I cocked my ear and listened for any clue of his whereabouts.

"Jack, where are you? Come out from wherever you are."

I heard a noise in the dining room. I peered over the top of the buffet. Jack was playing with the extra plastic dowels that I used to cover phone cords.

"We have to leave now," I said. He threw another dowel up in the air. I hated it when he ignored me.

Glancing at the clock, I saw the time was 12:45. The party was supposed to start at 1:00 P.M. We were going to be late. Frustrated, I stamped my foot.

I retrieved the broom and rabbit carrier from the closet. With the broom handle I pounded the floor right behind his rump. Startled, he looked behind him. With the broom's bristles I nudged him into the rabbit carrier and slammed the door.

Leaving my home, I carried Jack's carrier in one hand and my purse and camera with my other hand. Arms full, I had to shut the door with my foot.

On the drive to the party, I sang along with Neil Diamond's *Song Sung Blue* from his Hollywood Bowl CD. Jack didn't make any trouble. Maybe he liked the music as much as I did.

Becky lived on a steep hill that overlooked the ocean in Redondo Beach. Her condo was on the top floor of a three-story building. Faded white stucco. Potholes in the driveway. The elevator was not working so I had to lug Jack up the narrow stairs. The gray carpet in her entryway was stained.

When Claire opened the door, I had the first glimpse of Becky's spacious apartment. It was a hot day, but a cool ocean breeze rustled the drapes that framed the sliding glass doors. Claire stood nearly six feet tall. She had long blond hair and a lean muscular body due to her interest in sports. Becky, a petite brunette, excelled in yoga and Tai Chi. Her ready smile and charisma attracted many friends.

Becky sat across the room on the white comfy sofa. She held Laura, age 3, on her lap. Laura, the picture of sweetness, had long blond hair, an upturned nose, and twinkling brown eyes. Claire's other child, Ryan, age 4 ½, released his extra energy by stomping on the pillows.

Everyone yelled all at once, "Happy Birthday, Judy!"

I hugged each person before setting Jack's carrier down on the dining room table. I scooped Jack out of the carrier and carried him over to the sofa, so I could introduce him to Laura and Ryan. They both came over to pet him.

Ryan asked, "How long have you had Jack?"

"Five months," I said.

"Do you know yet if he's a Jack and not a Jackie?" Claire asked.

"I wondered that myself. My vet did an exam and determined that Jack is a boy."

"If he made a mistake," Claire interjected, "there could be lots of bunnies in your home if you got another rabbit."

"Oh, I'd love to see lots of bunnies," chorused Ryan and Laura. "We could come and see all of them play together."

"I'll be very careful so that doesn't happen," I assured my nieces. They laughed.

"Do you keep him in the cage all the time?" asked Ryan.

"Can he eat what you eat?" asked Laura.

"Those are good questions. I have a cage where I keep his litter box and water bowl, but he is free to move around outside in an enclosed area that does not have any phone or electric cords. I mostly give him Timothy and oat hay in the morning and at night. In the mornings he gets dry pellets. At night I make him a salad of romaine lettuce, cilantro, curly and Italian parsley. He also likes carrots and bananas, but not the regular food I eat."

"Maybe we can try different types of food today," suggested Ryan. "If we have grapes and strawberries we could see if he likes them."

"That's a possibility," I agreed. "Today as a special treat, but not on a regular basis."

"I want to hold Jack now," Ryan insisted.

"Me too! Me too!" shouted Laura. I assured her that she would have a turn.

I gave Jack to Ryan. His face lit up with a smile.

"Oh, Jack's fur is so soft," he said. "He's happy I'm holding him."

Then Laura cuddled Jack, beaming with joy.

"Before we place Jack on the floor," I said, "let's put down the beach towel, litter box, and water bowl. And let's find more towels to put over the electric and phone cords. You see, rabbits will chew on anything including base boards and phone and electrical cords. They could get electrocuted, and we sure wouldn't want that."

Becky fetched some towels and put one down next to the dining room table. I set Jack on the towel. I liked that he would be eating his snack near us. I wanted him to be a part of my celebration.

"We're all going to need to watch him while we're eating so that he doesn't get into mischief," I said.

The table was decorated with three red balloons, fresh flowers, and a brightly colored tablecloth. Becky said a prayer of thanksgiving for our food. We ate our open-faced tuna melt sandwiches and a tossed salad with tomatoes and avocado. For dessert Becky served fresh strawberries while Jack ate his carrots.

"Aunt Judy, does Jack like strawberries?" Ryan asked.

"Yes, he does."

Ryan held out his hand holding a red, ripe treat. Jack stood on his hind legs to reach the strawberry.

Becky appeared in the doorway with my birthday cake. The carrot cake was rectangular. It held two circles of burning candles. A real carrot and green carrot tops decorated the center. Before I could make a wish and blow out the candles, Ryan's' hand grabbed the fluffy carrot tops off the cake. He tossed them over to Jack.

"Why did you do that?" Claire asked.

"So the carrot tops wouldn't catch on fire," Ryan replied.

I smiled. Ryan was a clever boy.

Everyone sang, "Happy Birthday, Dear Judy."

Ryan tried to blow out the candles. They would not blow out. He tried again. No matter what he did, they still burned. He pounded both of his tiny fists on the tabletop. The dishes bounced noisily on the table.

"Hey what's going on here?" he asked. All the rest of us tried blowing on the candles. Still they wouldn't blow out.

"See, you can't do it either," Ryan exclaimed, triumphantly.

"They must be trick candles," I said.

Becky came back from the kitchen with a bowl of water. She was laughing.

"Those *were* trick candles," she joked, "and that's why you couldn't blow them out." We all laughed, too. We dipped each candle into the water and finally the flames were extinguished.

I was licking the frosting off the candles when Laura put her face next to mine.

"Aunt Judy, how come your face is so red?" she asked. "Did you get sunburned?"

Darn. I'd almost gotten away with no one noticing my face.

"No, Laura. The doctor took off the top layer of skin," I said.

"O-o-oh," she said. "Does it hurt?"

"Not anymore. It's finally healing."

Claire and Becky looked up, surprised,

"Well," they said, "this is news. Did you have cosmetic surgery?"

"Yes, it's a procedure called laser resurfacing." I said.

"Do you think it was really necessary?" she asked.

Claire's critical response hurt my feelings. "

I was sick of paying the dermatologist's mortgage," I countered.

"Oh yes, you and your family with all your skin cancer," Claire said, as if just then remembering the family history.

"The doctor advised the treatment to deal with my skin problems once and for all," I said. "A nice bonus is getting rid of scars and wrinkles and looking younger."

Both of my nieces nodded. Maybe they finally understood. They were only in their thirties, without wrinkles now, but suddenly aware that they might have them at my age.

Becky cut generous pieces of cake and passed them around the table. Jack was not allowed to eat sweets but this time I made an exception. I set a piece of cake on a paper plate in front of him. When he sniffed it, a small dab of white frosting stuck to his nose. He sneezed. The frosting flew across his towel.

Then to my surprise his whole face disappeared into the frosting. He took a big bite. When he looked up again he looked like a tiny ghostly clown. We all laughed.

"Look!" Ryan said, clapping his hands with delight. "Jack likes cake!"

Becky posed us with the cake and candles and took a group photo.

The next day at Costco I had prints made. I looked great! No lines. All puffiness both above and below my eyes was gone. My skin had tightened. I looked younger. My face was still red, but it had been worth it. I sent copies of the photos to Claire and Becky. One day when the kids are grown, I hope they look at them and remember how much fun they had at the party with Aunt Judy and Jack.

I kept one photo for my dresser to remember that lovely afternoon. Yes, I felt like a new person both inside and out.

Claire, with Ryan and Laura   Photo by Becky

Chapter 19
A Day at the Beach

Two weeks after my birthday party, Becky phoned to ask whether I'd like to go with her to the Redondo Beach Wellness Community Center for a Tai Chi class. I jumped at the chance. I'd heard so much about the Center but never had a reason to go. Becky had started going there after her mastectomy a year before. Little did I know that one day I'd be going there for more than an exercise class.

"Wear comfortable clothes so you can stretch," she said.

"Oh my gosh! I don't know if I have any," I said.

She laughed and assured me that I must have something in my closet that would work just fine.

❄❄❄

On the morning I was supposed to meet Becky, I wore jeans because I couldn't find any athletic clothes in my closet. Becky's apartment was near the beach, close to the "World Famous" (according to the website) Redondo Beach Pier. Since Jack had never seen the Pier, I decided to take him on an outing there before I met Becky for the afternoon class. I fetched Jack from behind the couch.

"We're going to the beach," I announced. "It's like a carnival."

The weather was warm with a light tropical breeze. We parked on a road overlooking the ocean. It was going to be a fun adventure.

I dropped quarters in the parking meter. We had an hour. I decided to put Jack on a leash, so he could hop without running away. I didn't want to have to carry him. I took Jack out of his carrier on the back seat and put him on my lap while I tried to undo the knots in his leash. The leash was a halter and Jack wasn't happy about having to wear that contraption. He kept trying to jump off my lap while I wrestled with the knots.

Exasperated, I finally grabbed a towel on the back seat and dropped it over his head. Because he couldn't see what I was doing, he settled down. I slipped the leather straps of the halter over his ears and chin, but I wasn't done yet. There were still straps I had to finagle around his belly. He fought me on this. He kicked the towel off his head and tried to use his back feet to lift off.

"Stop already! I need your cooperation," I shouted. "At this rate we'll never get to the beach."

With my left arm, I grabbed him around his neck and used the leverage to tighten the belly straps. I felt all the air whooshing out of his mouth and stomach. I hated to manhandle him like that, but I couldn't risk having him escape.

On our walk to the Pier, seagulls flew over our heads. On the horizon, sailboats drifted slowly. There wasn't enough wind to fill the sails. The first building I noticed on the Pier was the police station with its American flag. This made me feel safe. Originally built in 1889, the Pier had been renovated several times, most recently in 1995. The City poured reinforced concrete so that the Pier would withstand the battering of waves for another 100 years.

Photo by K. Poehlmann

A major tourist attraction, the Pier had something for everyone. There were vendors selling balloons, pin wheels, pizza, saltwater taffy, popcorn, and hot dogs. There were nightclubs, bars, restaurants, and entertainment establishments with names like South Bay's Brixton's, Charlie's Place, Old Tony's, and Kincaid's.

This was a Monday, so the Pier wasn't as crowded as it was on a weekend. Thank God. I didn't know if Jack and I could handle so much activity and excitement. Even though it was a weekday there were still plenty of people around. They whizzed by on roller skates and bikes. Other people walked their dogs. On weekends there would have been fiddlers, street performers, dancers, and acrobats, all with jars to collect donations.

I hugged Jack and carried him down to a flat cement area right in front of the Ice Cream/Coffee Shoppe. Across from the store, people relaxed on the grass hill. They sipped coffee or water and talked with friends.

"Let's find a place where I can put you down, so you can explore," I said.

My peripheral vision caught a Doberman Pincher straining against his owner's leash. Instinctively I turned away and started to walk in another direction. It worked. He didn't see Jack. Dogs, especially hunting dogs, kill rabbits for fun and sometimes for lunch. I needed to be vigilant.

I walked to another section of the Pier. No canines in sight. I placed Jack on the ground. Unlike a dog, he didn't move immediately. Instead, he sat very still. His nose twitched. Alert. His ears flattened back against his head. That is always a sign of fear in rabbits. Suddenly he hopped and yanked on the leash hard. I had to run to keep up with him.

"Look!" a little girl yelled. "A rabbit!"

Jack stopped suddenly, confused by all the noise, or maybe he thought the little girl might be dangerous. If he escaped, he would endanger his life. A crowd gathered. Most of them had probably never seen a rabbit on a leash before.

Suddenly a cocker spaniel came around the corner. I saw him catch sight of Jack.

He bounded towards us. I scooped Jack up. The dog jumped up on my legs. He was barking. I turned my back to the spaniel and used my chest to shelter Jack.

A robust round-faced woman with curly gray bouffant hair bulldozed her way through the crowd. Clearly she was the cocker spaniel's owner. She grabbed the dog's leash off the ground and yanked his collar until he obediently sat down.

"This isn't the best place for you to bring a rabbit," the woman scolded.

I took a deep breath and puffed out my chest.

"My rabbit has just as much right to be here as your dog does," I retorted. "Besides, your dog jumped on me and could have hurt me. What is your dog doing off his leash? You're lucky I don't sue you and have your dog put down!"

She gave me a look as if she wanted to start a fight, but I turned my back on her. My heart was pumping fast. The whole situation had revved up my adrenaline. As I walked away with my dignity intact, a man in the crowd sided with me, saying, "Some people can be really rude." I nodded agreement.

Whew! A close call.

I carried Jack over to a refreshment stand and purchased a root beer and a corn on the cob. Hopefully the food would calm me. I found a picnic table near the fishermen. Small groups of men hung over the railing and watched their lines. When I finished my food, I was relaxed. I put Jack on the ground, so he could explore the wooden pier. We walked over to a man who was casting out his line.

Photo by K. Poehlmann

"What kind of fish do you catch?" I asked.

"Mostly mackerel," he said. He wore a jaunty cap that made him look like a sailor.

Jack's leash was seven feet long. As the fisherman and I talked, Jack's leash tangled around the man's leg.

"Oops! Sorry if my rabbit is bothering you," I said. "What's your name?"

"Roberto." He looked down at Jack and smiled.

"This is a first," he joked. "Caught by the leash of a rabbit."

I lifted Jack up and placed him on the other side of my leg, away from Roberto.

"What kind of bait do you use?" I asked.

"I don't need to use bait because the fish here aren't very smart."

We both chuckled. He cast out his fishing line far out into the ocean. A few seconds later there was a tug on the line. He reeled in three fish on one line, each on its own hook.

"How do you account for your success when your neighbor's buckets over there are empty?" I asked.

"I'm the only one who casts out his line."

I turned to watch the other fishermen, whose lines dangled limply off the pier.

"Look!" Roberto said suddenly, pointing to the sky. A hawk circled directly over us. Suddenly it went into a dive. I turned to see where the hawk was headed. Oh my gosh, it was diving towards Jack!

Jack hopped underneath a plastic chair. This was no dumb bunny. He knew by instinct to hide from danger. Still, I wasn't taking any chances. I sat on the chair, grabbed Jack and held him close to my chest. Another close call. I turned towards Roberto who seemed pleased that I had rescued Jack. I thanked him for the warning.

"What will you do with the fish you've caught?"

"They will be my family's dinner."

"Next time I'm down here I'll look for you," I told him. Then I picked up Jack's paw and made him wave goodbye to Roberto.

Our play date had passed quickly. I was glad Jack and I had spent time together on the beach. The ocean breeze had refreshed us both.

Jack and I drove to Becky's apartment and arrived on time. I hadn't told her I was bringing Jack. I hoped she wouldn't mind if I left Jack in his carrier at her place while we went to the Tai Chi class. When she answered the door, we hugged. She was very happy to see Jack. I took Jack out of his carrier and Becky held him while we talked.

✳✳✳

The Wellness Community Center is nestled between other storefront businesses on the top level of the Redondo Beach Pier. Subsidized by major corporations and donations from the community, they were able to offer lots of free services: lectures, classes, parties, food, and fun events. The building hosted several support groups for cancer patients as well as their friends and caregivers. They also offered free parking, which is good because parking is always at a premium at the beach.

Becky had originally joined her support group during her chemo treatments for breast cancer. Even though she'd finished her treatments the year before, she continued going to the weekly sessions to see friends she had met there. Becky led me to a large living room at the back of the building. All the furniture had been pushed back against the walls to allow freedom of movement.

She and I plopped down on a brown couch to wait for others to arrive. An attractive woman with an angular face and brunette hair that fell to her shoulders walked briskly over to greet us. She was wearing a sweat suit that seemed way too large for her,

Becky leaned over and whispered, "That's Joy, our teacher."

"We don't do that here," Joy said authoritatively.

Don't do <u>what</u> here? I wondered, staring at her, puzzled.

"When you sit, I want you to sit with conscious intent. I want you to move slowly and deliberately. No plopping or slouching," Joy said.

I felt peeved. I'd never met her before, and here she was ordering me around. I chose not to say anything. I didn't want to get on her bad side.

I studied her. She looked to be in her 20's. Her limbs moved effortlessly.

"Were you ever a dancer?" I asked her.

Poised and serene as if she'd just completed a meditation, Joy considered my question.

"I studied ballet in the past and was in a few productions in San Francisco. That was before I discovered Tai Chi and became aware of the benefits it had for my body."

The fact that she was a ballerina explained everything. In my opinion, people in ballet have a tendency to be a bit strange. Perhaps that's their artistic temperament.

By this time eight more women of various ages and shapes had arrived. Becky and the other women wore athletic clothes, stretch pants, or tights. I felt out of place in jeans. If I was going to continue this class, I would have to get some suitable attire.

The class began.

"Breathe through the movements," Joy said.

I lifted my left leg slowly. I wobbled on my right leg and almost lost my balance.

"Now, slowly and deliberately, raise your right arm," Joy said.

I flailed my arms. All these movements were supposed to be done in slow motion but my body refused to cooperate and move slowly. I felt like I was going to fall over.

Joy came over to assist me.

"Breathe slowly as you move. There is no need to rush. This is a time for you to become acquainted with how your body moves. We're not in a race with each other. You need to move at your own pace."

"Thank you, Joy. This is all new to me," I said.

"Maybe it would be easier to be closer to the wall just in case you need to brace yourself," Joy suggested.

"Good idea," I said, and moved next to the wall. Having the wall handy gave me the confidence to try the moves and helped me balance. For some exercises I did the whole move with one hand on the wall.

The hour passed quickly. She had us lie on the floor on a mat at the end of class. "Now close your eyes and rest for a bit," she ordered.

When I closed my eyes, I had a premonition – the awful feeling that I would be coming back to the Wellness Center and not just for Tai Chi classes. Would Becky have another bout with cancer? Would I come here to support a friend? Tears filled my eyes.

I remembered my sister Andrea, who had been eight years older than I. We'd been very close. When she died from ovarian cancer twelve years earlier I had felt devastated. When her daughter, my niece Becky, got breast cancer two years ago I'd been distraught.

There is a pattern developing, I told myself. *Who would be next? Would it be me?* A wave of fear shot though me. No, it wouldn't be me. I lived a healthy lifestyle. I tried hard to dismiss my frightening thought but failed. I began to cry and had no Kleenex to blow my nose.

Joy saw my tears and brought me some tissues.

"I'm sorry you're in pain," she said.

"Thank you," I mumbled. "But it isn't pain from doing the Tai Chi. I had disturbing thoughts during the meditation."

Even though Joy offered to talk with me, I didn't feel comfortable sharing. I felt I might be judged by her or that she'd say that what I was feeling was nonsense.

After our class ended, Becky and I thanked Joy for her kindness and helpfulness.

We exited the building and walked down the steps to get lunch. Becky and I passed some of the same restaurants that Jack and I had seen earlier that day. This time I felt anxious. Gone was the carefree mood of that morning. Now the dread of the premonition hovered over me.

We settled on Chinese takeout. We sauntered over to a wooden picnic table near the fishermen to eat our lunch. Roberto was no longer there on the Pier.

"The class is easier for me now," said Becky. "Each time it will be easier for you too, if you choose to continue."

I didn't tell her about my uneasy feelings. I felt anxious but figured it was all in my imagination.

❋❋❋

When I got home I cuddled and rocked Jack in my chair and told him about my premonition. He understood of course. He always did. I remembered friends who had pets and I could tell they bonded with them.

"Jack, you are indeed emotional support for me."

Then I prayed, "Okay, God, I don't know what the future holds for me, but You do."

The Bible verse Isaiah 41:10 came to mind. "*Do not fear for I am with you. Do not be dismayed for I am your God. I will strengthen and help you. I will uphold you with My righteous right hand.*"

Years ago, I wrote down that verse and always carried it with me. Whenever an anxious thought appeared, I envisioned God holding my right hand. I cried in relief. He promised to be with me and indeed He was.

Every day I found more verses that were comforting and wrote them down also. God was bringing me peace, joy, and the courage to deal with whatever lay ahead for me.

Chapter 20
Pothole #3: Scary Diagnosis

Three days later on a Friday night, I noticed when going to the bathroom that I was bleeding. This was not normal for a woman in her 50's. In my panic I called out to Jack.

"Jack, where are you? I need to see you now!"

Maybe Jack sensed my fear and ran away from me. Oh no, I thought. I need to be careful and not frighten him.

I sat on the sofa trying to decide what to do next. Only one thought came, to call my friend Elaine. Although I am older than she is, I always valued her wise advice.

"Hi, Elaine. Is this a good time to talk? I'm in a real panic right now."

"Of course, Judy. What's going on?"

"When I went to the bathroom just now I discovered blood. This is not supposed to happen, since I'm on both Premarin and Provera hormones," I told her.

"Oh, heavens, Judy! This could be serious. The sooner you see the doctor, the better," she counseled. "Don't call for an appointment. Just walk in and insist on seeing the doctor. Let me know what happens."

"Thanks a lot for your suggestions. I will follow through and call you Monday night."

After hanging up with Elaine, I went to look for Jack. I needed comfort for whatever I would face on Monday.

Jack was behind the couch. I crawled around and grabbed him, inhaling dust and coughing, and thinking, *I must do a good sweep back here, but not now.*

"Oh, Jack," I whimpered. "I don't know what's happening in my body. I can't even bear to think about all the things involved with possibly being really sick."

I carried Jack to my rocking chair. We stayed there a long time. My tears fell on Jack's fur, but he didn't seem to mind and didn't try to get free. He just let me hold him. He must have sensed I needed him just then.

✳✳✳

All weekend I was filled with dread. There was something going on in my body and I was afraid of what I might hear on Monday. The best I could do was to keep busy and try not to let my imagination run wild.

On Monday I took Elaine's advice. At 9:00 A.M. I rushed into my gynecologist's office.

"I have an emergency," I told the receptionist. "I need to see Dr. Salem right now."

"Sorry, you'll have to wait. The doctor is delivering a baby this morning."

"A baby?" I repeated, not wanting to believe her explanation.

"It might take hours," she replied. "Perhaps you should go to the emergency room."

"I'll wait."

I sat down on a hard leather chair that hadn't been designed for long periods of sitting. I looked around Dr. Salem's waiting room. Why hadn't I noticed the play area before? Puzzles. Coloring books. Plastic toys for toddlers. I picked up a magazine. It was for expectant parents. On the wall, there were several photos of pregnant women in different trimesters. Why had I thought he specialized in menopausal women?

Time passed extremely slowly. The chair grew increasingly uncomfortable. Finally, three hours later, Dr. Salem, white coat flying, dashed through the reception room.

As always, I was struck by how handsome he was. Maybe that's why he had so many women waiting to see him. Six feet tall. Strong jaw. His muscular arms had probably been developed by wrestling reluctant babies out of his patients. Dark, kind eyes. He reminded me of Charlton Heston in *The Ten Commandments*. Perhaps his good looks had distracted me from noticing that he specialized in babies rather than women my age.

✳✳✳

"Doctor, I had some bleeding," I told him as I sat across from him in his office. "This is not supposed to happen."

"No need to be concerned," he said. "It's normal for ladies your age to bleed."

"Not for me. I'm taking both Premarin and Provera. When I take both hormones I'm not supposed to have periods anymore," I complained.

"You're fine," he said.

I remembered a conversation I'd had with him three years earlier. I decided to refresh his memory.

"After my sister Andrea died of ovarian cancer, I went to the Gilda Radner Clinic for an ultrasound test. The clinic said that the lining of my uterus was too thick. I asked you then to take me off the hormones and you refused."

My heart was beating fast. I didn't want to contradict him, but I was genuinely afraid.

"Since your family has a history of osteoporosis, I thought it best," he said. "Hormones keep the bones strong."

At this point I raised my voice and demanded, "I want all the cancer tests. If you refuse to give me those tests, I will find another doctor and I won't be back. I will tell my friends that you failed to disclose to me the risks of taking hormones. I will tell them you're a bad doctor." I knew I was almost becoming hysterical, but I couldn't help myself.

"This is foolish," the doctor said. "You will see what I mean when you get your test results back and they are negative."

"I trusted you to know what was right for me and I feel that you've let me down," I said, near tears.

"Calm down, Judy. Let's wait for the test results before you get so upset."

He summoned the nurse and ordered the tests. She drew my blood to send to the lab.

***

On Friday of that week, Dr. Salem called.

"I'm so sorry, Judy," he said sheepishly. "The test results are positive. You have cancer of the lining of the uterus."

I screeched at him. "You were so sure of yourself. I wish you had told me the dangers of hormones three years ago. I would have gone to another doctor to get natural hormones."

"You will need a hysterectomy," he said, ignoring my rage. "I have contacted Dr. Lamb, a head surgeon at UCLA. I will assist him in the procedure. The nurse will schedule you to come in and do the paperwork. What about coming in next Wednesday?"

"Five days? That's a long time to wait," I complained. "Besides, how can you be sure the test results are accurate? You gave me the wrong diagnosis before. Why should I believe you now?"

He ignored my question.

"The test results are reliable," he said. "You need this surgery. Perhaps the nurse can fit you in late Monday afternoon."

"That's a little bit better," I conceded.

This is all a dream – like Jack's adventure at the Hollywood Bowl. I will wake up shortly and none of this will have happened, I told myself. But deep down I knew it was real. I was angry at the doctor, at God for allowing this to happen to me, and at myself, that somehow perhaps I could have prevented this awful situation.

Exhausted, I hung up the phone. I needed some comfort. I needed Jack. I found him crouching by the piano pedals. I sat on the floor, picked him up and cradled him on my lap.

"Jack, I've just been diagnosed with cancer and I'm very, very scared," I said. "That doctor is not taking any responsibility for his mistakes."

Jack's expression looked blank. I needed him to understand. I lifted him onto my shoulder so that his face touched mine. When I looked into his eyes, he knew that I was feeling sad.

"How can I trust that doctor to help me now?" I wailed.

Over the weekend I pretended that the results were wrong. Things like this happen to the lady across the street, not me. My body had betrayed me, and I was mad.

Jack and my good friend Fran consoled me over that long weekend. But Jack was my closest confidant. He patiently listened to my complaints and didn't talk back.

✳✳✳

On Monday, when I met with Dr. Salem and filled out the paperwork, grim reality hit me harder.

"Before I commit to the surgery, I need a second opinion," I said. I wasn't going to make the same mistake my sister Andrea had made. She'd procrastinated, and her cancer had spread. Even though Dr. Salem had seen me quickly, I wasn't convinced that his diagnosis was correct, so I would do some research.

I sprang into action. While I was looking through the Blue Shield directory for OB/GYN doctors, the phone rang. It was my friend Sonya. I hadn't heard from her in three years, ever since she moved to Florida.

"I felt very strongly that I ought to call you," she said.

I explained that I'd just been diagnosed with uterine cancer and said, "I need a second opinion. Do you know someone here in Southern California?"

Amazingly, she did. She referred me to Dr. Hawkins, who had given her a partial hysterectomy before she moved away.

I called Dr. Hawkins' office immediately. The receptionist said it would take three months to get an appointment. Three months?! The cancer could grow and get worse. Much worse. I didn't even know how far along it was now.

I had promised to call Sonya back. When I did, I asked, "How did you happen to call me this morning?"

"I just felt a prompting by the Holy Spirit. Somehow, I felt that we needed to talk."

Sonya and I had first met each other at a college briefing cruise with the Hollywood Presbyterian Church back in 1965. We became friends, and later, roommates. It was at her counsel that I left my job with USC Medical School at the County Hospital of LA to pursue my master's degree in education.

We shared an apartment, first in East Los Angeles and then in Palos Verdes where we both taught school for the same school district. She was one of the fortunate women who met their husbands through either Hollywood Presbyterian or Bel Air church. I had visited her at her home in Florida on vacation.

I relayed the bad news I had received from Dr. Hawkins' office, that it would be three months before I was able to see him.

"I've known Dr. Hawkins for years," she said. "His son and my son are friends. I have his home number and will call him tonight."

At 8:00 P.M. Sonya called with very welcome news. "Dr. Hawkins can see you tomorrow at 11:30 A.M."

This was a miracle! What a relief! Soon I would know the truth about the lab results.

✳✳✳

Speaking with Dr. Hawkins was the catalyst that helped me face reality. Because of his kindness as he confirmed the diagnosis, my confidence was restored that I was in good hands. He reassured me that Dr. Lamb was a superb surgeon and said he would contact my doctor to schedule the operation as soon as possible.

I called Sonya to thank her.

"You were right, it was by the leading of the Lord that you called me yesterday. You saved my life. I am so grateful. I really liked Dr. Hawkins and if it hadn't been for his three-month wait, I would have wanted him to be my surgeon. By the way, how is Jonathan doing?" I thought I remembered that her son was in college, but wasn't sure.

"He's in his sophomore year. Thanks for asking. He has a double major already. I'm really proud of him."

We chatted some more, catching up on events since we'd spoken last three years ago. She had given me hope that God wasn't done with me just yet.

"Let's keep in touch, Sonya. I really appreciate all your help here."

"I'll be praying for you," Sonya promised.

"Thank you. You're a good friend."

Dr. Salem's office scheduled the surgery for Oct. 31st. Oh, no! Halloween! Such a weird date. I'd be fasting and would miss out on all the chocolate candies. Darn it!

Chapter 21
A Dismal Halloween

Two weeks before the surgery, I finished filling out all the paperwork, including the dire death warnings that come with consent for anesthesia. They also took a pint of my blood in case I needed a transfusion, so I was feeling a bit woozy when I went home to Jack that night. I needed some comfort and found him behind the credenza. I carried him to my rocking chair out on the patio.

Together we watched the sun set. The blood red colors and brilliant yellows usually made me happy. Tonight, they made me feel sad. I didn't want to go through the surgery. I didn't want to be in pain. Mostly, I didn't want to die.

Okay, God, how am I going to do this? How do I know what Your will is for me? If I have the surgery and treatments, will I be able to live for many more years?

I prayed and waited and listened but didn't get any sign that He had heard me.

I squeezed Jack tighter. He tried to wiggle away from me, but then he settled down when I stopped holding him so tightly.

✳✳✳

My surgeon, Dr. Salem, said that I needed to meet with an oncologist, Dr. Green, and a radiologist, Dr. Hass, before my surgery. Apparently, Dr. Lamb was only my surgeon in the hospital, so Dr. Salem would counsel me on getting an oncologist. Then he would be out of the picture.

I met with Dr. Hass first. He had the face of a friendly beagle with intelligent eyes and a light easy manner.

"After you finish with your chemo treatments with the oncologist, we'll see each other every day for three weeks. I've been doing this for fifteen years. I'll always be available to answer your questions," he assured me. "Call my service anytime."

"I'm glad you're on my team," I said.

✳✳✳

Four days later I visited the oncologist, Dr. Green. His office was one block west of my real estate firm on Torrance Blvd, which made me happy, since it was such a convenient location. Becky went with me to the appointment. She wanted to take notes and give me her opinion of the doctor.

Dr. Green's waiting room had putrid green walls. Not a good sign. The doctor had sloppy gray hair, a sullen look, and heavy jowls. He looked at Becky and me but didn't say hello. Instead, he got right down to business.

"I don't know how to treat you," he said curtly while skimming the paperwork.

If he'd looked up he would have seen me biting my lip and looking nervously at the floor, but he was more interested in the paperwork. The next words out of his mouth were not exactly comforting.

"There's not much research on your type of cancer. The treatment may or may not work, as your cancer is Stage Three."

Startled, I just nodded. Did he even know which one of us was the patient? Becky and I looked at each other. Her expression mirrored the disgust I felt. Wow. This guy was dreadful. It wasn't just the words that I didn't like. His voice and manner were too detached.

"I'll take your case before the tumor board. There's a meeting in this area next week," Dr. Green said. "The best oncologists in the state will be there. Maybe they'll have other ways to handle your type of cancer." He picked up his calendar. "I'm scheduling your chemo treatments every three weeks," he announced.

"I was hoping to go to the mountains over Thanksgiving with my family," I said.

"Forget taking a trip on Thanksgiving," he said.

"What? Can't we be flexible?"

"I'm in charge. I know what's best for you," he announced.

"But...."

"Let's just do things my way."

Becky and I gave each other another look. This time it meant *Let's get out of here.*

"We've learned as much as we need to know from you," I said. Hopefully, he'd heard the edge to my voice. Others might find his approach comforting, but I didn't like him. Not one little bit. What a bully.

After we left the office Becky said, "Judy, there must be other oncologists."

I shook my head and blinked back tears. *Why did everything have to be so hard?*

Becky hugged me. I drove home feeling more miserable with every mile. I'd gone into his office feeling optimistic, but now I felt deflated.

By the time I reached the front door to my home I felt angry, discouraged, and depressed. I desperately needed comforting.

"Where are you, Jack?" I pleaded. "I want to see you." I spotted him in front of the stereo.

"Now!"

He looked up but didn't move toward me. I stamped my foot. He disappeared behind the credenza.

"You're like everybody else," I whined. "Not there when I need you."

I raced to the refrigerator and grabbed a large chunk of dark chocolate. Usually I didn't allow myself to indulge this early in the day, but under the circumstances I deserved it. I grabbed the sports section of the *Daily Breeze* from the coffee table and stomped up the stairs to my bedroom.

When I was at the side of my bed I imagined Dr. Green's head on my pillow. With the rolled-up newspaper I hit the pillow over and over again, as hard as I could.

Several minutes later my rage turned into tears. I was furious. *How dare he ignore me and treat me like a child!* Exhausted, I collapsed on the bed and fell into a deep sleep.

On waking an hour later, my first thoughts turned to Jack. I felt bad that I'd yelled at him earlier. I tiptoed downstairs.

"Sorry Jack," I said, my voice soft and apologetic. "Where are you, my sweet Jack?"

No movement. If I don't see or hear movement, then he's probably hiding. I didn't blame him for being mad at me. When he still didn't come, I played some music on the stereo and sat on the sofa to wait. Five minutes passed. No sign of him. Fifteen minutes passed. Still no sign of Jack. Surely it wouldn't take that long for him to stop being afraid of me. He had to show his face sometime.

Thirty minutes later he finally poked his nose out from behind the piano.

"I don't blame you for being cautious, Jack. This is the first time you've seen me so angry."

I stood up slowly so as not to startle him. If I made any quick motion he would run away again. Slowly, I walked towards him still speaking softly.

"I'm so sorry, Jack. Mama was mad at the doctor. It had nothing to do with you."

He looked up at me with a tentative expression on his face but didn't move. Thankfully, when I reached for him, he let me pick him up. I lay down on the couch and held him on my lap, stroking him.

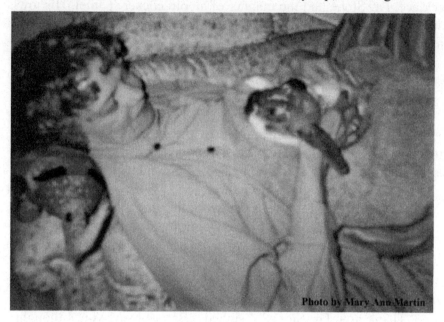

Photo by Mary Ann Martin

"Dr. Green is a great big bully. He has no sympathy or understanding. He didn't treat me right. I never want to see him again," I confided. "There must be another doctor who's better for me."

Maybe it was my imagination, but I could have sworn Jack nodded in agreement. "Jack, you've given me an idea," I said.

"Let's call Dr. Hass, the radiologist. Maybe he can recommend a better oncologist."

The receptionist transferred my call directly to the doctor.

"There's got to be a better oncologist for me," I pleaded.

"What happened?" Dr. Hass asked.

"Dr. Green is mean and negative. I need an oncologist who will be positive and more cheerful. Someone who can be a suitable member of our team."

"I know just the man – Dr. Stone," he said, without commenting on Dr. Green's lack of basic human kindness. He gave me his phone number.

✳✳✳

Two days later Becky went with me to meet Dr. Stone. Whereas Dr. Green reminded me of a bulldog, a man who wore negativity like a necklace, Dr. Stone had the manner of an old cocker spaniel. His jowls had drooped some, but he had kind eyes, and bushy eyebrows. I liked him immediately.

"If you need me," he assured me, "call my service in the evenings. As I always wear my pager, they will be able to reach me anytime, day or night."

"If I have surgery on Halloween, I want to schedule my first treatment so I will be well enough to travel with my nieces to the mountains over Thanksgiving. Dr. Green insisted that I must stick to his schedule, but I don't want to be bossed around by him."

"I'm not that rigid," he assured me. "We'll schedule the first chemo on November 15th. Does that work for you?"

I looked over at Becky. She gave me a wink and smiled.

He looked again at my paperwork and reassured me, "I am confident that the chemo will work. I don't want you to worry."

I was so relieved, I cried. He looked at me with a compassionate expression on his face.

"Thank you, Dr. Stone," I sighed. "Before I saw you, I thought I was doomed. I'd like you to be on my team along with Dr. Hass."

We all stood up. First, I impulsively and gratefully hugged him. Then both Becky and I shook his hand before we left.

"I don't usually eat steak," Becky said, "but this is a special occasion. Let's celebrate."

We went to The Sizzler. The only thing that could have made the celebration more perfect was if Jack had joined us.

After my wonderful consultation with Dr. Stone I was thrilled because I'd never have to see the sullen, bossy Dr. Green again. Later that day, his receptionist called.

"Doesn't he know he's not my doctor anymore?" I asked, puzzled.

"He has some information for you about the meeting he had with the state oncologists."

"Put him on the phone, please."

Without any sort of greeting, such as "Hello, Judy," he said abruptly, "All the oncologists agreed that two different treatments will work for you – Taxol and Carboplatin."

136

He'd followed through and did what he said he would do. What a surprise. I didn't say anything.

"I heard you're seeing Dr. Stone. Is that correct?" he inquired. His unanswered question hung in the air – *Why did you choose another doctor over me?* He deserved an explanation. Maybe it would help him be kinder to his other patients.

"Yes, that's correct. You're too much doom and gloom for me," I replied, bluntly. "As I see it, doctor and patient are supposed to be a team, and the chemistry just isn't right between us. Thanks for the treatment information, though."

"Sorry about that," he said, but he didn't seem upset – or sorry – at all.

After we hung up I turned and said to Jack, "Maybe I was too hard on Dr. Green." I paused to think that over. "On second thought, no, I wasn't," adding, "The big bully."

It felt so good to release my rage against Dr. Green that I wondered whether the same method might work whenever anger at my mother bubbled to the surface and gave me feelings of guilt and shame and fear. *Could beating up a pillow get rid of those corrosive feelings?*

I decided to keep an old pillow and rolled-up newspaper handy in the closet for the next time my mother's hurtful words made me feel bad. A cheap alternative to pounding a punching bag at a gym. I sure wouldn't want to be sued for breaking the bag. That's how angry I felt at times. And I made a mental note to close the door so the loud noise wouldn't scare Jack.

❋❋❋

That night as I cuddled Jack, I realized that I had moved through the Five Stages of Grief. I was grieving for myself, knowing that cancer had killed my sister Andrea and my best friend Dorie. I could be next.

Stage One (Denial) had been disbelief and protesting, *Why me?* Stage Two (Anger) – there was plenty of that! Anger with incompetent, uncaring doctors. Anger with myself for failing to do something to prevent the cancer, and even with God, for allowing it to happen.

How was I able to bypass the third (Bargaining) stage of grief? I didn't make any deals with God to let me survive the cancer by promising to do something (like go to church more often) or give up something I loved (like chocolate). I knew that lots of people did this, but it was silly to think that you could bribe God. I believed in His plan. If it was His will that I lived through this ordeal, that would be great. If not, well, I'd see Dorie and Andrea in heaven sooner than I thought.

Stage Four (Depression) was what I had felt for the past few weeks, dwelling on the thought that this was the beginning of the end for me.

"Jack, I have a bunch of top-quality doctors scheduled to perform the surgery. Friends are praying for me. God sent me Sonya to arrange an earlier appointment with Dr. Hawkins. Dr. Green met with world-class doctors who suggested treatments that would work for me. God provided another oncologist who was not only available, but more flexible and more positive than Dr. Green.

I'm going to take these as signs that He heard my prayers.

"You and I will have to trust in the Lord, Jack. We'll face this together, no matter what comes."

I was at Stage Five – Acceptance.

Photo by Cheri Burcham

Chapter 22
Finding Out Who My Friends Are

"I wonder," I said to Jack as I was brushing his fur, "how my friends will react to the news that I have a life-threatening illness. I must confess, I feel a little anxious. Will they be supportive, or will they shun me?"

When I finished brushing Jack, I went to the gym. The first person I saw was Connie, a woman I had met at a church in Redondo Beach.

Even though I had her phone number I was reluctant to contact her, since I considered her more of an acquaintance. Yet I thought perhaps she'd like to join me to see *The Anonymous Four*, a vocal ensemble of four women who specialize in performing medieval music found in ancient monasteries and abbeys. They have given concerts in the USA and internationally since the late 1980s.

They have recorded and toured with the Chilingirian String Quartet, fabled harpist Andrew Lawrence King, Darol Anger (violin) and Mike Marshall (mandolin, guitar) and other accomplished musicians.

"Have you heard of this group and would you be interested in joining me if I get tickets?" I asked.

"Yes, a friend at church has talked about them. I'd love to see them!" she said with enthusiasm. "When you get the tickets let me know how much I owe you."

***

After I purchased the tickets I called her to confirm the date to see the show. When there was no answer, I decided to go to the gym at about the same time I saw her before. She was just getting on the treadmill and about to punch in her heart rate settings when I arrived.

"Hi Connie, I went to the box office at the Shubert Theater to buy tickets for their concert on Saturday," I said as I climbed onto the nearby treadmill.

"That's great!" she exclaimed. "I'm really looking forward to this."

Then I blurted out, "By the way, I just got the results of my blood test back from the testing I told you about before. I have uterine cancer and will need to have surgery at the end of October."

Her body language signaled that this was not what she wanted to hear.

"Oh, that's awful. I'm sorry this happened to you," she stated. "Are you concerned about the prognosis?"

"Yes, I didn't think this would ever happen to me, and it's hard to deal with."

We walked on our treadmills in silence for a few minutes. Then she asked, "Are you sure you still want to go to the concert?"

"Oh, yes. I've wanted to see *The Anonymous Four* for a year now."

"But do you feel well enough?"

"Of course." More silence.

"I may have a problem with the date. I just remembered I'm leaving town the day before the concert," she said.

I wasn't sure whether to believe her or not but decided to give her some time to check her calendar.

"I'll call you later tonight about your schedule," I offered.

"Okay," she replied. "I'll find out when my trip happens."

On my drive home, I was confused, not knowing why she had changed her mind. Why had she been so eager to go initially, but once I shared my diagnosis, her attitude changed? Did my mention of cancer, a serious illness, trigger emotions in her that she was not ready to face? Was she afraid of her own mortality that she might also get a serious illness, and might die?

As I entered my home, I slammed the door. Jack watched me and cocked his head as I stomped around the room. I picked up the litter box, which needed to be cleaned, and emptied it into a plastic bag as I muttered to myself, "I'm not sure if I believe about her needing to check her schedule."

Startled, Jack looked up. His ears turned back on high alert. I went over to pick him up and we sat on the couch.

"This is so painful," I shared with Jack. "Am I imagining things about why she doesn't want to join me? Was my telling her about my cancer unsettling for her? Maybe she's not much of a friend after all and made up an excuse to avoid going to the concert with me."

Perhaps it would have been better if I'd gotten a commitment on possible dates before I purchased the tickets. Or perhaps her reaction was the belief that somehow my cancer was contagious. So silly. Like children teasing me about having "cooties" in elementary school. Was it all emotionally based?

Years ago, when I first started my real estate career, both my sister Andrea and I were depressed. She, because her husband, a doctor, was unhappy in the marriage so he took off to study in Paris for a year. At the same time, I was dealing with all the bad memories of my childhood and afraid to confront it all.

Andrea and I both had therapy with the same person, Keith. I was on medication for six months and then *voilá* – one day I felt much better, decided that I was healed, and didn't need to take it anymore. Our therapy ended when Keith moved to Australia.

Maybe I was having a dose of depression again, and I was deliberately ignoring it. This time, I was depressed about the prospect of dying too early.

I had grieved extensively when Dorie, Andrea, and my beloved Aunt Ruth had died of cancer. Was *my* cancer really the result of taking those hormones that Dr. Salem said I must take? I was angry at him because he was clearly not knowledgeable about ladies going through menopause. I was angry at myself for not being more assertive with him. I should have refused to take those hormones. This very week I had heard about an alternative to prescription drugs – natural hormones in the form of herbal remedies.

Did I bring this cancer on myself?

"What do you think of all of this, Jack?" I asked while continuing to pet him. He looked at me with his soulful eyes. I sensed that he was listening and understood exactly how I felt. My tears fell on Jack's head. He reached over and licked my hand.

"But you'll be here for me, won't you?"

I hugged him tight, probably too tight. He squirmed so I put him down and continued the nasty chore of cleaning out the litter box.

It still smelled like pee. Normally I cleaned it out every four days, but today was day six. The deodorizer wasn't working any more.

I fetched my plastic gloves from under the sink and carried the litter box outside. I rinsed it out, added some white vinegar to cut the odor and vigorously brushed the insides, leaving the box to soak for a while. In a half hour I would refill it with the litter bedding and fresh Timothy hay. Taking care of this and other chores temporarily took my mind off Connie's reaction to my news.

I called her that night to see what she'd found out about Saturday. Maybe she was really leaving town.

"I'm catching the plane Saturday afternoon," she responded. "I'm really sorry I can't join you. I hope everything works out for you with your surgery."

"Thank you, Connie. I appreciate that."

Was it my imagination after all, my thinking that all my friends would reject me when it's just my rattled nerves playing a big part? Or was it that Connie couldn't take being around someone who was seriously ill? If so, I needed to let go of her, as her fear of her mortality was her issue, and not mine. I couldn't afford to risk bringing any more negativity into my life.

Later that night I hesitated before calling Jean and Mary. They had been friends for many years, and I hoped that they would be understanding and supportive in my time of need and confusion. But I couldn't count on it.

I used the conference call feature and called them both at the same time. Mary answered first, and I put her on hold while I dialed Jean.

When they were both on the line, I said, as calmly as I could manage, "I have uterine cancer and will need to have surgery by the end of October."

"Oh, that's awful, Judy," Jean responded, "I'll call Bel Air Church and ask the deacons to pray for you at our next meeting."

"The deacons' group meets in West Los Angeles Tuesday night," Mary added. "Count on their prayers."

"I'd appreciate you doing that," I said. I felt relieved. More tears filled my eyes. Cancer sure was making me emotional. I heard a crunching sound behind me. I turned around and saw Jack take a bite out of the corner of my wooden coffee table.

"Hold on, both of you," I yelled into the phone. "Jack is acting out!"

Without waiting for their response, I dropped the receiver and commanded, "No, Jack!"

He looked up and then ignored me. I ran into the bathroom for the water bottle. He took another bite out of the coffee table. I fired the spray. The blast of water stopped him in his tracks, but only for a moment. He seemed to be assessing whether or not I was serious. But maybe he didn't even feel the water.

"Dang it, Jack!" I fired the spray again, this time directly into his face just as he was about to take a third bite. Startled, he shook off the water and then backed away from the table. I stood over him and shook my finger in his face.

"No, Jack!" I pointed to the cage. "Go there. Chew on your toys. That's why I bought them for you."

He looked up at me as if exasperated that I'd interrupted his fun.

"Jack, I'm serious. That's MY stuff!"

I put a pillow from the couch on top of the chewed corner. I would have to put some anti-stick tape on it later.

Oh my gosh, Jean and Mary were on hold on the phone!

"So sorry you had to wait," I explained. "I had to stop Jack from chewing the furniture."

"Does he often do that?" Jean asked.

"Unfortunately, yes. I'm having to keep a close watch on him, especially since my diagnosis. He seems to be misbehaving a lot more."

"I'm so sorry to hear this news," Mary said. "The Lord will be with you. Let Bill and me know how we can help you. Don't hesitate to call anytime."

✳✳✳

Mary and Jean were as good as their word. A week before my surgery they arranged for the members of the deacons' group to lay hands on me as they prayed for my healing. I felt the presence of God. It was so comforting.

At first, I only told two people in my real estate office that I had cancer – my best friend Margaret, and the office manager, Danny. I decided not to tell the other agents as I was afraid that they might tell my clients that I was sick and steal my business. Later, I confided in my friends Charlene and Susan.

Another friend, Verna, also gave me some unexpected support. She researched my type of cancer on the Internet. She told me that "endometrial" means cancer of the lining of the uterus. It seems one in thirty-eight women will have that diagnosis. In sixty-eight percent of the cases, it is localized or confined to that area.

"There is a 95.4% five-year survival rate," Verna said.

"You mean I might only live five more years?"

"No, it means that after five years if you don't have a re-occurrence, you're cured," she assured me.

I breathed a sigh of relief. She had made the unknown, known, and that reduced a lot of my fear.

"Thanks for your efforts," I said gratefully.

"I was happy to do it. Call me anytime. Remember, Judy, we're friends. And true friends are there to help when needed."

Maybe I've said this before, but it bears repeating. My friends were my lifeline during this crisis, and still are in times of trouble. I was grateful that the Lord would show me in the weeks ahead how many good friends I had who were emotionally supportive and praying for me.

They were able to assure me that the chemo treatments are a season in my life and will not go on forever. This news prevented me from moving back into any depression that might be lurking on the sidelines.

One morning I reached out to my dear friends Vi and Rose, who comforted me with their caring words. These two would turn out to be vital in my dealing with unknown potholes still to be encountered.

Chapter 23
Planning for Surgery

While I waited for my surgery date, I went back to the Wellness Community (now called the Cancer Support Community South Bay) at the Redondo pier to see what programs they offered while I was doing my treatments. The kind receptionist gave me the information.

"There is a cancer patient group that meets on Thursday night. It's for people with all kinds of cancer. You will need an initial meeting with the therapist and then you can join them. There's also a 'Writing for Wellness' group that meets once a month on a Saturday morning led by an accomplished writer. It's well attended. She assigns various topics to the attendees and encourages them to write quickly."

I was very interested in joining both the Thursday night group and Saturday class, so a week later I met for my initial appointment with the therapist, Jane, who would be facilitating the cancer patient group.

I went to my first writing class on the Saturday before my surgery. There were fifteen of us and Barbara, the group leader, instructed us to write on a specific topic for just five minutes. She called the topic a "prompt," and announced it just before setting the timer.

"Write continuously. Don't take your pen off the paper." She ordered. "Maybe you'll say you have nothing to write about, or maybe you don't like the topic. That's okay. Soon you will have something to say. Just let your thoughts flow."

She was right. I could do that. One prompt was "how did you feel when you first learned you had cancer?" I had plenty to say on that topic. I sometimes even changed the topic and wrote about Jack or about the weather. That was acceptable to Barbara.

Once she gave us a prompt on "what do you think is your purpose in life?" I had wondered about that all my adult years. After I left teaching I was involved in other jobs before I finally entered real estate. I wanted – no, I *needed* – to know God's purpose and plan for me. I loved listening to the others share their writing, and soon became friends with many of them.

Belonging to this group nourished my soul. It gave me a chance to spread my wings and gain confidence as a writer.

The week before my scheduled surgery, people continued to surprise me with their support. My niece Becky arranged for various friends to bring dinners to me for the fifteen days of my convalescence. I trained Chris, the twelve-year-old neighbor boy, to clean the litter boxes and prepare Jack's food. Jeri, my cleaning lady, offered to shop for groceries and check on Jack until I was through with my treatments.

Jack was not supportive, though. He raced around more. Things that didn't normally bother him, did. He must have sensed that something was going to happen. It made him hyper. The slightest noise set him off. When the gardeners started their blowers, he ran for cover faster than usual. He hid behind the couch so often that I had to constantly stop what I was doing and calm him. Maybe he'd picked up on my anxiety.

I'd spent hours journaling with God about how I felt. That helped me keep the fear away. I also journaled about the people who were projecting their own fears about cancer on me. My needing to remember it wasn't necessarily about me, but their awareness of their own mortality and recoiling from that unpleasant realization.

If there was negative energy around me, I needed to retreat to a better place inside myself. If Jack had been able to journal, maybe he would have been less anxious and more supportive.

❋❋❋

On Monday I went to a pre-operative appointment. The nurse drew blood and reminded me that enough blood would be saved for me in case the doctor needed it for a transfusion. Dr. Salem agreed to play the soundtrack of *Sense and Sensibility* in the operating room while I was under anesthesia. He warned me to avoid eating or drinking anything but water after midnight.

The night before the surgery, I decided to stuff myself. My friend Liz bought me dinner at Hamburger Hamlet. I ordered a one-pound hamburger with tomatoes, lettuce, pickles, Swiss cheese, and dripping with barbeque sauce. The platter came with onion rings *and* French fries. Dinner also included a mud pie for dessert. A real pig-out. I took my time chewing and kept eating even after I felt full. I wasn't going to deprive myself.

❋❋❋

Halloween morning, I woke up wondering how Dr. Salem could have scheduled surgery for 4:00 P.M. on a day that was meant for feasting on sweets. What a time to have to fast! Somehow, I would have to find the will power to resist all temptation.

Despite my pig-out the night before, when I woke I already felt hungry. It was only 9:00 A.M. and my mouth watered for more delicious mud pie. Not only that, my office was having a Halloween party at noon, with lots of sweets to share. It wasn't going to be easy, but I planned to go just because I love parties.

I sat on the edge of my bed and stretched. My upper leg and hip were bothering me. Darn. The pain was so bad I went to the medicine cabinet to grab a couple of Aleve pills.

Before I could pop them in my mouth, I remembered Dr. Salem's warning. *No medication the day of surgery.* The doctor was going to give me a test. If I cheated, and he detected it, my surgery would be canceled. Oops. I'd almost screwed up.

My hip throbbed. What was I going to do? Luckily, I remembered that I had some topical items I could use for pain. Biofreeze was one I used at the time I was running the L.A. marathon. I'd try that first. Later, if necessary, I could use either Orthogel or Aspercreme. I hoped that the doctor wouldn't care if I applied something on my skin. Anyhow, I was desperate. I rolled on the Biofreeze and it felt cool. I decided I'd wait a half hour or so and see if it helped. It did.

I went downstairs to the living room and couldn't see Jack.

"Hey, Sweetie Pie, Mama needs to let you know her plans for the next few days."

Silence. I wondered where Jack was. I called him again. Finally, Jack peeked out from behind the piano pedals.

"Would you like a carrot?"

His ears perked up. I knelt on the floor beside him. He scrunched down his whole body as if to prepare himself for being picked up. I carried him into the kitchen with my left arm. I turned on the hot water for coffee with my right hand. Then I remembered the doctor's warning against drinking anything other than water. I poured the nearly scalding water into my favorite mug and sipped it plain. Ugh! Without at least a squirt of lemon, it tasted awful.

In the refrigerator on the bottom shelf I found a bag with three tiny carrots. I juggled the carrots and Jack under my left arm while holding the cup of hot water in my right hand. I carefully lowered myself into the rocking chair as I fed Jack the first carrot. He chewed quickly. He must have been hungry. I fed him another as I sipped the hot water. I hoped it would help me feel full.

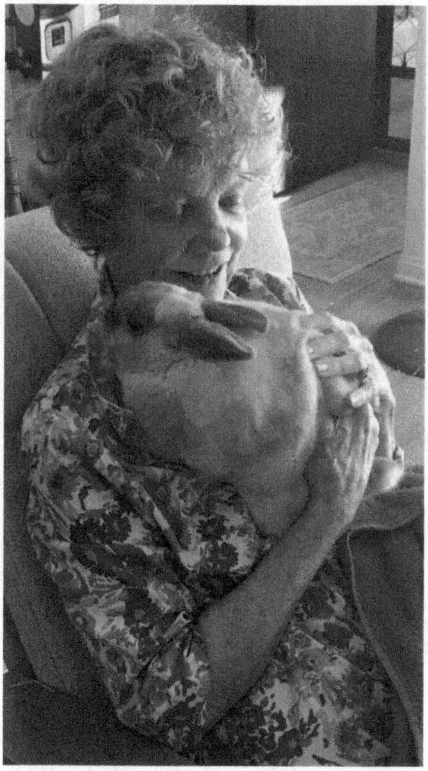

The motion of the chair was soothing.

"In a few hours," I said to Jack, "I will be going into the hospital for surgery. I am nervous because I don't know what to expect."

Maybe Jack was listening, but he didn't act like it. He just chewed on the towel he was sitting on. I kept talking and rocking us in the chair.

"The doctor is going to play our favorite tape during the surgery. Remember *Sense and Sensibility*, Jack? It's the tape I play for you almost every day."

Jack didn't seem to understand what I was talking about. He just kept chewing on his carrots and towel. I petted and rocked him for 45 minutes and it calmed me down. When I placed Jack back down on the rug he immediately ran to his litter box and peed. I didn't realize he'd been holding it. Thank goodness he hadn't peed on me.

I packed my suitcase. Then I dressed up in a work outfit: dressy brown pants and a ruffled plaid shirt. I wanted to look good for the office party especially since I would probably be the only person who wasn't dressed in a costume.

A few minutes before I had to leave I noticed that my hip felt better but darn it, now I had a headache. Time for one of my own remedies – something I discovered one day while cleaning out my freezer. I opened the freezer door and stuck my head inside. Inhaling a few deep breaths of the ice cold air cleared my head. Soon I no longer felt tired. My headache disappeared.

At 11:30 I fetched a bottle of water from the refrigerator and waved goodbye to Jack.

"See you later, Sweetie Pie."

***

At the office, the party was underway. Pirates, witches, milk maids, and baseball players ate barbecued ribs and sipped drinks from plastic cups. Laughter filled the room. The desks had been cleared of files and equipment and now held bowls of potato chips, M & M's, and fried chicken wings. All that delicious food and I couldn't eat a thing!

Then I spied a man who I had met on a singles' cruise last year. He was pouring himself some wine as I approached.

"Remember me?" I blurted out. "Judy?"

"Oh, yeah. Judy," he mumbled, swaying slightly, "from the cruise. I remember you running around the Ping-Pong table. You beat me."

"Of course I won the tournament. I was the only one who was sober." The sarcasm was lost on him.

Looking down, I noticed that his left hand holding a plate of spaghetti had tilted upward.

He asked, "Want some?"

At the same time I reached down to steady the plate, he lifted it up suddenly. The plate collided with my mouth (fortunately closed), causing me to sneeze as the sauce splashed up my nose.

"Oops," he slurred.

Danny, the office manager, came to my rescue with some napkins. Margaret strolled over.

"I see you've met James," she said. "You don't have to share. There's plenty of food. How about I get you your own plate? And how about a drink?"

"Just some water would be fine," I said, wiping sauce off my face and resisting the impulse to lick my fingers.

"Are you sure? There's wine, iced tea, and coffee. Come get some food." She grabbed my arm and steered me toward the buffet.

"Thanks, but I'm having a surgical procedure later today, so water is all I'm allowed." I hoped she wouldn't ask about the specifics of the operation. Thank goodness, she didn't.

Before I could even grab a bottle of water, Charlene and Susan greeted me.

"You *must* try my spaghetti and meatballs," Susan urged. "I spent all morning making it."

My mouth watered so much I couldn't look her in the eyes. I was focused on the serving bowl. I didn't tell her that I'd already inhaled some of the aromatic sauce, thanks to James. Maybe I couldn't eat the meatballs, but I sure had a good smell of them. I was glad noodles weren't hanging out of my nostrils.

"No, thanks. I'm not hungry, but would you mind if I could wrap some up and take it home for dinner?"

She was pleased and beamed a smile.

"Oh, that's fine, Judy." She scurried off to get some tin foil.

Margaret, seeing that a plate was being prepared for me, added some chips and chocolate cake. It was all I could do not to dip my finger into the frosting. When the plate was filled, I started to back off towards the door. I would put the food in the frig, so Becky could enjoy it later.

I had a flashback to childhood, when I was about seven. My sister Deborah would make chocolate chip cookies for a high school event and ask me to help. When the dough was ready to put on the cookie sheet, I'd get a spoon and we'd take turns. She'd put a scoop on the sheet and I'd take a scoop to eat. We'd make a double batch, and when we were done, I was full of cookie dough and very happy. I smiled at the memory.

Normally I enjoy myself at Halloween parties, but not today. Everything on the buffet table was too tempting. In less than fifteen minutes I slipped out, vowing that next year I'd eat lots of sweets to make up for being deprived this year.

Exhausted by all that mental anguish, I drove home and took a nap, and dreamed about chocolate.

Becky arrived at 3:00 P.M. to drive me to the hospital. Jack, the scamp, was so busy eating his hay in the litter box, he didn't even notice I was leaving. I knelt and gave him one last hug and a kiss on the back of his head anyway.

"Bye, Jack," I said. I hoped he would miss me, but I doubted it. He just took another bite of the hay.

"You'll be in good hands while I'm in the hospital. Chris and Jeri will take care of you."

❋❋❋

At the hospital the nurse checked my insurance card, then hustled me into a small gray dressing room. She pulled the drapes and told me to put on a hospital gown. I sat on a small uncomfortable bed. My legs accidentally touched the bed's cold metal legs and my bare feet shivered on the hard floor.

After Becky helped me put my stuff in a large white plastic bag, she took a seat across the room. A different nurse brought me slippers, then drew some blood. She put a drop of the blood on a slide and left the room.

I was glad that I had used the Biofreeze topically on my skin, which had helped the pain move from an excruciating nine to a tolerable five on a zero-to-ten scale. I had gambled that the Biofreeze did not go into my blood stream. A few minutes passed. The nurse came back. I couldn't read the expression on her face.

"All clear," she said cheerfully. I was relieved.

She directed me to lie down on the gurney.

As they wheeled me down the hallway to surgery Claire ran alongside the gurney.

"You look good in that gown," she joked. She was out of breath. We laughed.

Outside the operating room Claire continued talking as if she wanted to distract me.

"We're going to get a manicure and pedicure while you're in surgery," Claire said. "But don't worry, we'll be close by. The doctor will call us when you're in the recovery room."

A man in a white coat I'd never met before walked towards us. I imagined he must be the doctor who would be performing the surgery. My fear about what was going to happen suddenly surfaced. What if I didn't wake up?

"I'm Dr. Lamb, and I will be your primary surgeon." He shook my hand and smiled. "You'll do just fine, Judy," he said. "I've had 20 years of experience doing these procedures."

He did look kind. I relaxed just a little bit. As the attendant wheeled me into the operating room Becky said, "God is with you."

The anesthesiologist asked me to sign more paperwork. It outlined the risks of anesthesia. It was the second piece of paper I'd signed saying it wouldn't be anyone's fault if I died. *Whose fault would it be? Mine?*

After I'd finished signing my life away, he tapped my left wrist. He tried to find a vein. It took him awhile. He kept tapping.

"Oops – I missed," he said. "Oops – I missed. Oops. Missed again."

I was becoming increasingly alarmed, but what could I do? Was this his first time doing this? Was he impersonating a doctor?

Finally, on the fourth try he found a suitable vein and inserted the needle, saying, "I'm giving you some anesthesia now."

The medicine stung. Nurses wearing blue hospital scrubs, surgical masks and gloves peered down at me. My eyes slowly began to lose focus. The white walls and harsh, bright lights dimmed. I closed my eyes and concentrated on the humming sound of the machines. The familiar melody of *Sense & Sensibility* comforted me.

That was the last thing I remembered.

✸✸✸

When I woke up, my first thought was: *I'm cold.*

"Please, I need warm blankets," I pleaded.

My teeth chattered. Instantly, warm blankets enveloped me.

"Her blood pressure is coming up now," one voice said.

"Good," another voice added. There were several nurses in the room with me. Suddenly Becky and Claire appeared.

"Hey, Judy," Becky said. "How are you feeling?"

I sighed and tried to smile. Claire held up her nails. Becky held hers up, too.

"See how pretty our nails look," Claire bragged, with a grin.

I appreciated that they were trying to cheer me up.

"You look pretty good," Becky assured me.

"Glad it's over," I mumbled groggily.

The results of the surgery would come later, but I didn't want to think about that now.

Chapter 24
Pothole #4: Facing Painful Memories

After I'd been in the recovery room for an hour, a nurse wheeled me up to my semi-private room on the second floor. Outside the door, I heard a woman's loud voice. So loud, in fact, that I heard it over the television, which had been turned up to a very high volume.

The nurse assisted me out of the wheelchair and into my hospital bed. In the bed next to me there was a very private conversation in progress. I tried not to listen but couldn't help but overhear through the curtain surrounding my roommate's bed.

"My husband and I want a baby!" a woman's voice boomed.

"Yes, but I hope you'll agree to have the surgery first," a man said. The distinctive male voice sounded familiar. I thought it might be Dr. Hawkins. He was the other doctor I'd met when I was seeking a second opinion.

The nurse fluffed my pillows and brought me a glass of water. Still groggy, I lifted my head to see better, but my eyes slipped shut.

"I think I'm pregnant," the woman said.

My eyes popped open. Dr. Hawkins had moved a bit and I could see through an opening in the curtain. The woman was tiny and very young. Probably in her early twenties.

"You really shouldn't wait to have surgery," Dr. Hawkins insisted. "Your tumor is cancerous."

"I've made up my mind," the woman snarled. "Go away!"

Her thunderous voice jolted my whole body. Poor Dr. Hawkins was only trying to help. He was an excellent doctor. If it hadn't been a three-month wait to be on his schedule, I would have chosen him to be my surgeon.

Even though I didn't know the whole story I found myself taking his side. I could hear her noisily turn over in her bed as she repeated, "I'm *not* having surgery."

He shook his head and backed away from her bed. "We'll talk later," he replied, adding, "when you're feeling better."

"I've made up my mind," she repeated obstinately.

For the first time, Dr. Hawkins glanced over at my bed. I waved, a stupid smile plastered on my face. He smiled and waved back but I could tell he didn't recognize me.

After Dr. Hawkins left, I heard her moan intermittently. Aaarrrggghh! Between the moaning and the loud TV, I was going to have trouble falling asleep. I imagined that I wasn't the only one on the floor she would keep awake tonight. Surely our neighbors heard it too. After a half hour of misery, I rang for the nurse.

"I'm not able to sleep, as the TV is so loud. Please, could you turn it down?" I asked in a whisper.

She did. I hoped that my roommate would not make a fuss. Thankfully, she didn't.

With the noise dimmed, I found my cassette player and earphones. I listened to the soothing classical music of *Sense and Sensibility* and dozed off.

In the middle of the night a nurse woke me up to give me ice chips. My mouth felt like sandpaper. I would have liked to drink some tonic water but that wasn't allowed, so I bit into the ice chips. The coldness refreshed me. The nurse took my pulse and blood pressure and left.

Three hours later the same nurse woke me up to take my vital signs.

"Your blood pressure is lower than it was last time. I wonder why?"

"My blood pressure is always low. That's normal for me."

✳✳✳

The next morning, Dr. Salem popped in for a visit.

"There were cancer cells in your ovaries," he said. "The other surgeon and I gave you a total hysterectomy."

I raised my eyebrows. I'd expected that, but still, it came as a shock.

"I have some other bad news," he said. "One cell in your left lymph gland was positive. You need both chemo and radiation."

I sighed, dejected.

"Now for the good news. The reason there was pain in your right hip flexors was because your nerve cells were knotted like pieces of yarn. I took the time to smooth them out." He put his hand on my hip.

"See how flat they are now? You won't be in pain anymore," he stated with a proud voice.

"Thank you, I'm so glad!" I exclaimed. "This is certainly an unexpected side effect of the surgery. The hip pain has bothered me for years. Now it's gone! Hooray!"

"You will be here two or three more days," he continued. "You need to eat whatever you're served. I want to make sure you're digesting your food. When you pass gas, then you can go home."

What? Passing gas is a deciding condition for me go home?

"Take your IV stand and walk around the halls as much as you want. Drink lots of water."

Dang it all. Having been overnight in the hospital several years ago, I remembered how bland hospital food could be.

"OK, I'll do it," I agreed.

✳✳✳

Mid-morning, Paula, a friend from church, came to see me. I wasn't expecting anyone to visit.

"I brought you a present," she said, handing me a huge stuffed dog.

The furry canine had floppy ears, big paws, dangling limbs, and wore a red handkerchief around his neck. I cradled him in my arms. We looked at each other. His soulful dark eyes were sad yet comforting. We rubbed noses.

He was so tall, his tail hung down and tickled my knees. He reminded me of how much I missed Jack.

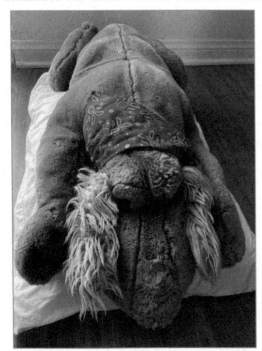

"I *love* him!" I exclaimed. "I'm going to call him Mr. Beagle."

"He'll help you feel better faster," Paula said, pleased that her gift was so cheerfully accepted. "On my way here, I passed by the newborns. Let's take a walk to see them."

Eager to be able to leave the room for some entertainment, I asked. "Is it okay to take Mr. Beagle with us?"

Paula gave me thumbs up. I set Mr. Beagle on the bed. She put her arm around me, so I could lean on her.

After my legs got used to standing, Paula handed me Mr. Beagle. When I held him against my chest my hospital gown fell open, exposing my rear end. Paula laughed at my embarrassment.

"Let's not give everyone a show, else we'll have to sell tickets," she observed. "Hold Mr. Beagle and the gown with your right hand."

I did as she suggested.

"Now hold the IV stand with your left hand."

Somehow, together we managed to recover my dignity. We walked down the hospital hall in the direction of the newborns. To steady me, Paula held my elbow.

"Any news yet?" a nurse asked as she passed by.

News? What did she mean by news? Then I remembered Dr. Salem saying that I had to pass gas before I could leave the hospital.

"No news yet," I reported, giggling.

Paula and I made it down to the newborn area and watched them in their bassinets. On the way back, we met Claire as she got off the elevator. I introduced her to Paula, and she was pleased that I had a friend come to visit. We chatted for a bit and then we all went back to my room. I hugged Paula and thanked her for coming.

"Sorry if I kept you awake last night," my roommate said, as Claire helped me into my hospital bed. "By the way, my name is Marie."

I introduced myself and Claire. We exchanged comments about the hospital.

"I overheard your doctor," I said at the first pause in the conversation.

"Then you know I don't want to be here," Marie said. "I want to be at home with my husband."

Claire interjected, "Judy, do you need anything?"

"A few hours ago, I asked the nurses for hot water and lemons for my tea. They've been busy getting everyone their breakfast. Do you think you can find where they keep the hot water?"

Claire loved having a mission. She rushed through the door.

"I also need batteries from the gift store. My cassette player is running low," I called out after her.

I looked over at Marie. She was cheering for a contestant on *Let's Make a Deal.* I'd been part of the audience of that show ten years earlier, but Marie seemed so intent on the game that I decided it wasn't the right time to tell her about my experience. Together we watched Bob Barker charm the ladies.

Ten minutes later when Claire returned, she put the pot of hot water and some lemons on my tray.

"Thanks so much, Claire. This will help me feel more at home, having my special cup and pot."

"What would I do without her?" I confided to Marie as Claire headed out on a mission to find batteries.

Let's Make a Deal ended with the contestant deciding among the three doors. She chose door #3 and didn't win the car.

During the commercial, I turned to Marie. "Aren't you afraid of leaving here after what your doctor said? Cancer can be deadly."

"Oh, no. I'll have the baby and think about the tumor later," she stated casually.

I hoped for her and her baby's sake that Marie was choosing the right door.

Thirty minutes later Claire came back with batteries in one hand and a wiggling bath towel under her other arm. She laid the bundles at the foot of my bed. The towel jumped, and Jack's head popped out. He blinked as if to say *Where am I?* Then he spied Mr. Beagle lying next to my feet. Was he jealous? I held my breath. He sniffed Mr. Beagle's paws and decided he wasn't any competition. What a relief.

Just at that moment Sharon, another friend from church, walked in and I introduced her to Claire and Marie. I was so glad she came. She sat on the edge of my bed where she could pet Jack as she told me about the latest news from the singles' groups.

"A couple we know got engaged and I can't imagine how those two will make it together. They are exact opposites in every way," she confided.

"Don't they say that opposites attract?" Claire asked.

"I'm not so sure," Marie interjected. "My husband and I seem to match on all levels."

I wondered about that, because that had not been my experience. I made a mental note: *Maybe I should be listening to some of my married friends and get feedback from them.*

I wiggled my toes to invite Jack to come and say hello. He didn't. He just sat there staring at me. Maybe I looked so pale he didn't recognize me. Claire scooped Jack up and laid him in my arms. I kissed his head and hugged him close.

Marie had been so engrossed with Sharon's news that she finally noticed Jack.

"A rabbit!" Marie clapped her hands. She jumped out of her bed and came over to pet Jack.

I kept my eyes on the door. We were having fun, but I was pretty sure pets weren't allowed.

When the nurse walked in, I pulled the towel over Jack's body. She did a double take and stared at the towel. The towel moved. Jack's head popped out. I thought she'd scold us, but she didn't.

"I'll come back in a few minutes," the nurse said, and smiled.

Five minutes later, Claire stood and picked up Jack.

"Sorry, Judy, I need to take Jack with me."

"But Jack just got here," I whined. I kissed him on his head again and gave him one last hug before reluctantly handing him over. Jack reminded me of home. I would miss cuddling with him before I fell asleep.

"I need to leave, too," said Sharon. "It seems like you're progressing OK, and I hope you'll be joining us at church real soon." She leaned over and gave me a hug.

"Thanks for coming, both of you. It means a lot to have you visit."

After they left, I hugged Mr. Beagle. I remembered the tapes I had received from Liz two days earlier and I was eager to play them. I inserted the new batteries into the cassette recorder and listened to my tape, *Why You Get Sick, and How You Get Well.*

Marie turned off the TV.

"Judy, would you mind turning the sound up on your tape recorder? I'd like to listen, too."

I turned up the volume and we listened to three chapters. I hoped these inspirational tapes would cause her to change her mind and stay in the hospital for the operation to remove her tumor.

❋❋❋

I must have dozed off and woke to the sound of the bathroom door slamming. My heart pounded. Then I saw Marie. She was packing her suitcase. I watched silently.

"I'm going home to have my baby," she explained.

I wished her well but felt sad about what I felt was a faulty decision. I would pray for her.

Marie might not want to listen to her doctor, but I would listen to mine. No matter what results Dr. Salem gave me tomorrow, I would choose life. God had a purpose for me to fulfill. His presence guided me.

A pastor from a nearby church came to visit and asked if I wanted to chat. He asked if I had any concerns.

"Yes, as a matter of fact I do," I confessed. "My Mom died a few years ago and we were never able to reconcile. She had been so mean to me as a child, but whenever I asked her if she wanted to talk about it, she said no. 'Past is past,' she'd say. I wish I could put all that behind me."

"Because you can't do this in person," he counseled, "I feel that the best thing to do to help release this anguish, is to pray for her and to thank her for being in your life."

"How does that work? She's in heaven. Will she be able to hear me pray for her? That will be hard to do, as I've been angry at her for a long time for treating me badly."

"Yes, that may seem hard to do, but I feel that by praying, God will help you to forgive her. I don't know for sure, but I think people in heaven are able to hear us. Are you willing to try that? Would you be willing to let me pray with you right now?"

I nodded. He led me in a prayer, asking that the Lord help me to forgive my mother.

"Thanks for coming in. I appreciate what you've said. Maybe God will understand that even if I'm angry, I will pray for her and I do have the willingness to forgive her."

My friend Rose came shortly after the pastor left to see how I was doing. I told her about my session with him. She sat down, held my hand, and stayed with me for over an hour.

Fortunately, the TV was off and in silence I was able to be with her in the peace and comfort her presence gave me. She understood, and I felt a healing take place within my soul. Later, we did a focusing session on the thought of praying for my mother.

A few years earlier, Rose, Vi, and I took a class based on the book *Focusing* by psychologist Dr. Eugene Gendlin, PhD. The author was curious about why long-term therapy patients achieved no results, yet others in therapy for a short time can greatly reduce or eliminate a psycho-emotional issue. In his research, he noticed that all the patients who were quickly cured were able to connect back to the original experience, whether it was long ago or a recent event.

Focusing is the process of a deep listening to the body – its sensations, feeling and emotions – in an open, accepting way. At the end of a session of listening intently, the unconscious will be revealed with its inner knowing. There can be both an emotional change that is directly felt and now is able to be expressed as well as an actual physical shift in the body.

After three years of practicing the skill of focusing, I have discovered that there are two parts of me. One is the adult who operates in my brain, the part that wants to pray for Mom and do away with any residual fears or anger I may have. The other part is my emotional inner child who resides in my heart, and who was both afraid of Mom and afraid to express my anger at her, even now.

When I began my session with Rose, she asked, "Is there anything in your life right now keeping you from feeling really good or really free?"

I closed my eyes and focused on how I felt in my body at that moment.

"My ears hurt really bad and so does my throat as I'm sitting in front of the mirror in my bedroom once again and Mom is about to say all those words I don't want to hear. My hands are clasped over my ears and the pain is so intense that I can't help crying out. I have no words to defend myself. My throat hurts as I want to talk back to her and say 'STOP!' but I'm afraid to say anything. I'm terrified that she will tell Dad and he will do what he has threatened to do – kick me out of the house. I'm only seven. I don't know where my dog Sandy and I would go."

"What words are you afraid to hear?" Rose asked.

"My mother is saying, 'Judy, I don't know what we're going to do with you. You have to accept that we wanted a boy and now that we're stuck with you, we're trying to cope. You should be ashamed of yourself. You're not pleasing to look at. Don't you see that? Therefore, you must be nice to everyone, or you'll never have any friends.'

"I was troubled by the words the pastor advised me to say in praying for Mom. My adult brain says yes, do it, but my inner child is still angry."

I took a deep breath and tried a prayer.

"OK, Mom, even though I'm angry with you, I shall try to pray that now that you're in heaven with Jesus and are reunited with Brittany, that you are healed of the heartache that it was your fault she died. Also, perhaps you're trying to get over the guilt of blaming Kevin for her death and giving Andrea and me such grief. I wish you well, Mom. AMEN."

As I prayed, I felt the shift in my throat as I found the courage to speak up to Mom. All the words that I had held back all those years were there for me to express.

I had finally found my voice.

At the end of the focusing session I had the feeling of a shift inside me. I had spoken my words to her and been angry. As Rose and I talked, it clarified for me that Mom was wounded, that she had never been able to handle her own anger, that she was insecure, and had both shame and guilt about Brittany.

In the days ahead, during my treatments, I was fortunate to focus with both Rose and Vi about what was happening around me. These sessions were a catalyst to help me move into healing my own wounds of the past.

***

During the next two days I took my doctor's advice and drank a cup of hot water with lemon every hour. Afterwards I took walks, usually down to the newborn area.

On one visit I stood at the window watching a couple waving to their baby. All the babies looked alike. Small, with wrinkled, reddish skin and wrapped in regulation white blankets. *How could they tell which one was theirs?* I wondered.

Every few hours a nurse stopped by to ask me, "Any news yet?" What she was really asking was, "Have you passed gas?"

"Not yet," I replied, "but hopefully soon."

I walked the halls and drank lemon water until I thought I might burst. At 4:00 P.M. on Monday afternoon, near the nurse's station by the newborn area, IT happened.

Finally!

"I passed gas," I shouted. "Did you hear it?"

A patient sitting by the nurse's station stared at me like I was nuts. Didn't he get it? This was a significant moment for me.

"I did it! I did it! I passed gas!" I exulted. I felt proud, like the times in high school when I had won a tennis tournament. Maybe the hospital should give trophies for passing gas.

"I'll call your doctor," a nurse said, amused and a bit disconcerted. "Looks like you might be able to go home tomorrow."

***

The next morning Dr. Salem came to see me.

"So there's good news," he said. "However, the nurses tell me that your blood pressure is too low."

"I thought you said I could go home when I passed gas." I was very disappointed, longing to go home and be with Jack.

He called the nurse in to take my blood pressure for a third time.

"It's still too low, 90 over 60, too low to leave," he said.

"Would you both please give me a minute?" I asked. After they left the room to confer in the hallway, I pumped my arms up and down and whispered to myself, "My blood pressure is rising, rising, rising."

I wasn't sure if it would work but hoped they would give me another chance. After a few minutes, I called them back in.

"My goodness," the nurse said, "Your blood pressure is now 105 over 70."

Dr. Salem smiled. I hadn't fooled him. He signed the release anyway.

Chapter 25
Childhood Abuse Still Haunts Me
to This Day

The surgery had taken a lot out of me. I felt sore. I felt tired. Becky drove me home from the hospital and I didn't want her to see me cry. Over the next two weeks I would need people to prepare my meals, get my mail, and take out the trash.

Becky and Claire had been frequent visitors at the hospital and I certainly didn't want to ask them for more help. They had already done so much. I hoped Becky remembered her offer to ask her friends to bring me meals. That was so thoughtful, as all my friends lived miles away, and Mary Ann was gone on another one of her business trips.

When Becky walked me to the door of my condo, I hung on tight. Home sweet home. Inside my condo it smelled stuffy. I asked Becky to open the window. Where was Jack? Probably hiding. Why couldn't a rabbit be more like a dog? A dog would run to greet me, tail wagging. Jack would never do that.

I felt disappointed. The least he could do was show himself. After all, we'd only been apart two nights when I was at the Abbey. This time I was gone for three whole days. I'd hoped he would miss me as much as I'd missed him, but I guess he hadn't.

Becky noticed that I was upset and deduced the reason. She set my suitcase down by the door.

"I'll find Jack for you," she said.

I sat down in my rocking chair and watched Becky search under the piano bench and behind the sofa.

"Jack, where are you?" she called softly.

Finally, she glimpsed Jack behind the stereo. She bent down slowly so as not to scare him and picked him up, with one hand cupped under his head and the other beneath his bottom. She carried him over to me.

"Here's Mama!" she said.

I held Jack tight against my heart, maybe too tight. He squirmed. I tapped his front paws with my fingers.

"Stop that. Be still," I said in a harsh voice. "I was hoping you would be glad to see me."

"I'm making some tea," Becky yelled from the kitchen.

Soon the tea kettle whistled. She popped her head around the door.

"Do you want Mint, Orange Spice, Peppermint, or Good Earth?"

"Peppermint would be great," I replied, adding, "And a rice cake with some almond butter, please."

I wanted more time with Jack, but he wouldn't sit still. If I didn't hold on to him, he'd hop off my lap and disappear again. Why was he acting this way?

by Eloise Donnelly

Becky brought out the tea and rice cakes on a tray. She set them down on the table next to the rocker. When I reached over to pick up my cup, Jack hopped off my lap and scampered off to his hiding place behind the sofa. Becky sat down across from me and nibbled on a rice cake.

"I think I mentioned this before you checked into the hospital, that I've asked some of my friends to help you. They're going to buy groceries and make you meals for the next two weeks."

"That's wonderful!" I sighed with relief. "I don't think I'm up for cooking."

I teared up, overwhelmed with gratitude. I closed my eyes and leaned back against the sofa.

"I should have known you'd take care of everything," I exclaimed with delight. "You've been so loving and kind to me, considering my needs and gathering your friends to help me."

Becky cleared her throat as if to say, *No big deal*, but I knew she appreciated my words of thanks.

"You'll be visited by Lucy, Elaine, Anne, Sarah, and your neighbor Marian. Claire and I will stop by, too. That's one person for each day of the week," she said cheerfully. She handed me a schedule. "Here are all the women's names, their phone numbers and the days they're coming over. Do you want to rest now?"

I nodded. My whole body felt like it would collapse into my tea.

"Marian is coming at six today," Becky said. She tucked me into bed, and I fell asleep immediately.

***

When I woke, my home was pitch dark. For a minute I didn't know where I was. Then I heard a banging noise. I tensed up. Was a burglar downstairs?

"Who's there?" I yelled.

No answer.

More banging. I felt weak from the surgery and fearful about being alone. For a moment, I had a flashback to my childhood, when I experienced the same anxious feelings.

Counting Brittany, I was their fifth child and arrived late in their marriage. Our parents told my brother Kevin, age seven, to watch his sister Brittany, age three, during a party at a neighbor's house. Kevin got distracted, and Brittany fell into the pool and drowned.

Afterwards, because they had been drinking, our parents were unable to accept that they were at fault for her death. They unfairly blamed Kevin for the rest of his life.

Thirteen years later, I was born. A "surprise" baby.

When Kevin was 19 and I was 6, he started bullying me – chasing, tackling, and tickling me without mercy. There was no way to escape this 200-pound man. He devised creative ways to scare me, like sticking spiders in my hair and locking me in a closet. I'm sure it was his way of taking out his frustration for the guilt he felt about Brittany. Our parents never let him forget it.

They reminded me constantly that I was a big disappointment to them. They had hoped for another boy. It could be that a girl reminded them of their loss of little Brittany, and they wanted to even things out with two boys and two girls.

I feared my father when he'd been drinking. He would spank me so hard with a belt or hairbrush or anything handy that I always had bruises on the backs of my legs. I escaped from Dad and Kevin by hiding in the back yard with my dog Sandy.

My sisters Deborah and Andrea were a saving grace for me. They were kind and tried the best they could to help me out. When I wanted a tennis racket, Mom decreed, "No way."

I mentioned this to Deborah and heard her say to Mom. "You got me a racket and now it's time for Judy to get one, too." The next day Deborah presented me with a racket.

My parents went on lots of vacation trips. It was their way to escape the memory of the accident. When they were away they arranged for an adult to look in on us. The rules were flexible, and Andrea and I would stay up watching the late movies. This was a special time for me with her. Because she was also mistreated by Mom, we had a special bond. When she pouted and was sent away from the dinner table I would sneak food to her room.

My mother told me so often that I was repulsive and stupid, that I came to believe it. She made it clear that my only hope to be accepted was to pretend to be nice, otherwise I would be disliked and even shunned. If I developed a docile character, it would compensate for my ugly duckling looks.

In first grade, I made a friend, also named Judy, who invited me to visit her home. I remember the day I first met her mother, Mrs. Hubert. She was so loving and kind that I cried tears of joy just to be with her. I felt safe. She listened to all my troubles over milk and cookies, and then sent me outside to play with Judy in their big back yard.

I started to imagine that they were really my family. They invited me on family vacations. For once, I felt like I belonged. Judy's parents would tell me that I was important to them. They contradicted everything my parents had drummed into me. The Huberts said that I was pretty and smart, and that they believed I could accomplish anything I wanted.

Life at home was a different story. I would try hiding from my father, but he always found me and spanked me really hard for "being naughty," without explaining what crime I had committed. While spanking me, he would often say, "If you don't mind your mother when I'm not home, I'm going to send you back."

Back to where? I wondered where that place would be. I started wishing for that return trip to be true. Any place would be better than here.

One day I took Sandy with me when I visited the Huberts' and asked Mrs. Hubert if she'd adopt Sandy and me.

"We can't do that," she said gently, without explaining that the law wouldn't allow it. "I'm sure your family loves you."

"I'm not sure at all. At my house I can't do anything right," I said, my voice trembling. "They don't make me feel loved or wanted."

"Well, you can come visit us any time you want," Mrs. Hubert assured me with a hug.

I felt warm and comfy inside. It wasn't the solution to my problem, but it was a darn good alternative. Thank God, the Huberts became my surrogate family. Judy and I were tennis buddies and took lessons together.

Now I realize that God placed me in that stressful environment with my parents and brother to give me the coping skills to deal with psychological and physical abuse.

Maybe His plan is for me to teach others what I have learned, and to encourage them to have faith and hope, leaning on the Lord when times get tough,

✻✻✻

BANG!

The noise brought me back to the present moment.

BANG!

My ears went on high alert.

Again, another bang. *Oh my gosh! What was that noise?* I tried to calm myself down. The bandages on my stomach itched.

Suddenly I realized it must be Jack going in and out of his pet door. Then I felt silly. The pet door was a noise that I should be used to hearing. Sitting there in the dark, ruminating about my past had obviously made my imagination run wild.

I looked over at the lighted clock dial by my bed. It read 5:45 P.M. Marian was supposed to arrive at 6:00. Hopefully she'd be on time. To calm my nerves, I inserted the tape *How to Get Well* into my cassette player and pushed play.

"Pay attention to your feelings," the narrator said.

I knew my feelings. I was feeling scared. If the lady on the tape could tell me how to stop being scared, then I'd have learned something.

I looked at the clock again. Five minutes more had passed. I couldn't concentrate on the tape. Would Marian remember to show up or would I have to scrounge around in my bare cupboards looking for something to eat?

A knock on the front door! Even though I was expecting it, my heart jumped.

"Who's that?" I yelled.

"It's me, Marian. I brought you some food." A glance at the clock showed she was right on time, 6:00 P.M. sharp.

"Please be patient," I called out to her through my upstairs bedroom window. "I have to move slowly so I don't disturb the stitches." With all the bandages and sore muscles, it was an effort to walk.

Just as I opened the door, Marian's three-year-old daughter, Josie, ran past us. She was dressed in a red checked dress, red socks, and a red and white polka-dot bow in her hair. Apparently, she had been told about Jack, because as soon as she spotted him, she made a beeline for him.

"Hi, bunny!" Josie screeched.

When he saw her little feet running towards him, Jack's eyes grew wide as if to say, *Yikes! Get me out of here!* The expression on his startled face made me laugh.

He scampered off. Josie ran after him. He made a lightning-fast U-turn and ran in the opposite direction.

I suddenly realized that if Josie caught him, she might try to pick him up by the ears. I didn't want Jack to get hurt but in my present condition I couldn't move fast enough to intercept a three-year-old.

"Stop!" I shouted. I felt helpless to do anything but yell and motioned to Marian to grab Josie. Marian sensed the danger to Jack and ran after Josie. Unfortunately, Josie reached Jack first. She grabbed for Jack's ears. Luckily, he moved faster than the little whirlwind toddler. She tumbled over and let out a wail.

"Watch out, Josie," I warned. "If you scare him and grab him, he might bite you."

Josie stopped crying. She looked up at me and smiled, then ran after Jack again.

He zoomed across the room and cowered in the corner, but she caught up with him. She scrunched down beside him and tried to pet his head. Thankfully, she bought my bluff and didn't try to grab his ears.

"Don't try to touch him until I introduce you. He's not used to strangers and gets very afraid. Stay still, please."

Josie obeyed me for the moment but looked over at her mother skeptically with her big brown eyes as if to ask, *Do I have to listen to this lady?*

Marian quickly scooped Josie up in her arms.

Talking quietly to Josie, I said, "You have to move slowly around Jack. Otherwise, you'll scare him. Give him some time to calm down. After we eat, I'll introduce you to Jack and you can hug and pet him all you want."

I was tempted to scold the child, but I realized that a toddler couldn't be expected to understand rabbit psychology. Also, I didn't want to annoy Marian by coming on too strong, or else that might be the end of my meal deliveries.

I took a seat at the kitchen table and pointed out the location of dishes and utensils to Marian. I smelled the delicious aroma of the chicken casserole she brought for our dinner. She also heated up some tomato soup.

"Are you going to eat too?" I asked Marian.

"No, but Josie will have some soup."

As cute as Marian's daughter was, I felt happy that I would never have any mischief-makers of my own. Unlike most girls I'd grown up with, I'd never wanted to be a mother. Once when I was twelve years old, I had to babysit a neighbor's child for an hour on a Sunday afternoon. When the child screamed, not knowing what else to do, I called 411 for advice. Luckily, the information operator had a little time on her hands. She patiently explained how to calm a fussy child.

I had never, even when I was a kid myself, been comfortable around smaller children. Now, I did want to be able to tolerate Josie since she and her mother would be coming another two times in the next two weeks. Josie was part of the meal delivery deal.

After we finished eating, I asked Marian to find Jack. Marian stood up and put Josie on her chair.

"You wait here, honey. Mommy's going to get the bunny. If you're good, maybe Miss Judy will let you pet him."

Marian looked around.

"Where are you, Jack?" she called. The blinds fluttered.

"Over there by the window," I whispered quietly so Jack wouldn't hear.

Marian tiptoed toward the sliding glass door where Jack remained hidden. She kneeled in front of Jack, so he couldn't escape. Gently she gathered him in her arms and spoke to him in a soothing voice. Although she was a stranger, and I was afraid he'd struggle against her, Jack remained calm. Marian placed Jack on my lap. Josie slid off her chair. Her movements were big and bouncing.

"Shhh. Move slowly and quietly," Marian coached.

Josie stood still and watched my hand. I showed her how to pet Jack lightly on his head and back. Gently, I guided her tiny hand towards his fur. She moved it back and forth very lightly on his head barely touching his fur, never once touching his ears.

"Very good, Josie!" I praised. "He likes you when you're kind to him."

✳✳✳

That night, after Marian and Josie left, I climbed into my bed utterly exhausted. I thought of Jack downstairs in his bed. I wondered if he'd felt lonely lately. With all my health problems I hadn't paid nearly enough attention to him. I hugged Mr. Beagle, the stuffed dog Paula had given me in the hospital.

It was easier for me to worry about Jack now than when I'd be starting chemotherapy. I'd have even less energy for him then. Mr. Beagle felt soft and cuddly. Far more affectionate than Jack had been that afternoon.

I resolved to make attending to Jack's needs a top priority as soon as my two-week recovery time was over. Figuring out how to do that would be a challenge.

❊❊❊

I was so grateful for all the women (Becky's friends) who came nightly to give me dinner, encouraging words, lighthearted conversation, and most of them prayed for me (and with me) before they left. At the end of the two weeks I felt I'd made lasting friendships with all of them, and felt loved and buoyed up by their care for me.

❊❊❊

One morning my sister Deborah called.

"What are you doing for lunch?"

"I'm having leftovers, and I'd love to see you."

She came bringing her lentil soup. It was delicious and I asked for the recipe. As we chatted I mentioned all the times in the past she'd been there for me.

"I'm so grateful that you came today. I'm feeling anxious about being cooped up here for the next two weeks. I don't know how – or if – the treatments will work for me. I've been praying and need to trust that God has a purpose and a plan in all of this happening, but right now I'm feeling that my faith is so weak."

"Judy, I'm glad you shared all your concerns, otherwise it might just fester inside of you and make you miserable. Let's pray right now for God to give you the courage and strength to endure all of this."

Her faith helped me immensely.

Both of my nieces, Becky and Claire, came over on one of the Saturdays when USC was playing UCLA with their yearly football rivalry and we had a good time watching the game. Becky promised that we'd go to the game the following year. (And we did.)

Left to right: Judy, Claire, Becky   photo by Deborah

Chapter 26
Pothole Number Five: Chemo

I was so grateful that Deborah came early so that we could go to the park and pray together so I'd have courage to face my first chemo treatment. Ugh.

We had waited in the doctor's reception room until our 10:00 AM appointment time. On entering the chemo room, I found a chair that pleased me and soon a nurse presented me with a warm heating pad to put over my left hand and wrist in the hope that a suitable vein would puff up enough so that the IV could be inserted easily. It was all hooked up to a stand that moved with me in case I needed to use the restroom or get a drink at the water cooler.

Drip. Drip. Drip. I watched the clear goop trickle down through the transparent tube into the two-inch needle sticking out of the large vein in my left hand. What a strange feeling. Weird. And there was nothing to do but sit there and wait.

And wait.

And wait.

Deborah waited with me. We both read our books and drank coffee. I listened to my cassette tape, wrote a letter, and watched TV. We chatted.

Still, the time passed very slowly.

Very slowly.

Later I went to the bathroom. On the walk back, the walls seemed to move. My brain clouded over, and my body began to wilt from under me. I couldn't avoid collapsing into the arms of two nurses. The stocky dark-haired one had baggy eyes and a big-toothed grin, but she wasn't smiling as she guided me back to the large leather recliner chair.

Deborah jumped up to help.

The other nurse, with shaggy blond hair, put up her hand in a firm *HALT!* Gesture. Deborah's face looked white and stark, but she sat back down, and gripped the wooden arms of her waiting room chair as she let us pass by. The nurses eased me into the recliner.

"Your blood pressure shot up," the blond nurse said. "We're going to have to give you just one medication at a time."

"Looks like you'll be here five hours instead of three," the baggy-eyed nurse remarked.

"Do you have a ride home?"

I looked over at Deborah. She shook her head. "Sorry, I have to leave."

Of course, she had to go. She'd already waited with me for over two hours.

"It's OK," I said. "I figured you wouldn't be able to stay the whole time, so I arranged with my housekeeper to pick me up later this afternoon. I'm sure one of the nurses will call Jeri for me." The blond nurse smiled and nodded *yes*.

"Oh, Judy, I should have known you'd have a contingency plan," Deborah said, relieved.

I hugged Deborah with my right arm. "Don't worry, I'll be fine. Your staying with me today meant a lot to me."

✳✳✳

When I finally arrived back home after that first chemo session, I found Jack sitting in the living room staring into the stereo glass. "Hi, Jack," I said, as cheerfully as I could.

He didn't move.

I walked over to the stereo to figure out what he found so fascinating. This wasn't the first time I'd caught him staring into the glass. It was happening more frequently. *Was he depressed? Did he think the reflection was another rabbit?*

I lay on the carpet next to him and put my hand on his head. "It's OK. I know you must be lonely. After Mama gets done with this awful chemotherapy, I'll see if I can find you a playmate."

✳✳✳

A week after my first chemo treatment, Becky drove me to a beauty conference for cancer patients at Torrance Memorial Hospital. We'd arrived late. I stood by the door of the enormous room surveying the scene. There were booths lining all the walls.

People were mingling and chatting. Some had bald heads. Others wore head scarves or flamboyant hats. Others seemed to be wearing wigs. Short. Long. Blonde. Brunette. Auburn. Many of the wigs were styled like the 1980's big hair. Yikes! Did their hair look like that before they lost it or were they trying to be someone new?

I leaned over and said in a low voice to Becky, "I think my hair is starting to fall out. While we're here maybe I should buy a wig. I don't want to walk around bald or with a scarf tied around my head."

We walked over to the nearest booth. On the table, Styrofoam heads showed off wigs for sale. Becky held up a bright red wig with shoulder length curls.

"What about this?" she asked.

"Yikes! I don't think so."

We visited almost all the booths, but most of the wigs weren't for me. They were outlandish. I tried on three hairstyles. I finally bought a blond one with curls that looked like my regular hair.

"Shall we go home and shave your head?" Becky asked. "That's what I did when I had cancer."

No way did I want to watch my hair fall out a clump at a time. On the other hand, I didn't want to shave my head either. I compromised.

At home, Becky cut my hair very short. Still, more hair fell out every time I shampooed. Within a week, I had only a fuzz remnant on top of my head. How fast it all happened.

The fuzz was blond. I'd wanted blond hair all my life and now there it was. I decided to start wearing my wig so that those in my real estate office wouldn't ask questions, or if they thought I was sick, try to steal my clients.

The next time I went to the office I wore my new wig. It felt loose. Hopefully it wouldn't slip to either side. Earlier that morning I tested the wig out while walking and even jumping around my home. Would it stay on my head? I bent over Jack and gazed down at him.

I asked, "Jack, how does my new hair look?" and then giggled.

Suspicious, Jack pressed his cone-shaped ears flat against his head. He moved away from me.

"Don't you recognize me, Jack?"

At the office, my manager Danny looked up and smiled when I greeted him with a cheery "hello." Just like always. He hadn't noticed I was wearing a wig. I'd passed the first test. One down. Whew!

The woman at the next desk nodded a greeting. Another good sign. She always noticed what everybody wore and made comments about it. When she said nothing, I relaxed.

For the rest of the day it was business as usual with my co-workers. On the way out of the door I patted my new wig,

"You did a good job." I said to myself under my breath. "No one noticed."

❋❋❋

Diane, my next-door neighbor, didn't like that I owned a rabbit, so I hadn't asked her for any help. Yet when she found out I was sick, she knocked on my door and asked, "Is there anything I can do for you?"

"You have such a busy social life, I don't want to impose," I said.

"What exactly do you need?"

"I need someone to drive me to the acupuncturist office for a treatment."

"OK, but how will you get home?"

"Margaret, my real estate partner, drives me from there to the doctor's office for my chemo treatment. Then Jeri picks me up after that."

Diane laughed. "Sounds like you will have a full day. Of course, I'll help. Let me know when you need a ride to the acupuncturist."

I hugged her impulsively for her unexpected kindness.

Becky had encouraged me to meet with Dr. Nancy, her acupuncturist. Becky said that those treatments would help me avoid pain and nausea during chemo. Dr. Nancy wasn't a medical doctor, but her methods and attitude were so professional that everyone called her "Doctor Nancy."

The day of the second chemo session Diane drove me to Dr. Nancy's office. I was wearing my blond wig again, for the tenth day in a row. I should have been used to it, but I still felt self-conscious.

The receptionist greeted me. If she noticed I was wearing a wig she didn't say anything. I smiled to myself while following her into the exam room. I sat on the treatment table.

As Dr. Nancy entered the room, she asked, "How are you today?" in a competent, friendly manner. She had long brown curly hair in a style that gave her an aristocratic look.

I whisked off my wig as if it were a top hat.

Startled, Dr. Nancy did a double-take in disbelief.

"How do you like the new me?" I asked.

She laughed out loud and I joined her. Then she patted my nearly bald head.

"The blond fuzz on top is cute," she said.

I gave her my wrist. Dr. Nancy took my pulses, first on the inside of my right wrist and then on the inside of my left wrist.

"We're going to prop up your system so that it will be receptive to the chemo's toxins," she explained. "By testing your pulses I'll be able to read your body." That reading would determine where she stuck the needles in my wrist, hands, feet, and chest.

I took a deep breath. All I had to do was to relax and let Dr. Nancy take charge. While she stuck the needles into my skin she told me jokes and asked me questions about my life. It didn't hurt at all. If anything, I felt comforted. When she finished inserting the needles, she turned on my favorite music and told me I should rest for forty-five minutes.

At the end of the session she told me to schedule acupuncture one hour before each chemo treatment, then again two days afterwards. She explained that acupuncture strengthens organ function to be ready for chemo treatments and helps reduce nausea.

✳✳✳

I left Dr. Nancy's office feeling much less apprehensive. I hoped her treatment would work because I hated how sick the chemo might make me feel otherwise.

In the parking lot, I saw Margaret waiting for me in her green Honda. Born in Canada and married to a British chap, Margaret had a gentle round face and a calming spirit that comforted me. She'd become a real estate agent the same year I did. Our clients liked her delightful English accent and so did I. It commanded respect, and that respect reflected well on me.

"Are you wearing a wig?" she asked, squinting at me.

I put my hand up to my head to remind myself that I was indeed wearing a wig. *Oh no! How could she tell?*

"Is it that obvious?" I exclaimed.

"No, it's good. It looks like your own hair. Honestly, I wouldn't have noticed, but it's just that the wig has slipped a bit. Here, look in the mirror."

She reached over and pulled down the visor on the passenger side where I was sitting.

I looked into the small mirror and with both hands straightened the wig so that it was in the center of my head.

"Thanks for letting me know."

"It's a pretty blond color," Margaret said in her charming British accent. "How was your treatment today?"

"She sticks needles all over me. They don't usually hurt. If they do, she moves them to a different area on my body," I said.

As Margaret drove me to my chemo treatment I double-checked my backpack to be sure I had everything I needed. A book. My lunch. Cassettes. A cassette player. My journal. A pen. Yep. Good to go.

With Dr. Nancy's treatment I was optimistic that I wouldn't get nauseated. I needed to have enough energy to earn my living as a realtor. Margaret dropped me at the hospital's front entrance. I straightened my shoulders and walked tall. *Here I come, chemo round two.* Many more rounds to go. I mentally psyched myself up to face this challenge. I would beat it.

In the chemo room, other patients were already seated in nine of the ten available recliner chairs. Some had already begun their drip. Most of them ignored me. Two people nodded hello. One lady grinned. She offered me the seat next to her.

I settled into the chair near the water cooler and bathroom. At least I wouldn't have far to walk when I wanted a drink. The blond nurse put a warm heating pad on my left hand as before, so a suitable vein would pop up to insert the IV.

I recognized the stocky dark-haired nurse from my first treatment. She said she needed a sample of my blood to be sure my blood counts were high enough for a treatment.

I held out my right arm. She poked the needle to find the vein.

"Oops! I missed," she said. She tried three times with no success. Was she related to the anesthesiologist who had the same problem?

"Ow!" I yelled. "That hurts! This is the third time you've struck out," I complained. "I need another nurse to do this."

Her dark eyes scowled. Her nose twitched but she said nothing. At that very moment the blond nurse walked by.

"I'm getting bruised," I complained to her. "Please help me." The stocky nurse glared. I didn't want to make an enemy here, but I had two more months of chemo and couldn't afford to be polite.

The blond nurse signaled to the dark stocky nurse, who got up and left. I was so relieved to have the needle attack stop that I couldn't help tearing up.

"She's okay," she said soothingly. "She just needs more practice."

"And maybe a better attitude," I added.

She inserted the needle into my vein on the first try.

"Thanks. Can you help me every time?"

"Sure, just ask for Johanna."

I took out my book, cassette player, and water bottle and put them on the table next to me. I had just gotten settled when a woman with ratty black hair walked in. She was a carrying a big duffel bag. She marched over to where I sat and stood in front of me with her hands on her hips.

In a menacing voice, she bellowed, "That's my chair!"

"Too bad," I said., trying to keep my voice firm. I didn't want her to know I was nervous and a little fearful.

She leaned over and gave me the look as if to say, *don't mess with me!*

"This isn't a restaurant," I added. "They don't take reservations here. You're going to have to get here earlier."

She moved in so close I could smell the onions she'd eaten for breakfast. As if that wasn't insulting enough, she shook her finger in my face.

"Time to move somewhere else, Missy!" she growled.

Johanna stepped between us.

"Let me get you a chair that's not taken," she said to the ratty-haired woman, who muttered under her breath. I figured she was in pain. That's easier to forgive than poor manners.

After the chemo treatment, I waited in the first-floor lobby for Jeri to pick me up. As always after a treatment, I felt extremely tired. Still, there was good news. Because of my acupuncture sessions with Dr. Nancy there was no nausea.

Dr. Nancy was a licensed acupuncturist and she may not be an M.D. but her Chinese herbs healed me more than any medications from a regular doctor. After so many mistakes, like the mis-prescribed hormones and delayed cancer diagnosis, I didn't have much confidence in doctors.

Losing weight would be dangerous, so Dr. Stone encouraged me to eat well. That night I ate a healthy dinner of meatloaf, peas, and mashed potatoes.

I also did focusing with Vi. We took turns. I listened to her work through what was going on in her life, and then it was my turn. Whenever I released my feelings, I felt a shift taking place within me. After two hours, I was emotionally drained, yet I felt better as I'd known that Vi had heard me on a deep level.

After my treatments, many friends called me to find out what my counts were for my white or red blood cells and platelets. Frankly, I got tired of reporting these test results each month. I was grateful for their concern, but suspected they were at a loss for words and asking for data was an easy way to start a conversation.

When Vi asked, "How are you? Are you up for lunch and a movie?" it was a welcome change from the specific health condition questions.

"You bet!" I replied enthusiastically. "Let's do it. I'm so glad you called."

At another time, I called my co-worker Charlene.

"Hey, my friend, I'm feeling weighed down by the world and need some cheer today."

"Oh, do I have a good joke for you!" After she delivered the punchline, I heard her infectious laugh and joined her. I felt my spirits rise.

"That's a good one! You are a tonic for my soul." We chatted a bit and I thanked her for pulling me out of my low mood.

Later that day, I felt anxious about my "geographic people farm," which is an area of about 550 homes that as a realtor I would walk through each month delivering newsletters and personalized scratch pads. I knew most of the owners living there and hoped that when they got ready to do real estate business, such as sell their home or buy another, they would call me. I needed to call Susan for some sage advice.

"Hi, Susan, I'm feeling stuck about what to pass out on my farm. I can't think of a good newsletter and don't have the energy to walk the streets right now. Any ideas?"

"Sure, Judy, I'll be glad to share my latest newsletter with you. How about getting one of the kids in your tract to help you pass them out? You walk on one side of the street and the kid walks the other side. That way, the owners will see you."

"That's a super suggestion! Thanks so much for your help."

I had learned that I could always count on Susan for wise counsel when I needed it. I was grateful that I had friends like Charlene and Susan to help me when I got into a tough spot at work.

I'm so glad that both Rose and Vi, my focusing friends, were available as I felt emotional support from them.

❋❋❋

Over the next three months I put on ten pounds. For the first and only time in my life, I was happy to gain weight. I still had one worry, and this one was in my home – JACK! I did not have enough energy to interview playmates for him. He looked so lonely. Every day he sat in front of the stereo, staring at his reflection in the glass.

"I know you're thinking there's a rabbit in there wanting to come out and play," I said to him one day. "You'll just have to wait a little while longer for me to find you a girlfriend."

Jack looked over in my direction. I could tell he didn't believe me. I had promised him a playmate too many times. He probably thought it would never happen. I hugged him.

"Mama will take care of you, as soon as she feels better

by Eloise Donnely

***

After a few chemo treatments, Dr. Stone, my oncologist, warned me that my red and white blood cells and platelets were dangerously low. If I didn't get them back up, I wouldn't be able to have another chemo treatment.

"You're going to have to come into my office every day, so we can give you the shots," he said.

"Every day? I can't do that!" I wailed. "Who will give me a ride? There's got to be another way."

The doctor insisted, so I said I'd figure something out.

That night I called my friend Liz. "I'm going to end up living down at that bloomin' doctor's office," I complained. "He says I've got to get daily shots."

"Don't worry," she assured me. "I can teach you how to give yourself the shots."

Liz came to my home the very next day. From her purse, she pulled out a syringe and an orange.

An orange? I stared at her in disbelief.

She thrust the syringe into my hand.

"Here, fill this with water," she said.

I filled the syringe with tap water and gave it back to her. She thrust the needle into the thick skin of the orange.

"The orange skin is like yours. It gives a little bit," she explained.

"Yeah, but the orange can't feel pain." I was dubious.

"Your turn," Liz insisted.

Determined to learn, I stuck the syringe into the fruit.

"It's one thing sticking it in an orange," I said. "It's another thing sticking it into my leg."

"It might sting, but you have to do this. Otherwise, you'll be going to that doctor's office every day, and I don't think you want that. Trust me, Judy, the more you do it, the easier it gets."

I made an appointment a few days later with Dr. Stone.

"I'm going to give myself the shots," I told him.

"Good for you," he said, "I'll give you a VHS tape to watch. It will show you how. Then we'll give you enough for one week at a time. That way, I can control your dosages."

I watched the VHS tape twice and then filled the syringe. The thought of putting the needle into my leg scared me. I held it above my left thigh for a few seconds before I finally pushed it in. It only stung for a second. The goop was cold.

That night there was a bruise, but I didn't care. The following day I gave myself another shot in the right leg. Bruises formed within two hours, but I didn't care. Not having to go to the doctor's office every day made it worthwhile. I wasn't going to be wearing shorts in winter anyway.

❅❅❅

Just before Christmas, my friend Verna wanted to host a potluck dinner party for our friends on my behalf. That way everyone could come together and pray for my speedy recovery.

On the morning of the party I took Jack to my veterinarian, Dr. Rosskopf, the owner of the exotic animal hospital. I was even more worried than I had been before. Jack was not eating. The doctor's diagnosis was that Jack had an infected front molar. He gave him a shot. On the way home Jack acted drunk. His eyes were unfocused. He passed out. Then he spent the entire afternoon sleeping it off.

When I dressed for the potluck party I noticed that Jack didn't seem to be feeling much better. I didn't want to leave him home alone. What if he had a delayed reaction to the medication? If he became sick, I wanted to be there to help him. Despite his wooziness, I gently tucked him into his cage.

Just before I left for the party, I decided to call Verna to find out if she had an allergy to rabbit fur. She did not, and I was relieved. With a towel wrapped around his tiny body we drove to the party together.

When I arrived, I put Jack's cage in a shady spot near the front door. When Verna answered the doorbell, I told her that Jack was with me and asked her to find out whether anyone in the group had allergies before I brought him into the house.

While she was doing that, I waited on the porch with my fingers crossed. "Jack, I hope your fur isn't going to be a problem. I want you close to me."

No allergies. Whew! That was lucky. Verna welcomed me in. She had prepared a place of honor for Jack. I set his cage on the towel-covered side table. Our 15 friends from the Bel Air Church greeted us and fussed over Jack but they were careful not to scare him. I laughed when they spoke to him in baby talk. Jack looked up at them with his big brown eyes as if to say, *Who are these crazy people? Do they think I'm a baby?*

"I've cooked a pot roast with roasted potatoes as the main dish," Verna said.

Since it was a potluck, everyone brought food. There were three salads including my good friend Bill Smith's famous spaghetti salad and several desserts. The food was scrumptious, and someone brought a relish dish with raw carrots that Jack enjoyed.

After dinner, I took Jack out of his cage and cradled him on my lap. People laid hands on both of us and prayed for our healing. I felt so loved. A warm sensation flowed through my heart.

"After you've finished praying for us to heal, would you be willing to pray for Jack to find a suitable playmate?" I asked my friends.

"I want a playmate, too," piped up one of the single men. We all laughed.

When they prayed I felt comforted and blessed. In the weeks that followed I was so grateful to Verna for planning that potluck party.

✲✲✲

After my third chemo treatment, Dr. Stone gave me anti-nausea medication to drink before my appointment. It tasted awful, but I could wash it down with tomato juice.

I asked him, "Do you really think I need to take this vile stuff when the acupuncture needles are working so well? "

"Judy, I understand your view, but I'd like you to take it home anyway, just in case you need it."

It turned out that I didn't need it, but I was glad to have it handy as a Plan B.

"Your CA 125 tumor marker was nine," said Dr. Stone. "That's normal. What I'd hoped for."

"I'm so relieved," I said, and gave him a high five.

✲✲✲

I continued giving myself the daily shots. On the morning of my fifth appointment I felt a bit queasy so I drank the anti-nausea medication with a tomato juice chaser. I felt drained and very tired.

In the chemo room the nurse took my blood and determined that my counts were not high enough for a treatment. I waited for Dr. Stone in an exam room, disappointed, since I'd been giving myself the shots as ordered.

I had a talk with God.

"I don't like skipping my treatment. Maybe this is Your plan for today, but I don't like it."

An hour later Dr. Stone arrived. He read what I'd written in my notebook about my frustration and hugged me.

"Sorry this had to happen," he said. "but I am confident that you will get through this. The shots are supposed to help the red and white blood cells and the platelets to increase, but sometimes it takes more time to strengthen the immune system as it has been compromised by the toxins of the chemo. You are really doing fine. This often happens. Please be patient. It's only a temporary delay."

I was reassured by his explanation. Because I was seeing Dr. Nancy, I was not getting the nausea I had heard about in the treatment room.

Dr. Stone's confidence in my getting well proved true. I finished my chemo treatments in February 1998. It was exactly five years after Dorie's passing and the same year that I got Patches.

Judy in the middle, green hat   photo by a kind passerby

I celebrated my recovery by entering the annual Revlon Run Walk for Breast Cancer in March. My friends walked with me.
They all wore signs that read:

I SUPPORT JUDY

My sign read:

IN MEMORY OF MY SISTER

AND MY FRIEND DORIE

And

IN SUPPORT OF MY NIECE BECKY & ME

The next week I was given the choice to start a course of radiation treatments or not. I opted for the treatments.

"An insurance policy for my future life," I told everyone.

It lasted for three weeks, five days a week. Becky, unfortunately, had not chosen to have radiation and her cancer returned within two years, leading to her death nine years later.

✸✸✸

I noticed that Jack was not looking as healthy now. He needed his own insurance policy. If he was to have a long satisfying life, he needed a companion.

And soon.

Chapter 27
Matchmaking for Jack

I found Jack behind the couch and scooped him up.

"We have another appointment with the wonderful Dr. Rosskopf. It's time to get you more Laxatone and hay."

I opened the door to the carrier. When I tried to put him inside, he jerked free and jumped out of my arms. Fortunately, I caught him before he landed on the floor.

"Stop this nonsense, Jack. You don't have a choice. We need to see if your front molar has healed."

On the stairs leading to the parking area, Jack hopped around inside the carrier and the unexpected force of the movement made me lose my balance. I gasped. By holding the carrier up against the iron railing I somehow managed to keep my footing.

"Stop fussing," I ordered. "I am the boss and you are going to do what I say."

Safely settled in the front seat of my car I took a few deep breaths. Jack was wearing me out with his antics.

We entered Dr. Rosskopf's reception area and couldn't find the receptionist. She wasn't behind the counter. I placed Jack's carrier on a chair in the waiting room.

"I'll be right back," I whispered. "I'm going to sign us in."

The lady in the next chair was petting her turtle. She didn't look up.

At the reception desk I found the sign-in sheet and picked up the pen. Something flew behind me and ruffled the back of my wig. I was in the middle of writing down my name.

"SCREECH!"

The pen slipped across the page.

"SCREECH!"

I gasped and ducked. "What was that?" I yelled.

"SCREECH!"

A two-toned parrot with orange stripes landed on top of the attendant's shoulders.

"They shouldn't allow flying animals to attack paying customers," I grumbled under my breath while I finished signing the register. Because I'd been so startled by the bird, I didn't notice a white dog stretched out on the waiting room floor. On my way back to my chair I tripped over him. A man coming through the door grabbed my arm before I fell.

"Thank you," I muttered, embarrassed.

I decided not to pet the dog. Most of his ear had been torn off. There was a gaping wound.

"Sorry," a woman said. I looked up and recognized the receptionist holding the white dog on a leash.

"He was in a fight with the neighbor's dog and lost. I couldn't leave him at home," she explained.

I sat down in the seat next to Jack's carrier. The lady petting her turtle was crying. Her poor pet's shell looked as if an ice pick had cracked it open. I winced.

The receptionist came to the window.

"I'm here to get some Laxatone and hay," I announced.

"I'll get some for you after your appointment," she replied.

Across the room I saw a young girl who looked to be around 18 years old. Long straggly hair. Torn jeans. An oversized shirt. She was petting an animal that appeared to be either a rat or a snake. I couldn't tell which. I shuddered. Whatever it was, I didn't like it.

Suddenly the creature jumped out of her hands. It jetted straight towards me. My feet involuntarily rose up off the floor.

I screamed, "What is *that*?"

"A ferret," she explained, heading after it and scooping it up.

Embarrassed, I put my feet back on the floor. If Dr. Rosskopf didn't see Jack and me very soon, we might not make it out of here alive.

A lady with gray hair and lots of wrinkles cuddled a black rabbit on her lap. It was bigger than Jack and had white pus oozing from its long, leaf-shaped ear.

"I heard you ordering Laxatone," she said. "Would you consider adopting another rabbit?"

"Perhaps," I answered vaguely.

I didn't want to commit myself, but I moved to sit in the chair next to her.

She handed me her card that read "Pet Foundation Rescues Rabbits." She introduced herself. "My name is Karen."

"Judy," I said, shaking her extended hand. I felt excited. Maybe I could finally find Jack a playmate at her Foundation!

"We don't give our rabbits to just anyone," she explained.

A little presumptuous, I thought. *I hadn't even said anything about adoption. Yet.*

"We have an application to fill out, and there would be an interview."

No way was I going to beg her for a rabbit. I instinctively didn't like her.

She bent over her rabbit and whispered soothing words.

I felt uneasy, as if she was disqualifying me as a candidate before I even filled out an application. However, I decided that she was just being careful. I was curious.

"How many rabbits do you have?" I asked.

"Seventy rabbits live with my husband and me. They've taken over the patio and living room."

"Maybe my rabbit Jack would like a playmate."

"You'll have dozens of choices. They're all caged separately until they're bonded. We put the rabbits in a cage together to see if they get along with each other."

My opinion of Karen went up. I respected the fact that she didn't want any of the rabbits to get hurt.

"You could bring your rabbit to stay with us. Let's see if there's a female rabbit he could bond with," she suggested.

"I will ask Jack if this is what he wants to do," I said.

"In the meantime, you can fill out an application for me to review. We only give our rabbits to proper parents."

I wasn't sure if I liked her attitude and wondered if she'd find a way to disqualify me.

"Do you keep your rabbit inside the house?" she asked.

"Yes. But he goes outside on sunny days."

"Do you think that's wise? There are coyotes and cats around," she admonished.

I bristled at her questioning.

"I haven't seen any coyotes in my condo complex, Karen. We have a secure front door. In my patio I have a high fiberglass fence. There's no way a coyote could get in. We have only indoor pets in this complex. In the 20 years I've lived there we have not had that problem. Besides, I put netting over his outside cage to protect him from predators."

I was convinced that this explanation was enough to reassure her. At least I hoped so. Karen frowned and gave me a skeptical look. I figured I had flunked her test.

"It must cost a lot more to raise two rabbits," I inquired.

"Not really. Just a little more hay and pellets."

"But what if they both get sick at the same time? That could be expensive."

Before Karen could reply, the receptionist called my name. Good thing. I jumped out of my seat, eager to leave behind Karen and her prying questions. Jack and I hurried into the examining room.

The doctor said that Jack was healing well but I still needed to continue giving him Laxatone. I paid my bill at the reception desk. With Jack in one hand and a large package of hay in the other hand I tried to open the door.

"Here let me get that for you," Karen said.

Darn. Had she been waiting for me? I thought I'd lost her.

"I like to be certain our rabbits go to good homes. In the past we've had unfit parents. So, please understand my being cautious."

"That's for sure," I muttered under my breath. I turned around as she was still watching us, and waved goodbye.

"Maybe I'll give you a call sometime," I said.

In the safety of the car I said to Jack, "She's certainly persistent, isn't she? I guess it's because she has so many rabbits that need homes."

I opened his carrier, so we could look into each other's eyes. "What do you think? Would you like to go visit her and see whether we can find a playmate for you?"

Since he couldn't nod his head, I couldn't tell what he was thinking. Yet this seemed an opportunity for him.

"If Mama gets you a playmate, we'll have to be sure she fits through the rabbit door that leads out to the patio. No plump girlfriend for you," I assured him.

Jack nudged my hand with his nose. A good sign.

"You'll have to teach her. OK?"

He looked at me as if he was concentrating on what I was saying, but since I got no clues from his expression, I decided to follow through with my hunch to investigate.

I was busy with real estate work for most of that week, yet each time I passed through the living room, there was Jack, staring into the stereo glass, seeing his reflection and imagining another rabbit trapped behind it and out of reach.

✳✳✳

On Saturday, I decided to go to Karen's home. My mother had always cautioned me about doing the proper thing like calling first before visiting someone. But I decided not to call, thinking I'd just show up instead. After all, she was running a business, right?

Her business card showed an address just north of me and close to where a friend from the Bel Air church singles' group lived, so I knew the area.

She lived in a medium-sized house, around 1500 sq. ft. The bushes by the windows had been trimmed perfectly. She probably kept the rabbits behind the house. I walked up the driveway and didn't see anyone peeking out the windows. No rabbits in the back yard. I rang the bell on the back door.

A stout lady with large jowls frowned down at me from behind the screen door.

"Karen's away," she growled.

"She gave me her card. I want to look at the rabbits."

"Do you have an appointment?"

"No, I don't. Sorry to bother you." I thought about asking to go in, but she seemed so stern that I decided to go home and make an appointment for later.

Driving home, I thought, *Judy, why are you challenging authority? You know better than to go to a place without an appointment.* Yet now I know there was a rebel in me, probably suppressed as a child by being constantly ordered to do this and do that. All those rules!

I was often thinking of ways to break rules, but fortunately my inner wisdom and the Holy Spirit prevented me from getting into mischief. I remembered Mom saying "Always do the right thing. Do not embarrass yourself." Here I had almost done that.

On arriving home I placed a call to Karen and was relieved to speak to her and not an answering machine.

"Would it be okay for me to come take a look at some of your rabbits?"

When I arrived 45 minutes later Karen was waiting for me in the front yard, watering her plants. She let me in through the patio door where I saw four tables, each about fifteen feet long and five feet wide. On top there must have been at least fifty cages filled with rabbits of every color and size. Amazingly, it didn't smell bad.

The room was filled with light. Large windows and overhead fans kept the air flowing. There were brooms and supplies in the corner. Not a piece of hay was out of place. Squeaky clean. I wasn't surprised how neat everything was, since at the vet's office Karen had come across as very meticulous.

I walked down the rows between the tables. Some rabbits shared a cage. Other rabbits had their own cages. As I passed each cage, I held up a 6X6-inch piece of cardboard to check the size of the rabbits to be sure a candidate companion for Jack would be able to fit through the pet door.

by Eloise Donnelly

"I like this one," I said.

"No, that's a male," Karen said. "You must pick a female. That's how we do it here because we've found that two males don't bond."

I felt uneasy, as I wanted to be able to pick the rabbits myself, but now I realized that this might not work out. Still, I found seven female rabbits that could be possibilities and seemed to be the right size. Hopefully, if I chose to return, Jack would agree.

After about 20 minutes I said, "Thank you, Karen, for letting me come take a look at your rabbits. I will think about all of this and give you a call if I want to proceed."

"If you choose to return with Jack, I will need him to stay here for three to five days, so I can determine which of the female rabbits will bond with him."

"Okay, thank you," I said, as I closed the patio door. I left, considering that if I returned, I might not have a say as to which female rabbit she would choose. As I had walked the aisles there were definitely ones I preferred. What if she chose one for Jack who didn't like me? What then? Yet who was I doing this for – me or Jack? He was the one who would be making the choice. I would have to live with the consequences.

As I drove home, I decided to talk with Jack and get a response from him whether to pursue this with Karen or possibly find another rabbit rescue place where I could pick out my own rabbit.

I read in the paper the next morning about a pet adoption taking place on Saturday up at a park in Westchester. If I went there, I could pick out a rabbit I liked and introduce her to Jack. I went to find Jack and continued thinking about this option.

"Jack, I could go to the park on Saturday and find a rabbit for you. Would you like that?"

He gave me a look that I interpreted as, *what if I don't like the rabbit you pick out for me at the park?*

I realized for sure that he wanted a playmate and wanted to choose one by himself without my interfering. That all made sense. I called Karen.

"Why don't you bring your rabbit at 7:00 tonight?" she suggested. "Then we can get started."

"Get started?" She made it sound like a major project.

Karen told me not to bring anything. She had supplies.

I went over to Jack at the stereo where he was looking into the glass. "Tonight, you will meet Karen and some possible female playmates. Let's hope the one you choose can fit through our pet door."

He gave me a look but I couldn't tell if he was pleased or not.

Karen opened the door immediately as if she'd spied us coming up her walkway.

"You're right on time. That's good. I have another client coming in an hour," Karen said.

As soon as I entered her home with Jack I felt nervous. There was a contract that I'd be signing which would commit me to taking care of this new playmate forever. I followed her to the patio and placed Jack's carrier on a card table. When I reached in, he retreated to the back. If he'd really wanted to be there, he would have come out.

"Let me get him for you," she said.

She reached into the carrier. I held my breath, hoping Jack wouldn't bite her. He hadn't bitten anyone before, but I wasn't sure he'd trust her. He came to her and she pulled him out easily.

"Oh, he's a cute one," she said, and held him close to her heart.

I'll bet she says that to all prospective clients, I mused, cynically.

She pulled out the contract. I read it thoroughly. I didn't want to miss the small print and leave anything to "trip me up" later.

"Any children at your house?"

"No children. I live alone," I said.

"Read here." She pointed to a section of the contract that stated I'd have to keep the bonded rabbit for life.

I gulped, thinking, *here's hoping for the best.*

"I'm sure we can find a suitable playmate for him," she said. "I hope he's fixed, that way he won't be territorial."

"He's fixed," I said. I held up the 6 X 6-inch piece of cardboard as a reminder. "Remember, his playmate needs to go through a pet door this size."

I followed her and Jack along the rows of rabbits.

"Do you see any girl bunnies that you like?" Karen asked Jack.

"What if they don't get along at my home?" I inquired.

"Don't worry. If they bond here for five days, they'll do just fine."

"How much will this cost me?"

"It will be $50. Make the check payable to 'Rabbit Rescue Foundation.' We exist on the little fees from rabbits we bond and also from contributions from the community."

I decided to write the check, hoping that Jack would succeed in bonding with one of them.

At home that night I felt lonely without Jack. I missed our playing together. On Tuesday I telephoned Karen.

"I know five days haven't passed yet, but can I visit Jack anyway?"

She didn't seem surprised that I'd called early.

"Sure. I'll be home," Karen said.

I drove right over. The first thing I saw was Jack and Shirley in a pen together. He was chasing her.

"Gadzooks! Jack is so horny!" Karen said. "He won't leave Shirley alone."

I told Karen about the basketball the previous owners had given me, and how they said Jack liked to push it around with his nose. At first I thought it was cute, but then he started humping the ball. Giving it away seemed to solve the problem.

"Judy, you obviously made a big mistake. Jack never had a chance to explore his sexuality," Karen said.

Now he was driving Shirley, his potential bunny soulmate, crazy. Shirley was a big white-ish beige rabbit who didn't look like she'd fit through the pet door. Her black, beady eyes seemed to bore deep into me.

"Jack, cool it," I commanded. "Or you'll never get a playmate."

"Not sure if this is a match made in heaven," Karen said. "We'll know in couple of days. I'm planning to sleep on the couch tonight and see if they seem right for each other."

Jack and I hadn't seen each other for days. He didn't even notice me. He only had eyes for Shirley. My feelings were hurt. I'd known him first. Was Shirley stealing him away from me? Sure, she'd only known him three days, but Jack was smitten. He chased her nonstop.

Shirley, on the other hand, wasn't so enthusiastic. When she got sick of him chasing her she stopped abruptly and nipped him on his behind. Jack didn't seem to mind.

I felt guilty, like it was probably my fault that he was so horny. Jack's health had been stalling, but with Shirley his strength and energy perked up.

"Call me Thursday at noon. I'll let you know if they are a love match," Karen said.

It was OK with me if they loved each other but I didn't want to end up feeling left out in my own home.

❋❋❋

As agreed, on Thursday I telephoned Karen, who announced, "The loving couple is ready to be picked up."

"Do you want to hold Shirley?" Karen asked when I arrived at her house.

Shirley squirmed in my arms. Then, for no reason, she turned around and bit my hand.

"Ow!" I wailed. "That hurts!"

"She'll get used to you. She's really quite friendly," Karen said as she finished clipping Jack's nails.

I had a premonition that Karen's prediction might not be true for me, but I set that thought aside as I handed Shirley back to Karen. We put Jack and Shirley inside the carrier together and after a few seconds, we overheard Jack humping her.

He might be fixed but he didn't know it.

Chapter 28
A Stressful Honeymoon

With two rabbits inside, the carrier was even more difficult for me to tote. They both moved around, shifting the weight of the carrier. Navigating the steps up to my unit was like swimming against the rapids.

Once again, I wondered if I'd made a big mistake bringing Shirley into our peaceful household. What if they fought each other all the time? What if they both fought *me*? Karen's home, like Switzerland, had been neutral territory. Here, Jack was the alpha male.

I opened the carrier door. Shirley couldn't escape from Jack fast enough. She raced across my vinyl floor and hid behind the sofa.

Jack's affections undiminished, he took off after her. Is this what they call in rabbit terms "hanky-panky"? *Was she flirting with him?*

They are both "fixed" but don't seem to realize it. He cornered her in the small space between the sofa and the wall there.

I didn't want them to get tangled up in a phone cord. I raced off to the sofa. When Jack saw me, he stopped humping her.

Shirley ignored me and turned her attention to a phone cord. She chewed it before I could stop her. I grabbed a newspaper and swatted both their behinds. They ran into their cage and I snapped the door shut. They'd just have to stay there while I prepared dinner.

❋❋❋

I thought it couldn't get worse, but it did. The next day Shirley attacked the baseboards. CRUNCH.

I dropped my yogurt dish.

"STOP!" I took off after Shirley. I knocked over a chair and a waste basket before I finally trapped her.

"Got you!" I yelled triumphantly.

Jack watched Shirley struggle to free herself. I wasn't about to loosen my grip. Unceremoniously, I dropped her back in the cage and locked the door.

"You had better watch out or you'll never get out of here."

On my way out the door to go to work, I noticed Jack standing in front of their cage. He and Shirley were looking at each other longingly. Or was that my imagination?

I sure hoped he wouldn't pick up Shirley's bad habit of chewing the cords and baseboards. Hopefully, he saw what would happen if he misbehaved. Like Shirley, he'd be locked up.

Unfortunately, I couldn't leave Shirley locked up in the cage all day. That would be a hardship on both of them.

"Aaarrrgggghh! Now I'm going to be late for work."

The instant I opened up the cage door, Shirley raced out and hid behind the couch.

"Bad Shirley!" I scolded. Even though I was running late, I waited to make sure she behaved.

One minute passed peacefully. Two minutes. At three minutes I heard another CRUNCH. I ran over and looked behind the sofa. This time it was Jack eating the baseboard. Because he'd seen Shirley chew, he figured it was also okay for him to gnaw on everything in sight. Now I'd have to correct both of them of this bad habit. But how?

Yikes! I took him directly to the cage for a "time out." Was I ever going to make it to the office? I had my doubts. Finally, at 10:45, exasperated, I locked them both in the cage together. They would have to suffer each other's company until I got home.

❋❋❋

That night when I came home from work, they were just lying there, ignoring each other. They looked forlorn. I felt guilty and let them out of their cage.

Hopefully they'd learned their lesson. After I ate dinner, I was exhausted and went right to bed.

The next morning when I opened the lace curtains in the living room the first thing I saw were holes in the fabric.

What? No! Can't be! Those holes had not been there before Shirley's arrival. Oh, I was mad! I stomped around my living room scolding both of them.

From my sewing kit I got a needle, thread, and scissors to mend the curtains. In the dim light I had a hard time threading the needle. I gritted my teeth. When would this madness end?

Desperate for solutions, I skimmed through back issues of the *House Rabbit Society* magazine. I fantasized that a Mr. Fix-It taught a behavior modification class for my two little delinquent bunnies. The reality was that I had to be Ms. Fix-It. Only I didn't know how. I needed help, but who could help me?

I telephoned a few friends, neighbors, a couple of co-workers, and even my hairdresser, to ask for advice.

"How can I curb their chewing?" I asked each of them.

"Try perfume."

I hated perfumes.

"Try baking soda."

How could I get baking soda to adhere to my curtains or the ruffles on the chairs? Make a paste? That would probably stain the fabric.

"Try apple cider vinegar."

Surely the acid in the apple cider vinegar would hurt the wood on my end tables and chairs. I had to try something. I decided that apple cider vinegar was the least of three evils. The vinegar smelled sour. It made my nose twitch. As an antidote I burned some Piñon incense from Mexico. It smelled like a sour fireplace. Yuck.

After I sprayed the vinegar, both Jack and Shirley took turns investigating the end tables. Their little pink noses sneezed delicately and that made their bodies twitch. They didn't like it. That was good.

However, how was I going to live in a home that always smelled like a sour fireplace? Plus, I couldn't very well spray vinegar on electrical cords. I still had to find a solution that would keep them from being electrocuted.

"Try plastic dowels from the hardware store," my neighbor Trudy advised.

An electrician friend recommended covering the most vulnerable cords with metal coils.

It worked. I wrapped the dowels and coils around the phone and light cords. Shirley and Jack could chew away to their heart's content and never touch a live wire and be hurt.

Another problem solved.

However, that lingering vinegar smell was still nasty. A few days later I was so sick of it that I returned to the hardware store. There had to be another way to stop them from chewing on the wood.

I bought tape with two sticky sides. I taped the entire length of the baseboards and around the edges of the tables. It took two and a half rolls for this experiment.

Shirley was the adventurous one. She approached the tape first. After she sniffed the end table from a safe distance, she decided it was edible. She tried to put her mouth on the tape, but her nose got stuck for a moment.

I giggled watching her.

Shirley tossed her head. Her nose pulled away from the tape. She decided to back away from the end table.

Jack watched her and must have decided he didn't like what he saw. He backed up and hit the tape on the baseboard. It pulled his fur. He shook his whole body as if to get a bug off. His right side hit another baseboard. He squeaked.

Shirley ran towards him but didn't know how to help.

I grinned and put my hand over my mouth. I didn't want them to know how pleased I was that my solution was working.

I'd like to say that all my efforts solved the problem and that they'd learned their lesson. However, I often found bits of fur stuck to the tape and had to replace it. But this happened less and less.

Just to be doubly sure they would behave, I sprayed diluted Listerine on the wood. Still, it took about three weeks for them to finally leave all the wood baseboards and tables alone.

Maybe I would send this tip to the *House Rabbit Society* magazine, since I always dreamed of being published.

Chapter 29
The Rabbit Whisperer

I had solved the chewing problem but hadn't solved Shirley's biggest problem, which was Jack. He wouldn't stop humping her. All day long. All night long.

The poor girl was exhausted from running away and I was exhausted from watching her run away. Although Jack had been neutered, that didn't slow down his sex drive. He was 8 and a half years old (middle-age in rabbit years) but had never lived with a female.

One day just before noon, Jack was getting ready to pounce on Shirley. I grabbed Jack by his head and his bottom. A look passed between Shirley and me as if she understood that I was on her side.

"Shame on you, Jack! You're giving Shirley such a bad time, she's going to want to divorce you." I pushed him back into the cage. "You need another time-out, young man."

Hopefully this would slow him down.

When Shirley saw he was safely incarcerated, she let me pet her nose for the very first time. Unfortunately, the time-out was only a temporary solution. I had to make Jack stop chasing and assaulting her.

Claire and I met for lunch at Bristol Farms restaurant in Palos Verdes that day. She suggested we visit the library. I came across a book that would change everything. On the shelf, oddly enough at eye level, was the book titled *Conversation with Animals.*

After only reading a few pages I knew I'd stumbled across the solution to the Jack-Shirley dilemma. Claire encouraged me to check the book out. I finished reading it that night and was so excited I immediately wrote a letter to the author, Lydia Hiby. The next day I mailed it and included recent photos of Jack and Shirley.

When I told Dr. Nancy that I'd written the letter, she was excited for me and the rabbits. An animal communicator in Hermosa Beach had helped her fix the problem with her dogs.

"You *must* find her!" she said. "What Lydia is doing is a method like that guy Monty Roberts uses to train horses by listening to them. He finds out what they're afraid of and what they need to be happy and safe. Judy, you did not find that book by accident. It was meant to be."

That reminded me of something I'd done at a party. A lady had a person in the audience think of a color and send a mental image to someone else in the audience. That second person was supposed to guess what color had been sent. I tried it with a partner. We got mixed results. It hadn't really worked for us because we were amateurs. Lydia, like Monty Roberts (the Horse Whisperer), was getting great results with her communication technique, developed over many years of experience.

✳✳✳

A couple of weeks after I'd sent off the letter and photos to Lydia, I followed up and left a phone message on her answering machine.

"I want to schedule a reading for Jack and Shirley," I said.

It took Lydia two weeks to finally return my call.

"The charge is $60 for me to read the two rabbits," Lydia stated.

Another two weeks passed before we spoke again. Lydia had received my money but had misplaced the photos.

"No matter," she said. "I can do the readings anyway. Describe both rabbits to me."

I wondered how she could do a reading without seeing the rabbits in person or even in photos, but she seemed confident. I decided to trust that she knew what she was doing.

I described Jack first. "He is 8 ½ years old. Spotted brown and white. His ears stick straight out and he weighs about five pounds. Shirley is bigger than he is. Her fur is a dishwater blond. She is 1½ years old and has white paws and a brown nose."

There was a long silence on the phone. I began to wonder if Lydia was still there.

More silence. I drummed my fingernails on the table. I waited expectantly for her to begin.

Finally, Lydia spoke. "I'm ready to do the reading now. Do you wear hand lotion?"

How odd. I wondered why she was asking me questions instead of Shirley. Wasn't she was supposed to be an animal communicator?

"Yes," I said.

"Shirley says it smells good," Lydia said. "Shirley also says she's anxious, since Jack hasn't given her a moment's rest. He chases her continually. She always has to find places to hide. She's getting very, very tired."

I hadn't given Lydia that information and I was impressed.

"Shirley also says she likes living with you. She says you've been nice to her," Lydia said. "It's not your fault that Shirley isn't social."

That was good news. I thought Shirley was mad at me because I had scolded her for chewing the baseboards and furniture. I had figured she blamed me for allowing Jack to hump her constantly.

"How do you know all this?" I asked.

Lydia said, "Shirley sent me mental pictures."

"Before coming to live with you, Shirley was confined to her cage," Lydia said. "Someone had tried to purchase her, but Shirley says they wanted to keep her for breeding. She was glad that it didn't work out because she never wanted to be a mother."

I'd never wanted to be a mother either, so I understood how Shirley felt. Luckily, both rabbits had been fixed. She would never have to worry about having babies.

"It's taking time for Shirley to get used to things at your house. She needs time to herself. She especially needs time away from Jack," Lydia said.

"What should I do?"

"Cordon off an area just for Shirley," Lydia suggested.

"What about Jack? Is there anything you can tell me about him?"

"Jack really loves you very much, but he worries that he's not pleasing you lately."

I had scolded him repeatedly since Shirley moved in with us. No wonder Jack was worried.

"He understands that there is something not quite right with him. He wants you to know that it's not his fault. He gets super-charged with hormones. When the doctor neutered him, he left behind a few of the sex cells. That makes Jack a loose cannon."

All this talk about their sex life was making me hungry. I took a bite of a ripe tomato. The juice squirted across the kitchen table. What a mess.

"Jack told me he likes to use his rabbit door and sit outside on the patio. He loves running free outside."

The more Lydia talked the more impressed I was with her communication skills. Jack spent as much time as he could outdoors.

Holding the phone between my ear and shoulder I wiped the tomato mess off the table. I peeked around the corner of the kitchen into the living room. Jack was staring at himself in the stereo cabinet again. Shirley was nowhere to be seen.

"When he sits in front of the glass in the stereo cabinet he notices that he is quite handsome," Lydia said.

How strange that she'd said that just as I noticed Jack doing it. Synchronicity!

"You're amazing," I said. "How I wish I could do what you do! That way I'd be able to prevent them from being naughty."

"Anyone can do it, Judy. I'm offering a class on Sunday morning at the Humane Society in Pasadena. You'll learn whether you receive communication from Jack through mental images or through feelings."

"How much is the class?"

"It costs $300. That gives you lifetime access to the classes. I allow just one animal per family, but you may come as often as you like."

I was broke. But Jack and Shirley had to start getting along. Even if I didn't learn how to read their minds in the first class, I could attend once a month forever. I really wanted to know what Jack and Shirley were thinking.

"You may want to bring Jack to the first class," Lydia said. "He has an outgoing personality. The class will enjoy him. It will be easier for them to read his mind and tell you what mental pictures they are receiving."

"Maybe," I said. "But first, let's focus on Shirley. Tell me exactly what to do to curb Jack's humping."

That night I followed Lydia's instructions. I set up a fiberglass fence to separate the living and dining rooms. I placed a second litter box in the dining room with water and pellets for Shirley. That way she wouldn't have to share her most private moments with Jack anymore.

Satisfied that I'd solved Shirley's problem, I sat on the sofa to read *Clean Your Clutter*. I was in the middle of reading about throwing away paper and books when I heard a crunch.

The dreaded noise from behind the buffet meant Shirley was chewing the baseboards in the dining room.

Darn it. I would have to buy more double-sided tape and do what I'd done in the living room. In the meantime, Listerine would have to do. I grabbed the diluted Listerine spray bottle and raced towards the noise. Behind the buffet I caught Shirley in the act.

How dare she! I thought. *After all my efforts to help keep Jack in line, this was how she was repaying me.* When I pushed back the buffet she saw the spray bottle and ran away. I saturated the baseboards with the spray solution. *Take that, you rascal!*

Satisfied that I'd won that round, I returned to the couch and got cozy.

Two minutes later, another CRUNCH. Gosh darn it. I jumped up and sprayed more Listerine everywhere. Now that must be the answer. This time, Shirley got there before I could even sit down. CRUNCH!

Clearly, if I was going to win, I had to change my tactics.

Shirley would see who was the boss when I locked her up in the bathroom for the night. But I had to catch her first!

She ran fast and knew how to hide. Behind the plant stand I finally cornered her. To make sure she didn't escape, I got down on my stomach like a soldier crawling across the battlefield.

The dining room chairs were in my way, so I squeezed my body into the small space around them. I took a deep breath and reached out to grab Shirley, but she was too fast for me.

On my hands and knees, I tried to follow her to the other side of the dining room. My hand hit the plant stand. Yikes! A tray of demitasse cups on the metal stand almost fell over. When I steadied them, I hit my head. Ouch!

Shirley watched me with a curious smile on her face. Was she enjoying my misery?

If it was the last thing I ever did, I was going to wipe that smile off her face.

Suddenly I devised a plan to trap her. Next to the buffet, I rigged a cardboard box by putting some carrot tops inside. Shirley was too smart to be fooled and scampered off.

"Dang it! I really don't like you very much, Shirley. I might take you back to Karen," I threatened.

Then I remembered what Karen had said. Things would work out between Shirley and Jack, because they'd been bonded. Also, I'd signed a contract stating I'd keep her for life. Oops, I almost forgot that part.

But what about *me*? I needed to be a part of this equation, too. If Shirley didn't start being nice with me (the mother-in-law), the girl didn't stand a chance of surviving the honeymoon.

Eventually I managed to herd Shirley into the bathroom. Quickly I set the fiberglass fence across the doorway.

"Got you!" I yelled triumphantly. "See how you like spending the night by yourself."

Shirley peered through the fence with a woebegone expression on her face. At least the smirk was gone.

I had won, at least this round. But matching wits with a rabbit is not much to brag about.

A few minutes later I caught Jack gazing at her through the fiberglass.

"She's getting the night off, Jack. You need to cool it," I chided, while shaking my finger at him. Jack looked at me as if to say, *What's with you? You are ruining my fun.*

"I really don't have to keep Shirley, you know," I reminded him. Then it was as if I heard my mother's berating voice.

"Judy, since you did read all the small print in the contract, you don't have a choice. You are stuck with keeping Shirley. It's time to change your attitude and make this work."

Anger and resentment started to build inside me. If I wanted to break the contract and send Shirley back, that was my business, not my mother's.

I headed for the closet and retrieved the pillow and newspaper. As I beat the pillow as hard as I could, I found the voice to confront my mother, something I hadn't been able to do as a child. The bedroom door was firmly shut, so Jack and Shirley didn't hear my shouting and unladylike words.

As I learned through focusing, there is a transition of feelings from a general negative emotion to a location in the body that is the true source of the pain. I started out with anger and my tensed arms were ready to beat the pillow.

I pounded energetically and sensed the angry feelings moving to my heart as I remembered my mother telling me I would never amount to anything, that I was ugly, and would have to work extra hard to make friends.

As I child I was overwhelmed with sadness and couldn't find a voice to tell her how deeply her words were wounding me, knowing that she would keep doing it. All I could do was stand there and listen to her cruel insults and criticism. Later I would hold onto my pillow and rock back and forth to comfort myself.

Thanks to focusing, I knew of a way to recognize the source of the pain and deal with it directly. The anger usually moved to my heart, as I relived the sadness and emotional pain of being ignored and treated like an object, as with Dr Green, or with Mom, my heart hurting, knowing that she would always treat me badly

Sometimes the feelings would be fear or anxiety, as I did with both my dad and brother when I tried to hide so they wouldn't find me. Focusing shows the fear is in my chest and throat because I have no words to defend or protect myself. Feelings of fear that the situation at home would never change drove me to escape to the Huberts'.

Focusing helped me deal with the feelings of shame as my parents and brother said I made too many mistakes or was not worthy to be in the family.

I could start with an emotion and trace it to a particular location in my body, but sometimes the body pain comes first, as with my brother's constant bullying. Focusing explained that the anxiety caused my neck to hurt because when I was a child, my brother was a pain in the neck.

Before I learned focusing, I couldn't identify the reasons for my rage and tears. I find many social situations, words, or actions that are triggers to nasty childhood memories. Whenever I feel negative emotions for no apparent reason, I turn to focusing to reveal the source of the pain and deal with it.

Once you define the problem, you can solve it.

I found the focusing technique very useful at decision points too, such as whether or not I should agree to the laser resurfacing procedure.

By Eloise Donnelly

Chapter 30
An Unusual Love Triangle

The next morning, I was so angry that I phoned Karen.

"What's this about you wanting to breed Shirley?" I demanded.

"What are you talking about?"

"An animal communicator said you planned to breed her. I thought you said she'd been spayed."

"Breed her? That never happened, Judy. She was spayed at three months."

Who was I to believe? Karen sounded sincere. But Lydia had read me Shirley's thoughts. Should I trust this Lydia? Did I waste my money? Then again, maybe Karen was hiding the truth from me. I changed the subject and told Karen that I had to give Shirley a time-out from Jack's humping her.

"I locked her in the bathroom."

"Judy, remember: don't separate Jack and Shirley for long periods," Karen said. "You must keep them together most of the time or they will have to be bonded again."

After hanging up with Karen, I opened the gate to let Shirley out of the bathroom. She didn't want to leave her sanctuary. She grunted from behind the toilet. I reached for her. Her nostrils flared. I'd never seen a rabbit get angry. She settled back on her haunches ready to pounce. Her look said, *Leave me alone!*

I grabbed a broom to prod her. Out she came from behind the toilet. Luckily, I had more intelligence than she did. Otherwise we'd have been there all day. As it was, I was already late for work.

As I drove to the office I realized that I did not want a repeat of what had happened the night before. Perhaps Lydia's class at the Pasadena Humane Society on Sunday was a good idea, although it was a real splurge.

Would this class help? That remained to be seen.

✱✱✱

Sunday at 6:00 A.M. the clock radio blared Beethoven. I bolted from my bed and tripped over the laundry basket. Darn. I needed more sleep, but I needed to mend the Jack-Shirley dilemma more. I could only take one of them to Lydia's animal communicator class and Lydia had suggested Jack because he was more open to new experiences. Besides that, Shirley had a terrible attitude.

I stumbled into the shower. Afterwards, I put on the clothes I'd laid out the night before. For Jack and Shirley, I prepared a breakfast of hay, pellets, and apple slices. For my breakfast I prepared toast with peanut butter and a big banana.

For my lunch I packed an antipasto salad and root beer. Jack would have to snack on his hay. No special lunch for him.

At 7:45 A.M. I hustled Jack into his cage. On the first trip out to the car I settled Jack into the back seat. On the second trip I arranged food and green tea on the front seat, so I could snack during the drive. At 8 A.M. I was finally ready to go. Shirley was standing at the front door with a look that said, *What about me? Can't I go too?*

"Not this time," I said and turned the lock.

❋❋❋

The drive to Pasadena took 1½ hours. I was afraid that I would get lost, but Lydia had faxed a map and the directions were easy to follow. I found a parking space directly in front of the Humane Society building. Lucky!

As I turned off the engine I noted the time was 9:25. Thank goodness I was on time.

Built in 1915, the Pasadena Humane Society had two stories and modern beige siding. Towering trees grew behind the building. I heard lots of barking dogs but didn't see any. They must be inside. I guessed that about 500 dogs stayed there.

A woman about five feet tall with a self-assured, powerful presence approached me. This must be Lydia. I felt assured that she projected this confidence when she dealt with her animal clients. Her long brunette hair whipped about in the wind. She smiled a greeting and I relaxed.

"Hi, Judy," she said. She seemed to know who I was without my telling her. "Let me help you with the cage."

"I'll get it," I said. I opened the car's back door and pulled on Jack's cage. The water bottle was so heavy I couldn't budge the darn thing. Lydia reached in and pulled out the cage easily. What amazing strength she had. I felt envious. My muscles never wake up before noon – if ever.

"The class is on the second story," she said.

"How many dogs live here at the Humane Society?"

"About 300."

I wasn't too far off on my estimate of 500. *Gosh, that's a lot of dogs to feed and care for while they wait to be adopted.*

The office door was on the right, but Lydia took me through the wrought iron gate. I would have expected a heavy dog smell, but there was none. There were several staff members on the grounds and volunteers who helped keep the pens clean.

I peeked around the corner before we went up the stairs and saw an enclosure that was 12 feet wide by about 15 feet long. A huge dog saw me, barked excitedly and jumped up as if to encourage me to come closer. There was a large water bowl in the back but not a trace of dirt anywhere, and no dog toys available. His only entertainment would be visitors passing by who might talk to him, pet him, and hopefully adopt him.

Lydia explained, "Volunteers come here every day. They take good care of the animals. They bathe the animals and tell them they are loved. Some rescues have been badly mistreated. The public isn't too aware of the plight of some of these creatures. We feel so good when we find loving homes for them."

She opened the door of the classroom. Around ten animals and their owners were already settled in the room. *How could there be so many animals in one room and not be bedlam?* I wondered.

A German Shepherd by the door was the first to greet us. He stood up to his full height – about four feet tall – and lunged towards Jack's cage. Jack shrunk down in a futile attempt to hide. His eyes grew large and his ears flattened.

"Oh! Oh!" was all I could say. I lifted Jack's cage higher and quickly made my way across the room and sat down near the windows. After I checked on Jack to make sure he was okay I went back and talked to the German Shepherd's owner.

"I hope you plan to keep your dog on his leash. I don't want my beloved rabbit to be scared."

"You don't need to worry about Eric," she assured me. "We have two rabbits at home, two other dogs, and a cat. It was Eric's turn to come this time."

"Do you come often?" I asked.

"I've been here before and each time I learn new things. By the way, my name is Sally."

I introduced myself, then noticed the class was about to begin, and took my seat. Lydia passed out several handouts. They listed each animal's personality traits and abilities.

Lydia was in the middle of telling the class that cats can't be trained to sit up like a dog, when Eric snapped at a tiny black terrier. The terrier's owner, a petite young girl, tugged on the terrier's leash to keep him from trying to counterattack the bigger dog.

"Eric, that is NOT how we behave in this classroom," Lydia said. "When you misbehave you must come and sit by me." She marched over to Eric and led the big dog up to the front of the room. Eric resisted her by pulling back on the leash. He wanted to return to the safety of Sally. Lydia thumped him on the rump. She was not to be disobeyed.

"Sit!" she commanded.

Eric sat down, but his big eyes pleaded with Sally to come and rescue him. Sally looked like she wanted to save him, but she didn't move. Eric tried to stand up. Lydia's feet were touching him and kept him in check. He sat down again. This happened several times.

It took a few minutes before Eric eventually realized who was boss. Eric stayed up in front of the class for 45 minutes and Sally didn't interfere. Finally, Lydia released him, and he raced back to Sally. She threw her arms around his neck and kissed him on the forehead. It was wonderful to see the love between them.

Later every pet owner introduced themselves and their pets. Besides Eric there was another German Shepherd in the class, plus a terrier, a cocker spaniel, three cats, a parrot, a turtle, a snake, and of course, Jack.

At noon Lydia announced an hour break for lunch. Since Jack was caged I left him in the empty room. The pet owners who didn't have a cage had to take their pets along. Some opted to go to a deli nearby but the rest of us had brought food. We ate outside together.

At lunch some of us went on a tour to see the dogs eager to be adopted. Almost all were friendly, seeking to make a good impression on every visitor. We passed by the rescue bus which is used to round up strays and take them off the streets. We also saw the hospital for the spaying and neutering of all newcomers. After lunch it was time to communicate with our animals.

"Take a deep breath and get quiet inside," Lydia instructed. "That way you'll be able to read their minds."

Jack was the third animal to take his turn and I sat with Lydia in front of the room. I propped him on my lap.

"He's 8 ½ years old," I said. "I'm his second owner."

Lydia led the silent meditation and directed all the people in the room to transmit their questions silently to Jack. I wondered if Jack would be able to answer all their questions at once. Apparently, he was able to do this.

I heard some giggles. Sally cleared her throat and said, "I see Jack chasing another rabbit."

"Yes, I got that, too," said the woman who owned the parrot.

"Oh, my!" the owner of the turtle murmured. "He's humping the other rabbit."

More giggles. "I'm getting that, too," someone concurred.

It was amazing that so many people were able to see what was going on with Jack and Shirley, even though they'd never seen them together.

"Do you have white walls at your place?" someone asked.

"No. I have light-colored wallpaper."

"Jack told me you have slippery brown floors."

"Yes, I have vinyl floors that he could think were slippery."

"Do you have furniture with webbed feet like an elephant?"

This was a very odd question. Elephants don't have webbed feet. But I suppose the scalloped edges around the feet *could* appear vaguely like webbing, so I answered, "Yes, the coffee table in my living room has webbed feet."

This mental telepathy or mind reading or whatever it was, seemed to be working. There was no way ten other people could know what they knew otherwise. Lydia had explained earlier that animals are not limited by time. Their thoughts are instantaneous, not in a slow form as when someone is talking. Even so, it was hard for me to grasp all of that.

After Jack, it was a cat's turn. I tuned in, and in my mind's eye I saw the interior of her owner's home. Mostly, though, I just listened. This was my first day of trying Lydia's method and I didn't have a lot of confidence in my skills.

"You did great for your first day," Lydia assured me as I packed up to go home.

"I'm exhausted," I said wearily. "All that concentrating challenged me mentally."

What I didn't say was that I was worried about whether I could do this with Jack and Shirley if Lydia wasn't around.

✳✳✳

In the days after the class, Jack acted less aggressively towards Shirley. In turn, Shirley became more aggressive towards *me*. When I set down the food and water bowls she tried to bite my hand. Once she tore my shirt sleeve. When I tried to pet Jack, she ran towards us as if to head off the competition.

It was an odd sort of love triangle. Jack and Shirley were buddies. Jack and I were buddies. But Shirley and I had become enemies.

"How awful you are behaving," I said to Shirley one day. "I adopted you as a playmate for Jack but that does not give you the right to be mean to me."

She threw me a sullen look that clearly said, *I couldn't care less about you. I like Jack.*

Shirley was obviously jealous and trying to break up the relationship between Jack and me. It didn't matter to her that I'd known him first. Was I anxious that he might stop liking me?

Time would tell.

by Eloise Donnelly

Chapter 31
Jack Slows Down

Months passed. Thank God, Shirley and Jack's honeymoon was over. They settled into being an old married couple. Jack had stopped chasing and humping her all the time. Shirley had stopped fighting him off all the time. Once she let down her guard, they both relaxed together.

Instead of avoiding Jack, Shirley groomed him. She licked his ears, face, eyes and all the places he couldn't reach by himself. Sometimes I even think she knew when his cataracts were bothering him. Now that I didn't have to police them anymore, I sat in my rocking chair and read a book, so we could all hang out together.

I loved watching the contented couple put their heads together. Sometimes Shirley laid her head by Jack's bottom. You couldn't have stuffed a pea between them, the curves of their bodies hugged so close.

More months passed and if I was growing older, so was Jack. I couldn't move around as well. My joints felt stiffer. My vision was less focused. There were pains down in my knees and sometimes in my shoulders. My concentration wandered. Jack never jumped much anymore. Instead of running, he moved slowly. His appetite wasn't what it used to be. His hair had grown as gray as mine.

"When was the last time you saw Jack chase Shirley?" I asked Mary Ann, who was home from her latest business trip.

"Hmmmm, must be six months now," she said, "although I've only been here off and on."

❋❋❋

A few days later, when I caught a winter cold, Jack caught one too. I heard him sneezing. To combat our colds, I fed aloe vera juice to both of us twice a day. My cold went away, but Jack's symptoms worsened.

Then one day he got diarrhea. I called Dr. Rosskopf's office. They told me to bring in some of his poop. I scooped it into a plastic dish. Over the next few days, Jack's cold seemed better. I imagined he'd even gained a little weight. Everything was going to be fine.

Just when I felt confident that all the danger had passed, I found him spread out, his legs skewed. His whole body lay flattened against the vinyl floor. There was poop and urine all around him. It was early morning, so he must have been lying there for hours while I slept upstairs, unaware of how much he was suffering.

His eyes sent me a desperate look for help, but I felt helpless. He looked so miserable. He couldn't sit up by himself. Not knowing what else to do, I picked him up tenderly. I didn't worry about my clothes getting dirty. I didn't care about anything but making him feel better. *Maybe a sitz bath would help*, I thought.

I filled a shallow pan with warm water in the kitchen sink and held his small body upright, so he was standing on his hind feet. That way I could clean the feces off his small, trembling body. I wrapped him in a heavy bath towel and dried him off.

"It's okay, Jack. I'm taking care of you," I assured him tenderly. Tears rolled down my face. "You'll be okay," I whispered again and again. I knew that I was lying but it made us both feel better.

Because he had diarrhea, I put towels down in the living room and quit feeding him so many greens. By the time I said good night, I felt he was doing much better.

Suddenly at 3 A.M. I woke up with my heart pounding. Sensing something was dreadfully wrong, I hurried downstairs. Sure enough, there was Jack who had tried to get into his litter box but couldn't. He'd collapsed into a small heap, squeaking faintly.

Eeeeck! Eeeeck!

When rabbits squeak it's a sign they're really frightened. I picked Jack up.

"Shhh... Mama's here. You're not alone."

I placed him on a little cushion on my lap. In the rocking chair we rocked back and forth. Back and forth. For almost an hour. I was crying because I didn't know what else to do to make him feel better. When he dozed off, I placed him back in his cage and went upstairs to get some more sleep.

❋❋❋

The next morning when I set him on the counter to give him another sitz bath, he couldn't sit up at all. He crumbled over onto his left side. His right leg was useless. I fed him his meds as usual. At least it was something I could do for him. Then I called the hospital.

"I need an appointment with Dr. Rosskopf to see Jack right away," I said.

"Dr. Rosskopf is not in today and Dr. Weinstein has a full schedule. If you like, you can drop him off."

Drop him off? How could she even suggest that I drop him off?
"No, that won't work for us," I shouted, and slammed down the phone receiver. We would have to wait until the next day to get some help. I left for the office worried about what I would find when I came home that night.

✳✳✳

After work when I saw that Jack had not moved from the position I had left him in that morning, I knew he hadn't been able to drink any water or eat his food. Desperate, I called the hospital again.

"This is an emergency," I said. "I don't care if Dr. Weinstein is busy. I need to bring Jack in now."

"Just a moment, please," the receptionist said in a cool, detached voice. Then she put me on hold before I could say anything else.

Jack was dying. If Dr. Weinstein wouldn't see us, I didn't know what I would do.

"Come in at three o'clock tomorrow, but you'll have to wait," the receptionist warned me. "We'll see if the doctor can squeeze Jack in."

I sighed a big sigh. I felt grateful. Everything would work out. I just knew it.

✳✳✳

In the hour before the appointment, Jack finally ate some food. He was too weak to drink the water by himself, so I propped him up. He drank a few drops. I looked over at his rabbit door and wondered if he'd ever be healthy enough to hop through it again.

I had to face up to the truth. Jack might not return from the doctor's office. I was not ready to say good-bye. *Would I ever be ready?*

I fed Jack some carrots and carrot tops hoping it would not be his last meal. I tried to sweet talk Shirley into going with us to the doctor's office, but she ran behind the couch. There wasn't enough time to catch her.

I placed Jack's carrier on the passenger side of the car and raced to the doctor's office. I was out of breath when I rushed through the door of the reception room. The nurse reminded us that we'd have to wait for a gap in the doctor's schedule. So, we waited.

And waited.

And waited some more.

218

Frustrated by the delay, I started to cry. I hoped Jack would stay alive long enough for the doctor to help us. Although the animal hospital required animals be kept in a closed carrier, I opened Jack's door, so I could pet him.

While we waited I must have sniffled my way through an entire box of Kleenex.

"The doctor will see you now," the receptionist said. She had a bouncy ponytail that matched her big-toothed smile. I followed her into a cubicle where we waited again.

At least in the cubicle I didn't have to follow the hospital's rules. I took Jack out of his carrier and held him on my lap. He looked scared.

I didn't particularly like Dr. Weinstein. His manner was gruff. With his overbite, he reminded me of a mean Bugs Bunny. My last rabbit, Patches, had been afraid of him.

Dr. Weinstein entered the room. He put his hand on Jack's head and gave him a warm smile.

"Jack is not doing well," I said.

"Let's weigh him," Dr. Weinstein said. "We can't use the baby scale anymore because it measures pounds. Since he's lost a lot of weight, we need to weigh him in grams now."

"Is this the end, doctor?"

"It doesn't have to be. It's up to you. How old is Jack?"

"Jack is 12½ years old. I've had him for nine years."

"The normal age range for rabbits is six to nine years," Dr. Weinstein said. "In rabbit years, he's in his mid-90's. But that doesn't mean he can't live longer."

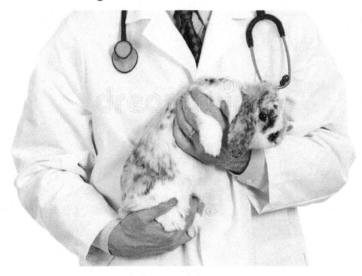

The doctor paused sympathetically before asking, "My question for you is, are you willing to go the distance? Do you feel that his best years are over? If you want me to help him end it, I will."

"That's not my first choice."

"If not, you must be ready to give him lots of quality care. It will be time-consuming and messy," he explained.

"But still he'll be alive," I insisted.

"If you commit to the extra work, then we'll go that way. However, don't tell me you'll go the distance and then not do it. That would not be fair to Jack. If I were to see that happening, I would be an advocate for the animal," he announced in a stern voice.

I gulped. This was a harsh reality.

"You need to make a decision, one way or the other."

Dr. Weinstein sure didn't mince words. I was on the hot seat.

"Are you telling me that Jack could still have more years to live?"

"I'm telling you that the times ahead may not be easy. You will have additional responsibilities. There will be costly medicines and you'll have to learn how to administer them. You will need to pad his cage, so he doesn't get saddle sores on his haunches."

"I'm willing to go forward," I said. "But perhaps a week at a time. Let's see how the treatments work."

"Fair enough. I will give him an injection today for his spine and legs. He's dehydrated, so I'll also give him IV fluids."

As we left the office he said, "We will know within 24 hours if this treatment will work. Or not."

by Eloise Donnelly

Chapter 32
The Worst Pothole of All

On the drive home, I remembered that I had some big foam pieces in storage. I cut four-inch layers and placed them inside his cage. I placed his food bowl closer so that he could raise his head and eat out of the bowl without moving his body.

After awhile I noticed he couldn't change positions. That meant he couldn't reach the water bottle. I turned him over. He resisted. Finally, he drank a few drops.

At around 11:00 P.M. he struggled to his feet and tried to leave his cage.

I cheered.

Shirley came over from behind the sofa and watched him totter down the ramp. When he fell, Shirley backed away. Then he picked himself up and sat at the bottom of the ramp.

Shirley snuggled beside him. Satisfied I had done all I could do, I went to bed.

The next day, I came down the stairs and Jack had used the litter box. He was moving about in the cage. Shirley ran from the sofa to the window and back again as if to say, *Look! Look! Look! Jack is better!* I patted Shirley on the head.

I was amazed at how well Jack was doing. I was also amazed that Shirley let me pet her. For almost three years, she'd simply endured my touch and treated me like a rival for Jack's love.

This day, though, she seemed to like me. Maybe it was because she was happy about Jack's recovery. Maybe she was finally accepting me. Maybe she and I would finally become friends. I sure hoped so. If something happened to Jack, would Shirley and I be compatible enough for her to continue to live with me?

I wondered about that.

Even now it isn't easy for me to write about what happened to Jack, but I want my family and friends to understand how I felt. I admit that writing about traumatic events is also a release.

Dr. Rosskopf was still out of town when I took Jack in for his follow-up appointment with Dr. Weinstein.

"I'm amazed at how well Jack is doing," Dr. Weinstein remarked.

"Yes, he's doing so much better."

"Just to be safe, I think it would be a good idea to do an x-ray of his spine today."

In the exam room, Jack sat on my lap while we waited for the results. They came back in less than ten minutes. Dr. Weinstein pointed to the x-ray.

"The discs in his spine have degenerated greatly, but this happens with rabbits his age."

Jack wasn't interested in the x-ray. He focused his attention on Dr. Weinstein's other hand. Maybe he thought it held a treat, and he was going to get a carrot. Or an apple.

"The problem is that Jack is still dehydrated. He needs another injection. More fluids."

Jack shook his body as if to say, *No! Not another shot!*

I stroked his forehead until he calmed down. He stayed still while the doctor stuck the needle in the back of his neck.

"Make a follow-up appointment with Dr. Rosskopf for Monday. He's Jack's regular doctor. I need him to evaluate his progress," Dr. Weinstein said as he walked us out.

I paid the bill. These visits were becoming more and more expensive, but it was worth it because the shots were keeping Jack alive. I just hoped that he wasn't in too much pain. It would be selfish of me to keep him alive if he were suffering terribly.

Over the next few days my hopes for Jack's recovery faded. He pooped and peed everywhere. He couldn't control his bowels or bladder. To protect the floor, I put towels down, but the smell still overpowered me. Even the cat litter box deodorizer didn't help.

Every time I walked through the living room something else needed to be done. Morning and night, I checked Jack's bottom and gave him a sitz bath. I gave him Laxatone every other day, so he wouldn't get hairballs. He couldn't eat on his own. I spoon-fed him small helpings of baby food – spring vegetables or bananas. Pears were his favorite.

From her usual place in the corner, Shirley often watched us. I wondered if she knew Jack was sick. If she did, she couldn't communicate how she felt. I called Lydia and left the message, "I need to know what's now happening with Jack and Shirley. Please call me."

Two weeks later, when Lydia still hadn't returned my call, I decided to ask Shirley using the techniques I learned from Lydia at the Pasadena Humane Society. I sat in a chair close to Shirley, and asked her, "What are you thinking and feeling about Jack right now?"

Right away I received a response. *Look, I don't like what's going on right now with Jack. I just want you to leave me alone.*

That was pretty much what I expected from her. I had a feeling that the other people in Lydia's class would have come to that conclusion as well.

I often remembered what Dr. Weinstein said about how much work it would be to take care of Jack. That warning had been an understatement, but I didn't care. I wanted Jack to live as long as he could. The thought of waking up and not seeing him downstairs was more than I could bear.

I was devastated seeing that he couldn't move enough to drink or feed himself. His legs seemed to be paralyzed. Every night, I picked him up and we sat in front of the fireplace. Shirley always joined us. She snuggled next to Jack and didn't pay any attention to me.

Then Jack's appetite returned. My hopes soared. To celebrate, I put out bowls of pear baby food that Jack liked. Shirley tipped over her dish and ran away as if angry.

"What's wrong with you?" I yelled after her. "You should be happy he's doing better."

At the next appointment I told Dr. Rosskopf how Jack whimpered when he moved.

"That's arthritis," he observed.

"He seems to be in so much pain," I wailed.

"That's the disintegrating disk on his spine. The one Dr. Weinstein showed you on the x-ray."

I bowed my head. More and more I had to accept that Jack would not be with me much longer.

In the next three weeks, Jack stabilized, and I pretended the worst part of the illness was behind us.

Early on a Wednesday morning I came down the stairs and saw Shirley grooming Jack. That wasn't unusual. What was unusual was how she was sitting on top of him, licking his head. Curious, I tiptoed up to them. Shirley stopped licking and looked at me suspiciously. I knelt down to get a better look at Jack. With her paw Shirley batted my hand away.

"Eeeeck!" she squeaked. "Eeeeck! Eeeeck!" Translation: *Stay away – he's mine!*

"He's mine too, Shirley, and he was mine before you got here," I told her. I reached under Shirley and pulled her off Jack.

Oh my gosh! His legs had become trapped between the foam and the litter box. Jack tried to move but when he couldn't, he looked at me with a helpless expression on his face.

I turned my back on Shirley and went out to the patio. Rocking myself in the wicker rocker I wondered how much of this I could take. A half hour later, I heard Jack whimpering inside.

Now what?

I found him lying in a heap with Shirley standing guard. She tried to stare me down, but I wasn't having any of her attitude. I ignored her and picked Jack up.

When I rocked him in my arms tears flooded my eyes. It was time to make a decision, no matter how much I wanted to keep him alive, I had to consider his quality of life.

But not yet. I wasn't ready.

✳✳✳

The next day I returned home from work and saw that Jack was in the same position I'd left him in the morning. That scared me so much that I immediately called the hospital.

"Jack is in too much pain. I just can't allow him to suffer anymore," I told the receptionist. "It's time to put him to sleep."

"Dr. Rosskopf is not here today. Why don't you just drop him off?"

"What? I can't believe you said that."

"We're very busy right now."

"No way! He's not garbage to be dropped off. He's my precious pet who needs to have a proper send-off."

"I don't know Dr. Rosskopf's schedule for tomorrow. Call us in the morning. We'll see what we can do." Her voice had softened. I could tell she was trying to be kind.

After I hung up the phone I rocked Jack for an hour. It was hard to imagine what life would be like without him.

When Mary Ann came home from work that evening she found us sitting in the dark. Jack's head was tucked under my arm as if he was trying to hide. I was shivering.

She turned on the light next to the couch. She sat down next to us and petted Jack.

"This is going to be our last night together. I wish I had more photos of him," I said. "Most of the photos of the last three years are of him and Shirley together. I'd like some of him alone. I'd also like one of him and me."

As Mary Ann went to get the camera, I turned on the gas fireplace and positioned Jack on his cushion in front of the hearth.

"Let's party," I suggested.

I fetched some almonds and raisins from the kitchen. Offering the treats to Jack inspired him to raise his head.
Mary Ann snapped a few photos of him chewing.
The promise of treats got Shirley's attention.

"Be sure to get photos of Shirley and Jack together," I said.

I held out an almond. Shirley took her time but eventually came over to sniff it.

Mary Ann took more photographs. There was one with Shirley nuzzling Jack.

"Good girl," I praised, and fed her another almond.

I was grateful that Mary Ann was with me on the last night of Jack's life. She shot a whole roll of film in ten minutes. It wasn't until I had them developed that I realized that there was only one of Jack and me, but by then it was too late to get more of us.

After the photo shoot, Mary Ann asked me if I needed anything else. When I said no, she went to bed and Shirley returned to her corner of the room. I turned on some music. *Lumen De Lumine (Light of Light)* by Joseph Michael Levry.

On the CD cover it said, "The highest prayer for opening the heart, touching the soul and bringing light." The beautiful music of a piano, guitar, violin, and flute soothed us.

"You will be healed by Jesus," I assured Jack. He looked up at me as if he understood what I was trying to tell him. Maybe he didn't mind dying as much as I minded him dying.

We sat there together, Jack and I listening to the same CD over and over again. For hours, we barely moved. Although I knew I'd be tired at work the next day, I didn't care. I couldn't stop crying.

Finally, at 4 A.M. I tucked Jack into his bed. I left the music on. Maybe it would comfort him through his last night on earth.

When Shirley saw me walk toward the stairs, she hopped over to where Jack was lying. The last thing I saw was her nestling up against his warm body.

I expected Shirley to want to come with us to the hospital and say her last goodbye to Jack. It took thirty minutes to capture her. Maybe she suspected what was going to happen and that was why she was giving me so much trouble.

After I captured Shirley, I picked Jack up. He whimpered. The poor baby had soiled himself again. I didn't mind giving him one last sitz bath. While I dried him off with two fluffy towels, he sat quietly in my lap. When we were finished, he licked my hand.

"I'll get you to the hospital as fast as I can, Jack. I'm going to help you stop suffering," I said in a soothing voice. "Everything will be okay, you'll see."

"Are you sure you want to do this?" the receptionist asked. I nodded then paid for the final injection. The receptionist escorted me into the cubicle. On a table inside the exam room I set the carrier down with Jack and Shirley inside.

For the first time I did not have to wait. Dr. Rosskopf appeared immediately. I gently retrieved Jack from the carrier and sat him on my lap. Although I left the carrier door open, Shirley stubbornly stayed inside. With my other hand, I had to pull her out by the head. Hay spilled onto the floor.

"You have to witness this," I commanded her.

A friend had once given me wise advice about having a pet be present when a playmate was put to a final sleep. Otherwise, the surviving pet would always wonder, *where is my playmate?* and experience great stress searching for him and never finding him. I suspected that Shirley sensed that Jack was in his final hours and didn't want to accept reality. That's why she strongly resisted going with me to the vet's office and tried to stay inside the carrier.

With tears in my eyes I turned to Dr. Rosskopf. "This is so hard for me," I said.

"This is the right thing to do, Judy. The degenerative disk in his spine will only get worse. You're doing this because you love Jack so much."

He took Jack from my arms and petted him on his head and back. "You've done such a good job taking care of him," he said.

I nodded because I didn't know what else to say. Dr. Rosskopf cleared his throat as if he had to let go of his feelings in order to do what he had to do. He placed Jack on the table and picked up the needle.

In a more business-like tone of voice he declared quietly, "It's time." He gave Jack the lethal injection in the back of his neck, the same place he'd given all the lifesaving shots.

When the needle pierced through Jack's skin, I felt the prick through my heart. He might as well have been giving me the shot. That's how much it hurt.

"You'll notice Jack becoming sleepier and sleepier. Remember, he won't feel any pain. You will know the end has come when his eyelids stop twitching." He put his hand on Jack's head and cleared his throat again.

"I will return in ten minutes," he said as he left the room.

Our little family of three was left alone. Jack lay on the table. I put my hand on his head. Shirley kept her distance and stayed near the carrier. She looked at me, then looked at Jack.

"That's right, Shirley," I said. "It's time to say your final goodbye."

Still she didn't move. She just kept looking back and forth between Jack and me.

"I'm sorry I can't be there for you right now," I told her.

I petted Jack, but he didn't seem to know I was beside him.

"I'm so glad you came to live with me," I said in a soft voice. "I have loved you and you have loved me more than anybody ever has."

I fondly recalled the many times Jack had been there for me.

"Jack, you were with me when I was dating Bernie and Martin and looking for Mr. Right. You listened and didn't judge me. At Francine's you comforted me during my recovery. When I had my cancer treatments, you were there to help me cope with the chemo. You filled a spot in my life that human beings couldn't."

As Jack became more and more still, his face became more peaceful. I felt grateful that he wasn't suffering.

"Look!" I pointed toward heaven. "Do you see Jesus yet? His arms are stretched out to welcome you."

I sensed Jack's spirit leave the room.

"I will see you in heaven someday," I murmured softly.

I looked over at Shirley. She still hadn't moved. She just wasn't getting it.

"Jack's in heaven with Jesus now," I announced to her.

Dr. Rosskopf returned. "Jack's legs are twitching," he said. "That's what happens at the end. He's gone now."

I looked over at Shirley. Abruptly she turned her back on me. Then she hopped back into the carrier and only peered out from behind the bars when Dr. Rosskopf wrapped Jack in a towel.

"I'm willing to give you permission to do research on Jack," I said. "Perhaps what you learn will help other rabbits live a longer life."

Chapter 33
Shirley Goes Home

I drove Shirley home. When I let her out of the carrier she ignored me and ran to her usual spot in the corner. Shirley wasn't a cuddler like Jack. The prospect of a future with Shirley was unpleasant. I decided to call Karen.

"Hi, this is Judy. About three years ago, I brought Jack in and you had him bonded with Shirley. They were playmates for those years, but this morning I had to put Jack to sleep."

"I'm sorry," Karen said sympathetically. "But there's no more suffering and pain for him." Then her tone changed. "What about Shirley? You might consider getting her a new playmate right away. You need to do what's best for Shirley," Karen admonished, sounding like a schoolteacher reprimanding a delinquent student.

I couldn't believe how cold and heartless she was. Jack was dead and that's how she was treating me? The sympathy was phony. All she could think about was *Shirley's* needs. Infuriating! I hung up the phone in disgust.

Clearly, Karen and Shirley were two of a kind. Arrogant. Haughty. Dismissive. Selfish. I looked over at Shirley. She lay in her corner, curled up like a lump and with her ears tucked in, as if she wanted to make herself invisible. Maybe she sensed that I really wanted Karen to take her off my hands. Maybe she missed Jack. Maybe she was angry because she now had to live alone with me. I wondered what bothered her most.

I tried Lydia's communication method with her but got no answers. In the five days that followed she barely ate or drank anything. I called my friend Marilyn, who also had a pet rabbit, for her advice.

"Judy, I think that she is so lonely without Jack that it might be best for her to return to her previous owner at the Rabbit Rescue place where you first got her."

"Thanks Marilyn, I was considering that option, but I wasn't sure."

✷✷✷

Because Mary Ann liked to shop rather than pay for her living expenses, she fell behind on her rent. I had a paper we had both signed showing the amount she owed me, which would be paid when her recently deceased sister's estate was settled.

I was away at the Abbey for the weekend and when I returned on Sunday, I noticed a note on the table along with the keys and garage remote.

Sorry, the note said, *the money from my sister's estate is not happening so I'm leaving. I will pay you when I can.*

I called her at work several times, but she never returned my calls.

Good grief! I thought. *One more monkey wrench in my life.*

I was so very lonely without Jack. I forced myself to eat. Most days I felt like a robot and barely noticed what was happening around me. Each night I held Mr. Beagle close and cried myself to sleep.

Jack's passing triggered memories of others I'd loved and lost. My sister Andrea. My beloved Aunt Ruth. My best friend Dorie. Sandy, my sweet dog from childhood.

The next day when I tried to feed Shirley she stood up on her hind legs and nipped my fingers. Clearly, she was making a statement. She did *not* want to be with me.

"Shirley, I think it's time for you to go back to your first mama. You have a special bond with her and will have a better life there."

I called Karen.

"It's not working out with Shirley. I think she would be happier with you. She and I don't get along. When she isn't ignoring me, she bites me."

"I told you to get another rabbit as a playmate," Karen reminded me.

I interrupted her, "Look, I'm still grieving for Jack. I'll be there in an hour."

"According to your contract, you're not allowed to do that," her voice was snippy.

"I can take her to the pound," I said, bluffing. Of course, I would never do such a thing, but Karen didn't know that.

"Bring her here and hurry."

I wasted no time fetching the carrier from the closet.

"Come, Shirley, you're going back home."

As I reached out to pick her up, she bit me hard on the back of my hand.

"Ooww!" I yowled. Was that her way of saying, *Thanks for taking care of me*? What an ingrate!

"You're going home to Karen and this will be better for both of us. She will find you another playmate."

Karen greeted me with a sour expression.

"You told me you'd keep Shirley until the end of her life. We had a contract," she reminded me again.

"The contract also stated that if for any reason I couldn't keep Shirley I could return her," I said.

"I have over 200 rabbits now. Taking in another rabbit, and especially one that is not adoptable, is not helping me."

"If I had had an opportunity to interview Shirley before she bonded with Jack, I would NOT have chosen her."

Karen gave me her superior look.

"She bites," I added.

"Well. She never bit me. Maybe you weren't treating her right."

"Nonsense. I lavished attention on her but she didn't return my kindness."

I pulled out my checkbook before she could say anything else.

"How about a donation?" I scribbled a check for $50 and thrust it at her, betting that this would shut her up.

The thought of money softened Karen's mouth around the edges as she took the check.

"I suppose Shirley is used to living outside the cage now. She'll have to be caged here. How do you think she's going to feel being locked up all the time?"

I had made up my mind not to feel bad. That was now her problem.

"Good luck, Karen. Good luck, Shirley," I said.

Shirley snuggled into Karen's arms. She looked happier than I'd seen her look in a long time. I turned my back on the two of them and walked away without any regrets.

Away from the rabbit house, the newly mowed lawn smelled wonderful. I breathed a deep sigh of relief.

It was spring. Time for new beginnings. I looked up at the white clouds moving across the baby blue sky.

"I'm sorry to see you go, Jack, and yet I will see you again someday. You're free to jump and hop in heaven and you are well again."

I closed my eyes, visualizing Jack as a younger version of himself, happy with a playmate in a meadow, and smiled through my tears.

In the days following, I would come down the stairs expecting to see Jack and he wasn't there. The house was empty. I treasured the memory of holding and petting Jack, a towel on my chest, as we watched movies together.

It was like losing a best friend. Even harder. Jack had never gotten angry and stamped his foot like a human friend would. He was always glad to see me and gave me unconditional love. I hadn't ever had that kind of bond with Patches.

Before this, I never understood how someone could grieve so much for an animal or love one so much. As painful as it was to lose him, I was grateful that I'd known Jack. My beloved bunny filled a big empty spot in my life that a human person couldn't. They're simply not capable.

Jack had been with me during my cancer treatments. I'd hold him close and share with him what I'd gone through. He listened, didn't ask questions, didn't judge me, just loved me.

He reminded me of my dog Sandy. Whenever I was afraid, I would hide out with him, safely away from my family.

The rabbits after Jack that I have loved and cared for are Sally, Sadie, Freckles, and Freddie.

Yet Jack will always have a special place in my heart.

by Eloise Donnelly

EPILOG

This memoir covers a time in my life where I faced incredible obstacles, both physical and emotional. With the invaluable help of family members and friends, and my unwavering faith in God, I was able to overcome them.

My cancer surgery was on Halloween 1997 and all treatments including radiation were completed by the end of March 1998.

I am a cancer survivor and want to give hope to those going through treatments now.

Some of the very deep "potholes" could be traced to negativity and fears I experienced in childhood. Facing them squarely and learning how to cope was an important step on my path to healing.

The reader may be asking, "Where are they now?" about key participants in my healing journey.

Reconciliation with my father.

When I was 45 years old I went to visit Dad at their home when Mom was in the hospital, having just had a stroke. Deborah had given me the movie *The Life of Jesus*. Dad and I watched it together. When it was over he asked, out of the blue, "Why don't you like Mom and me?"

This is it, I thought. *Finally – my chance to get it all out in the open. Here goes.* I took a deep breath.

"When I was a young child you spanked me so hard that I had painful welts on the back of my legs. When you'd been drinking and also angry at something or someone, you took it out on me and spanked me. I was frightened of you."

There. I told him the truth. Now the ball is in his court.

After several moments, he admitted, "I wasn't a good father to you, was I?"

"No, you weren't. I was always so afraid of you and also afraid of Kevin."

His eyes welled up with tears, and he choked out the words. "Is that why you never married, because the way your brother and I treated you made you afraid of men?"

"That's right, Dad. I learned about men from the bad example you and Kevin set."

I told him that between his harshness, Mom's constant criticism of my looks, and Kevin's teasing, by the time I graduated from college

I'd pretty much sworn off men for good. No way would I <u>ever</u> let a man make me miserable again.

He sat in silence, mulling over this revelation and considering the consequences of his actions. He started to cry.

"I'm so sorry I did that to you," he said.

I started crying too. I took his hand. He squeezed mine. We cried awhile together.

His eyes downcast, he rocked back and forth. Finally, he looked up. "I'm so sorry about everything that happened when you were a child," Dad said, with anguish in his voice. "It's all my fault that you never married."

"Your taking responsibility shows me that you care."

I scrounged in my purse, found a Kleenex and blew my nose before I spoke again.

"In the future, hopefully we can talk about things as they come up. Especially when it's hard."

Dad leaned forward and took my hand again. "Does this mean that you are willing to start over?" he asked, with some apprehension in his voice.

"Of course," I assured him, "Now that I can tell you're really going to be there for me."

After all those years, we were finally speaking to each other directly without Mom in the middle as mediator. All my life I'd wanted a relationship with him. I breathed out a long, slow sigh of relief.

The next time I saw Dad was six months later. Because he couldn't walk, he couldn't be at the same assisted living place where Mom now lived. This time I brought a pamphlet with me on *Steps to Peace with God*. We read it together and at the end I asked him, "Would you like to accept Jesus as your Savior?"

"Yes, I'd like to do that."

I led him in the steps to ask Jesus to fill his heart and we prayed.

"Dad, I'm so glad you did this," I said as I hugged him. When I left I called both my sisters rejoicing as we'd prayed for this to happen for over 55 years. Deborah went to see him the next day with a New Testament.

Closure with my mother.

Sadly, Mom and I never reconciled. I'd try discussing the past, but she would always change the subject. Such a loss for me. I don't think she ever apologized to my sister Andrea, whom she had both verbally and physically abused. Yet Andrea was the one who tried the hardest to get "connected" to Mom. Deborah and I gave up trying years earlier when we were in our 20's.

I think Mom's denial of her guilt kept her from admitting responsibility for Brittany's death. That's why she and Dad took all those vacation trips: to escape. Through the use of focusing and with prayer, I was able to forgive Mom and find spiritual healing.

Reconciliation with my brother.

Shortly after both my parents had passed, I confronted Kevin for his hurtful childhood teasing. He apologized, and I forgave him.

In 2015, when I received a call that he was seriously ill, I rushed to the hospital. On entering the room, I wasn't sure if he was asleep as his eyes were closed. I clasped his hand and said, "It's me, Judy." I had rehearsed what I wanted to tell him.

"It's awful that our parents treated you and me horribly. They shouldn't have told you to watch over Brittany. The accident was all their fault. You have lived under this false guilt all your life. Now it's time to let it go."

Just then I felt him squeeze my hand, so I could tell he was listening. Tears welled up in my eyes. I continued as memories from the past flooded through me.

"Mom shared with my sisters and me that when you were 20 you were drafted into the Army and you changed. She was proud of you as the Army straightened you out. You had become more responsible. A few years later you married an attractive, wise woman. She was a blessing and set you on the right track. I am grateful that she played a big part in your healing from the past and with our folks."

I kissed his forehead as I got up to leave, grateful that I had come. Kevin died the next day at age 88.

Reconnecting with the Huberts.

Somehow, I lost touch with the Huberts after my family moved away, even though they were so precious to me in my early childhood. It wasn't until Mom died in 1994, and Mrs. Hubert read the obituary in the newspaper, that she called her daughter Judy, my dear friend and childhood classmate. The obituary mentioned surviving children and their locations, so Judy tracked me down. She invited me to come for a visit.

Mrs. Hubert, now a widow, lived in the same home that I remembered as a child, all those years ago. Walking in, seeing that floor plan, I had *dejà vu*, heading for the breakfast nook off to the right. This time, I was served coffee and cookies instead of milk. I hugged Mrs. Hubert and cried with joy at seeing her again. I told her how grateful I was for their sharing their home decades ago when I was feeling unloved and desperate.

Mrs. Hubert passed away a few months later. Now I'm in touch with Judy on a regular basis. She's a real estate agent in northern California and we chat often.

My former roommate.

I was pleased that Mary Ann was available to help me with Jack and Shirley the night before Jack died, but shortly after New Year's Day 1998, she stopped paying rent. In March we set up a payment plan, where she would pay me as extra money came in. Her sister had recently died in a tragic accident, so I sympathized with her grieving and didn't pressure her. She claimed that she'd soon receive funds from the settlement of her sister's estate.

She moved out suddenly while I was at the Abbey on a weekend retreat. I left messages at her office, but she never returned my calls. A court official served papers from a jewelry store to Mary Ann. She had charged $750 and had run up bills for trinkets instead of paying rent owed to me.

Through small claims court I was able to win a judgment and finally, by getting a monthly stipend from her paycheck, I received most of the debt she owed me within six months.

Mary Ann was a complicated person and a mystery.

Other family participants in my story:

Sister Andrea and her husband Tom have three children. Andrea died in 1994 from ovarian cancer.

Sister Deborah married David. They have three children and reside in Southern California.

Niece Claire, her husband Mike, children Ryan and Laura, live in San Diego, CA.

Niece Becky died in 2005 after losing a courageous battle with cancer.

Aunt Ruth and Uncle Joe passed away several years ago.

Resources for healing.

I have continued with the writing group at the Cancer Support Center (now called the Cancer Support Community South Bay). It was and is a tonic for the soul. Barbara Abercrombie led the group at the time of my chemo treatments. Barbara Force is the current leader.

Caring for house rabbits has provided companionship as well as a calming influence when I feel anxious or nervous. There are several rabbit rescue centers in every State in the USA. Use the Internet or ask at a local feed store to find them. Knowledgeable staff and volunteers at these centers will help with adoptions. Some examples in California are:

Long Beach Animal Control (Care Services) is located in Southern California. Website is www.LongBeach.gov

Bunny Bunch Rabbit Rescue is located in Fountain Valley, CA. Website is www.BunnyBunch.org

Rabbit Rescue is located in Paramount, CA. Website is www.RabbitRescue.com

Rabbits and Bunnies Farm. Hobby breeders and sellers of pet rabbits, raised cage free in Apple Valley, CA. Their website is https://rabbitsbunniescalifornia.weebly.com/

Find a pet bunny in specific areas of your state using https://rabbitbreeders.us/state-rabbit-breeders-index/

...... Photo courtesy of Rabbits and Bunnies Farm

Retreats at St. Andrews Abbey have enriched my soul for many years. Retreats usually span a weekend (sometimes a few weekdays). They are led by a retreat master who offers a series of conferences or talks following a particular theme. Although the Abbey is a Catholic monastery, all Christians are welcome. Their website is https://saintandrewsabbey.com/

For another unique type of spiritual healing, contact Inner Relationship Focusing with Ann Weiser. Her website is https://FocusingResources.com/ The International Focusing Institute offers classes via Zoom. Their website is https://usabp.org/the-international-focusing-institute

ACKNOWLEDGMENTS

Sincere thanks to wonderful friends and family members who stood by me during a very challenging time in my life. Many of them played positive and influential roles in the development of this book over the last twenty years. I hope that they recognize themselves as they read the book and know that I owe them more than I can ever express.

Some names have been changed (including my own) on request to respect family members' and friends' sensitivities. I lovingly thank my sisters, my nieces, Liz Fry, Annette Tessier, Margie Chapman, Jean Worland, Mary Smith, Verna Griffin, Susan Nielsen, Charlene Glass, Margaret Higgins, Sonya Evans, Fluff McLean, Mary Russell, Claire Francis, Mary Visel, and Teresa Lin.

Special appreciation goes to members of the Bel Air Church and the Hollywood Presbyterian Church who provided a warm and welcoming venue for Bible study groups and singles' meetings. I have fond memories of Bible study sessions at Freda Mau's home.

I thank the Cancer Support Community South Bay's monthly writing group for providing valuable emotional support from the start of my treatments to this day. They offer many helpful services. For details, see www.cscsouthbay.org

Dr. Walter Rosskopf, owner of the Avian and Exotic Animal Hospital in Hawthorne, CA, offers unparalleled expertise and kindness to his patients and their owners. His staff is outstanding. I am among many fans who consider Dr. Rosskopf to be a national treasure. The hospital's website is www.BirdsAndMore.com/AvianHospital.html

Father Francis and the other monks at St. Andrew's Abbey in Valyermo, California helped me grow my faith as I faced the many potholes and challenges which led to my healing. Their website is www.SaintAndrewsAbbey.com

Lydia Hiby, Animal Communicator, has an uncanny ability to relate to animals. It's like witnessing magic in action. She offers seminars via Zoom and phone consultations in the USA and internationally. She is the author of *Conversations with Animals*. See www.LydiaHiby.com

Valerie at Sweetpea Foundation Rescue and Adoption (no longer operating) assisted me in giving four rabbits a place in my home over the years: Sally, Sadie, Freckles, and Freddie. She also provided supplies and skilled guidance in caring for them.

Kelly Morgan gave me valuable organizational guidance and mentored me as my editor for 19 years. She helped me document my life experiences in a form that would eventually become the foundation for this book.

My dear friend Katherine Poehlmann applied her editing and formatting skills to turn my manuscript into a publishable book. Her kindness, wisdom, and ability to brainstorm to reach creative solutions are amazing. I shall be forever grateful for the many, many hours she devoted to this project as my collaborator. She is the author of two award-winning nonfiction health books. Her nonprofit website is www.RA-Infection-Connection.com

Eloise Donnelly created all the lovely drawings in this book and the cover design. I am so grateful for her talent and generosity.

Marilyn Boussaid's eagle eye caught many elusive typos, grammar errors, and inconsistencies that I was able to correct before publication. Proofreading is her Super Power.

Thanks to David Lombard, Cheri Ann Burchiere, and Alicia Nelson for computer support that left me in awe of their incredible tech savvy and troubleshooting capabilities.

I bless the reviewers of the initial draft of this book for their helpful comments, insights, and suggestions: Alan Cook, Jane Persh, Mary Lichty, Margie Chapman, Helen Nah, and Angela Watton, as well as my family members.

Special thanks to cherished friends Rose Ramsey and Vi Olgun. We met as focusing partners in a class we'd all taken on learning the process of bringing awareness to the body in a gentle, accepting way. I discovered that the focusing technique helps me to discern what I really feel and to get in touch with my inner knowing. It has been a tremendous help for me to work with them, especially when I was feeling overwhelmed during chemo treatments and when dealing with bad memories of childhood. We continue to meet to this day. I owe them more than words can express.

About the Author

This memoir describes a true chapter in my life. Writing it has been sometimes painful but satisfying and cathartic. As a survivor of cancer treatments nearly 25 years ago, I was determined to share my story to help others overcome despair when diagnosed with a serious illness.

I appreciate all my friends and family members whose under-standing and loyalty helped me persevere through a series of major challenges (aka "potholes") that occurred over a short 4-year time span. We have become closer by sharing them.

The names and some places have been changed to respect family members and friends' sensitivities. Some played positive and influential roles. I hope they recognize themselves and know that I owe them more than I can ever express.

I thank God for the strength to carry on when I felt bullied, abandoned, abused, and unloved. He was by my side when I was battling cancer, constantly providing strength and hope.. He was with me in the depths of my grief. My faith in Him continues to help me cope with whatever obstacles present themselves.

I felt a surge of gratefulness the weekend I was at the Abbey as God's presence provided the comfort I needed and the high desert nourished my soul during my time there. The Lord blessed me with providing friends who brought food and gave their time and effort to provide comfort, care and emotional support for both Jack and me while at home after my surgery.

All of my house rabbits, especially Jack, have provided companionship, comfort, and entertainment. Their unique personalities, quirks, and antics have enriched my life.

Jack was a special blessing from the Lord as he provided constant, tangible comfort as I pressed through my various potholes towards my healing.

This is my first book, so I decided to write it under a pen name. I'd like to visualize my cherished bunny, Jack, running free in a green meadow in heaven.

Made in the USA
Columbia, SC
23 August 2022

65261321R00143